VOLUME 597

JANUARY 2005

THE ANNALS

of The American Academy of Political
and Social Science

ROBERT W. PEARSON, *Executive Editor*
LAWRENCE W. SHERMAN, *Editor*

Cultural Production
in a Digital Age

Special Editor of this Volume
ERIC KLINENBERG
New York University

SAGE Publications Ⓢ Thousand Oaks • London • New Delhi

The American Academy of Political and Social Science

3814 Walnut Street, Fels Institute of Government, University of Pennsylvania,
Philadelphia, PA 19104-6197; (215) 746-6500; (215) 898-1202 (fax); www.aapss.org

Origin and Purpose. The Academy was organized December 14, 1889, to promote the progress of political and social science, especially through publications and meetings. The Academy does not take sides in controverted questions, but seeks to gather and present reliable information to assist the public in forming an intelligent and accurate judgment.

Meetings. The Academy occasionally holds a meeting in the spring extending over two days.

Publications. THE ANNALS of The American Academy of Political and Social Science is the bimonthly publication of the Academy. Each issue contains articles on some prominent social or political problem, written at the invitation of the editors. Also, monographs are published from time to time, numbers of which are distributed to pertinent professional organizations. These volumes constitute important reference works on the topics with which they deal, and they are extensively cited by authorities throughout the United States and abroad. The papers presented at the meetings of the Academy are included in THE ANNALS.

Membership. Each member of the Academy receives THE ANNALS and may attend the meetings of the Academy. Membership is open only to individuals. Annual dues: $80.00 for the regular paperbound edition (clothbound, $120.00). For members outside the U.S.A., add $24.00 for shipping of your subscription. Members may also purchase single issues of THE ANNALS for $17.00 each (clothbound, $26.00). Student memberships are available for $53.00.

Subscriptions. THE ANNALS of The American Academy of Political and Social Science (ISSN 0002-7162) (J295) is published six times annually—in January, March, May, July, September, and November— by Sage Publications, 2455 Teller Road, Thousand Oaks, CA 91320. Telephone: (800) 818-SAGE (7243) and (805) 499-9774; FAX/Order line: (805) 499-0871; E-mail: journals@sagepub.com. Copyright © 2005 by The American Academy of Political and Social Science. Institutions may subscribe to THE ANNALS at the annual rate: $544.00 (clothbound, $615.00). Add $24.00 per year for subscriptions outside the U.S.A. Institutional rates for single issues: $96.00 each (clothbound, $108.00).

Periodicals postage paid at Thousand Oaks, California, and at additional mailing offices.

Single issues of THE ANNALS may be obtained by individuals who are not members of the Academy for $33.00 each (clothbound, $36.00). Single issues of THE ANNALS have proven to be excellent supplementary texts for classroom use. Direct inquiries regarding adoptions to THE ANNALS c/o Sage Publications (address below).

All correspondence concerning membership in the Academy, dues renewals, inquiries about membership status, and/or purchase of single issues of THE ANNALS should be sent to THE ANNALS c/o Sage Publications, 2455 Teller Road, Thousand Oaks, CA 91320. Telephone: (800) 818-SAGE (7243) and (805) 499-9774; FAX/Order line: (805) 499-0871. E-mail: journals@sagepub.com. *Please note that orders under $30 must be prepaid.* Sage affiliates in London and India will assist institutional subscribers abroad with regard to orders, claims, and inquiries for both subscriptions and single issues.

Printed on recycled, acid-free paper

THE ANNALS

© 2005 by The American Academy of Political and Social Science

Editorial Office: 3814 Walnut Street, Fels Institute for Government, University of Pennsylvania, Philadelphia, PA 19104-6197.

For information about membership° (individuals only) and subscriptions (institutions), address:
Sage Publications
2455 Teller Road
Thousand Oaks, CA 91320

Sage Production Staff: Joseph Riser and Esmeralda Hernandez

From India and South Asia,
write to:
SAGE PUBLICATIONS INDIA Pvt Ltd
B-42 Panchsheel Enclave, P.O. Box 4109
New Delhi 110 017
INDIA

From Europe, the Middle East,
and Africa, write to:
SAGE PUBLICATIONS LTD
1 Oliver's Yard, 55 City Road
London EC1Y 1SP
UNITED KINGDOM

°Please note that members of the Academy receive THE ANNALS with their membership.
International Standard Serial Number ISSN 0002-7162
International Standard Book Number ISBN 1-4129-1690-9 (Vol. 597, 2005 paper)
International Standard Book Number ISBN 1-4129-1689-5 (Vol. 597, 2005 cloth)
Manufactured in the United States of America. First printing, January 2005.

The articles appearing in *The Annals* are abstracted or indexed in Academic Abstracts, Academic Search, America: History and Life, Asia Pacific Database, Book Review Index, CAB Abstracts Database, Central Asia: Abstracts & Index, Communication Abstracts, Corporate ResourceNET, Criminal Justice Abstracts, Current Citations Express, Current Contents: Social & Behavioral Sciences, Documentation in Public Administration, e-JEL, EconLit, Expanded Academic Index, Guide to Social Science & Religion in Periodical Literature, Health Business FullTEXT, HealthSTAR FullTEXT, Historical Abstracts, International Bibliography of the Social Sciences, International Political Science Abstracts, ISI Basic Social Sciences Index, Journal of Economic Literature on CD, LEXIS-NEXIS, MasterFILE FullTEXT, Middle East: Abstracts & Index, North Africa: Abstracts & Index, PAIS International, Periodical Abstracts, Political Science Abstracts, Psychological Abstracts, PsycINFO, Sage Public Administration Abstracts, Social Science Source, Social Sciences Citation Index, Social Sciences Index Full Text, Social Services Abstracts, Social Work Abstracts, Sociological Abstracts, Southeast Asia: Abstracts & Index, Standard Periodical Directory (SPD), TOPICsearch, Wilson OmniFile V, and Wilson Social Sciences Index/Abstracts, and are available on microfilm from ProQuest, Ann Arbor, Michigan.

Information about membership rates, institutional subscriptions, and back issue prices may be found on the facing page.

Advertising. Current rates and specifications may be obtained by writing to *The Annals* Advertising and Promotion Manager at the Thousand Oaks office (address above).

Claims. Claims for undelivered copies must be made no later than six months following month of publication. The publisher will supply missing copies when losses have been sustained in transit and when the reserve stock will permit.

Change of Address. Six weeks' advance notice must be given when notifying of change of address to ensure proper identification. Please specify name of journal. POSTMASTER: Send address changes to: *The Annals* of The American Academy of Political and Social Science, c/o Sage Publications, 2455 Teller Road, Thousand Oaks, CA 91320.

THE ANNALS

OF THE AMERICAN ACADEMY OF POLITICAL AND SOCIAL SCIENCE

Volume 597   January 2005

IN THIS ISSUE:

Cultural Production in a Digital Age

Special Editor: ERIC KLINENBERG

FORTHCOMING

*The Rise of Regulatory Capitalism:
The Global Diffusion of a New Order*
Special Editors: DAVID LEVI-FAUR
and JACINT JORDANA
Volume 598, March 2005

Randomizing Place
Special Editor: ROBERT BORUCH
Volume 599, May 2005

*The Use and Usefulness of the Social Sciences:
Accomplishments, Disappointments, and Promise*
Special Editors: LAWRENCE SHERMAN
and ROBERT PEARSON
Volume 600, July 2005

INTRODUCTION

Cultural Production in a Digital Age

By
ERIC KLINENBERG
and
CLAUDIO BENZECRY

If you are like most contemporary American social scientists (in 2005), you are probably reading this volume of the *Annals* online, or you have downloaded it from a local network and printed this article from your personal computer. You would not have been able to find these pages in a digital library in 1995, or even in 2000, and so you would have traveled to the periodicals section of a university library to get them. If the journal was not there, you might have been able to borrow it from another institution, waiting days or weeks for it to arrive. The relatively slow pace of scholarly production means that this single delay would not likely have caused you much trouble. But when, upon receiving the text, you found citations to others that you needed for your research, and those articles were also unavailable in your library (or from its partners), then the problems began to mount. You adapted, learning to focus on journals stocked by your local institution rather than less accessible specialized literatures. Perhaps on occasion you left out relevant data because your deadline arrived before they did. Usually you just slowed down, and there is little reason

Eric Klinenberg is an assistant professor of sociology at New York University. His first book, Heat Wave: A Social Autopsy of Disaster in Chicago *(University of Chicago Press), won five scholarly book prizes and is currently being adapted for the screen and the stage. Klinenberg has published articles in journals including* Ethnography *and* Theory and Society, *and he writes often for magazines and newspapers such as* Le Monde Diplomatique, *the* Washington Post, *and the* London Review of Books. *His next book, on local media in a digital age, will be published by Henry Holt.*

Claudio Benzecry is a Ph.D. candidate at the Sociology Department of the New York University. He is also a member of the CECYP at the Fundación del Sur, Buenos Aires. His main interests are sociology of culture, sociology of intellectuals, and cultural studies and issues such as the relationship between literary practices, intellectual representations, and society in contemporary Argentina and the articulation between high art and popular culture in the Buenos Aires opera audience.

DOI: 10.1177/0002716204270420

ANNALS, *AAPSS*, 597, January 2005

to believe that scholarship suffered for it. Maybe the delays helped, giving you more time to research, reflect, and write.

But digital libraries and electronic communication networks can facilitate scholarly production. If, for example, you are interested in the theme of this volume, cultural production in a digital age, you can print these contributions; identify, link to, and download cited articles in other journals (and so on); search the network for academic, journalistic, and professional publications on similar themes; buy books (including texts you would never find in local bookstores); and assemble your own portable bibliography over the next few hours, all without leaving your seat. If your interest relates to a collaborative project, you can e-mail colleagues to keep them updated on your progress or provide direct links to useful articles (although you lose efficiency when you e-mail friends about unrelated matters in the process). When you begin writing and distributing your text via e-mail, colleagues and collaborators will use word processing software to insert edits, queries, and comments, returning the document to you electronically, and paving the way for an interactive intellectual exchange. The speed of communication facilitates collaboration in real time, but so does the standardization of formats, the ease of access to working files, the ability to record different iterations of the text, and the declining significance of distance made possible by digital networks.

We do not yet know whether technologies that reduce the barriers of time, space, and access help to advance social science or how they affect the outcome of intellectual work. But there is no question that digital technologies have changed the way scholars and academic institutions operate (Koku, Nazar, and Wellman 2001) and that the cultivation of novel research practices and the outcome of conflicts over the control, circulation, and application of advanced technologies in the university will shape the conditions of intellectual production. This volume of the *Annals* explores whether and how digital technologies and the actors who use and design them have altered cultural production more broadly, in fields ranging from journalism to gambling, social movements to marketing. We use an expansive concept of cultural production here since we are concerned with different kinds of symbolic, textual, and meaning-making activities. We include the news media, advertising, and emerging political cultures (particularly those generated by Web designers, net activists, and civic groups), as well as the traditional arts. The contributors work in different academic disciplines—sociology, anthropology, business management, and communications—and use a variety of theoretical and methodological approaches to assess recent changes in creative fields. But whether they analyze activists, media industries, or public policies, the articles in this volume cohere around a set of issues that are central to cultural producers, consumers, and citizens today. The authors disagree on some questions, such as whether, given the unequal access to advanced technologies (let alone more basic goods) within and among nations, it is appropriate to define the current period as a "digital age" (Norris 2001; Servon 2002; Zook 2005). Yet none use the concept to advance arguments for technological determinism. Rather, they share a guiding premise that social institutions, public policies, business organizations, and ordinary users adapt the products of software designers, engineers, and network architects to collectively, albeit contentiously, shape the conditions of cultural production.

Social scientists who rely on the Internet and other computer networks to conduct research know from firsthand experience that the most fundamental effects of digitalization on cultural production involve the restructuring of time, space, and place in daily work processes. This is not the place to document the numerous ways that digital technologies alter the spatial organization and temporal sequencing of creative labor. Because these themes have featured so prominently in previous publications (see especially Castells 1996, 2001), we chose not to make them the focus of this volume. Yet we must note that digital networks and the infrastructure systems that support them allow cultural producers to instantaneously transmit enormous amounts of information—audio, video, text, graphics, databases, and combinations of them all—across the globe, or simply across town. Those on the receiving end can add to or edit the contents, taking advantage of standardized formats and shared software to become coproducers (even when the original authors or copyright owners do not want them to), or they can quickly publish or broadcast the information, as media companies do with breaking news stories.

Digital Production

We are particularly interested in what happens to cultural products when they are crafted and distributed through digital channels (so, too, are major media companies and governments). Historically, the most influential new communications technologies have reduced the price of entry into a cultural field, creating openings for actors and organizations who were previously unable to get their work into the public. Today, for example, artists can easily alter and repackage digitally recorded music and video, sampling tunes or assembling images into new work, occasionally with high commercial or aesthetic value (as in DJ Danger Mouse's *The Grey Album*). Technologies such as SoundScan, which digitally tracks music sales figures so that commercial music companies can purchase market data in real time, allow big labels that can afford the service to increase efficiency, reduce opportunities for competitors (especially smaller, independent labels), and consolidate control over the field (McCourt and Rothenbuhler 1997; Anand and Peterson 2000). News companies can repurpose "content" (a term that is replacing "journalism" in some newsrooms) across platforms, adapting a single digital file to suit a newspaper article, Internet publication, or teleprompter script. This is a significant transformation (as Klinenberg argues in his article here) since it changes the meaning of cultural products and, in turn, the status of professional journalistic labor. In some companies, for example, reporters who are highly skilled at multimedia production (for on-screen television appearances and newspaper or Internet writing) have become more valuable employees, and they often get prime assignments because of their flexibility. Individual users can participate in the design of open-source software. But social scientists still know little about how producers in different fields use digital files in their creative processes.

Consumers can also repackage music and video into transferable files, as anyone who followed the news coverage of file sharing through software like Napster knows (McCourt and Burkart 2003). When the contents of electronic files are protected by copyrights, and the owners or producers object to outside manipulation of the work, innovative practices of digital cultural production can land someone in prison or in debt (as Siva Vaidhyanathan explains here). How nations and corporations define, control, and regulate this kind of activity is one of the major cultural and economic questions of our time, and collective interest in the issue has brought previously arcane debates over intellectual property law into the realm of popular culture as well as Congress and the courts (Lessig 2004; Vaidhyanathan 2001, 2004).

The Political Economy of New Media

There are high stakes in these and other disputes over the use of digital systems in cultural industries, so it is important to explore the relationship between technological development and the political economy of contemporary media, marketing, and entertainment fields. In some fields, such as video gaming, edutainment (as Mizuko Ito shows here), and casino gambling, designers have used digital devices to dramatically enhance the experience of playing, resulting in increased popularity and soaring profits. The short-term benefits for users can be offset by long-term costs, particularly (as Natasha Schull illustrates in her article) for gamblers, whose absorbing interactions with machines typically result in personal financial loss. In advertising, entertainment and retail companies are collaborating to blend interactive shopping opportunities with television and other cultural programming, taking product placement to new levels by giving viewers a chance to click and purchase clothing, furniture, and other products displayed on screen. Marketing firms are also using digital technologies to assemble detailed databases about consumers at the individual and group levels and to target campaigns based on information gathered through their surveillance. Surprisingly (as Joseph Turow shows here), consumers are often willing to exchange personal information for specialized services and elite status with certain companies, as with airline frequent flier programs or grocery and drug store discount cards.

New communication technologies create both threats and opportunities for major media corporations. Digital cable, for example, provides consumers access to hundreds of television channels, undermining the dominant position of traditional networks; and digital recording devices allow viewers to bypass commercials, potentially reducing the value of advertising and thereby the profits of stations. But the markets tell another story. As their stock prices and ad revenues show, big networks have become more valuable to investors and advertisers because established brands command attention in fields crowded by small players. Major media companies exploit digital technologies to expand their presence into different domains (they call this "extending the brand"), asserting themselves (their products as well as their logos) online, in print, over the airwaves, and through cable. Conglomerates have invested heavily in developing synergistic rela-tionships between their various media holdings, integrating their production pro-cesses into "convergence" systems that yield content for different outlets, "cross-promoting" programs in different media, and establishing lines of vertical and hori-zontal integration in production and distribution (Klinenberg 2000). Digitization facilitates these processes (Boczkowski 2004).

Historically, the most influential new communications technologies have reduced the price of entry into a cultural field, creating openings for actors . . . who were previously unable to get their work into the public.

In addition to the protections from copyright law, recent regulatory changes driven by the proliferation of new technologies in the media field have facilitated the growth of large conglomerates. Operating with the explicit premise that digital outlets (especially the Internet and cable) give consumers more choices than ever, the Federal Communications Commission raised the proportion of the national market that television companies could reach, cut restrictions on cross-ownership (for print and broadcast) in local markets, and gave away approximately $70 billion of digital spectrum to major media companies without significant public debate (Aufderheide 1999; Baker 2002; McChesney 2004). The period in which digital media developed has been marked by consolidation and concentration of owner-ship, not openness. This is true not only in television and radio but also on the Internet. Although users have virtually unlimited options for viewing information, audience ratings show that in the United States the most popular online news sources are Web sites from the largest media companies, including CNN, MSNBC, CBS, and *The New York Times*. (Even these sites rely heavily on the same wire services and photo agencies, so their stories are often identical.) According to a recent survey by Jupiter Media Metrix, five sites account for 50 percent of user time online. Thirty years ago, media scholar Ben Bagdikian warned about the dan-gers of a "media monopoly" in the United States because roughly fifty corporations controlled the industry. Today, according to the seventh edition of his classic book, the U.S. market is dominated by five conglomerates (Bagdikian 2004).

Cultural Politics Online

Yet digital technologies and the Internet have also allowed new voices to enter the media, in journalism as well as entertainment. Blogging, for example, has become a popular and increasingly influential form of online cultural production—so much so that in 2004, presidential candidates and other public figures began publishing their own blogs to gain publicity and attention online. Most bloggers are independent actors, usually journalists, techies, professors, and young people with free time, who post their personal experiences or daily observations online. Some technology experts and cultural critics have gained cult followings for their daily postings, and a few journalists have gained large readerships (especially among other journalists) by posting links to news stories and commentary about political issues on their blogs. Occasionally bloggers force reporters and political officials to address an issue that they had initially neglected. Most famously, bloggers repeatedly called attention to Trent Lott's inflammatory remarks about race, ultimately turning the issue into a major news story and forcing Lott to resign as the Senate majority leader. With a few notable exceptions, however, bloggers have not added much primary reporting to the journalistic field. (This may change as blogging evolves. In the summer of 2004, for example, U.S. political parties gave some bloggers press passes for their national conventions.) They offer opinion and, in some cases, insightful analysis of the issues that concern them (the media, technology, select political issues), and the most serious bloggers have emerged as important watchdogs of media and technology companies. But blogging is not a substitute for journalism, and there are real hazards in treating them that way. According to Alex Jones (2004), director of Harvard's Shorenstein Center for the Press, Politics, and Public Policy, "There is already talk of bloggers who would consider publishing items for cash and commercial blogs that tout products. Blogging is especially amenable to introducing negative information into the news stream and for circulating rumors as fact. Blogging's fact-checking apparatus is just the built-in truth squad of those who read the blog and howl loudly if they wish to dispute some assertion. It is, in a sense, a place where everyone has his own truth." While bloggers have enriched the cultural content of the Web, there is little reason to believe they will ever provide an adequate alternative to mainstream news.

Citizens, community groups, activists, political parties, and governments have also used the Internet to expand their reach, coordinate communication, and assert their presence in the political process. Political candidates established an online presence as early as the 1996 presidential campaigns (Klinenberg and Perrin 2000), and by 2004 the Internet had become one of the most important resources for fund-raising, advertising, and organizing. Professional Web design firms specializing in political sites have driven this process, not only helping candidates and parties post content but also (as Phil Howard's essay here shows) generating data about visitors. National, state, and local governments also use the Web to disseminate information, blending public relations projects that promote their programs with reports that citizens can use to learn about local conditions (such as crime rates, pollution levels, and school systems) or engage in political action. Many towns and neighborhood districts have set up electronic bulletin boards and discussion groups to help residents participate in civil society. Some cities use the Internet to interact directly with citizens, too. A recent national survey of local officials conducted by the Pew Internet and American Life Project found that 61 percent used e-mail "to communicate with citizens at least weekly," 56 percent claimed that their use of e-mail has "improved their relations with community groups," and 54 percent said the Internet has "brought them into contact with citizens from whom they had not heard before." Still, 38 percent believe that "community listservs and email cannot support public discussion of complex issues," and local officials are considerably more likely to use phone calls, letters, and meetings to communicate with their constituents. Federal officials, including congressional representatives, feel overwhelmed by e-mails and "often dismiss emails as not very meaningful" (Larsen and Rainie 2002). The early enthusiasm for the Internet as a source for new kinds of democratic interactions between citizens and officials has not only diminished in the United States. As Balazs Vedres, Laszlo Bruszt, and David Stark show here in their study of Eastern European civil society Web sites, even voluntary organizations working to advance democratic projects usually failed to use the Internet as a tool for participatory democracy.

Activist groups have developed more innovative and democratic uses of the Internet and digital networks. By the mid-1990s, as Castells explained in *The Power of Identity* (1997), dissident political actors of all persuasions (from the Zapatistas in Mexico to the right-wing militias in the United States, the anarchists in Europe to the Falun Gong in China) were adapting the network to break down communications barriers that had previously limited their reach. By the late 1990s and early 2000s (as Jeff Juris argues here), the network logic of social movements expressed itself in their public demonstrations as well as their electronic exchanges. The so-called antiglobalization protests, which in fact are not opposed to globalization but to the neoliberal versions of it, integrated a heterogeneous set of activists from throughout the world and yet were often organized without clear hierarchies or authority structures. The movement has been animated by the creativity and spontaneity made possible by horizontal networks and by participants' expertise in performing for and working with the media. Moreover, activists have digital photography, video, and text messaging to make their own media during protests, constructing temporary electronic communications centers to ensure that their experiences and perspective are disseminated online in real time, even before news outlets generate their own reports. Digital cultural production and novel forms of political expression merge whenever the network moves into action.

Digital Hubs

If international social movements reveal the ways digital networks enable the global dispersion of creative activity, innovative technology firms and cultural producers express the opposite tendency, clustering in small places such as Silicon Valley and (as Gina Neff shows here) Silicon Alley of New York City. Ironically, the technology workers whose products help other actors collaborate from a distance and the creative laborers whose work circulates through electronic networks reap special benefits from physical proximity to their colleagues and competitors. As in the film, music, and publishing industries, technology companies flourish in geographically concentrated "milieux of innovation" (Castells and Hall 1994), which facilitate face-to-face interactions between coworkers and blur the lines between social and professional spheres in ways that (managers believe) increase creative productivity. It is important to identify the prevalence of spatial clustering in certain fields of cultural production since the notion that advanced communications technologies have rendered place irrelevant is one of the leading popular myths of the digital age. Urban scholars such as Saskia Sassen (1991) and AnnaLee Saxenian (1994) have shown that banks, law firms, and other advanced service industries choose to cluster in particular cities not only because proximity to other business services yields economic advantages but also because executives and valuable employees (and potential employees) have strong lifestyle preferences for certain places. Recently, the geographer Alan Scott (1999) has documented similar trends in fields of cultural production, too; and in the spirit of Howard Becker's *Art Worlds* (1982), ethnographers are now beginning to explore the internal conditions of digital creativity clusters through observational research.

The Sociology of Cultural Production

In several fields, empirical research projects designed to assess the role of new technologies in cultural production are helping social scientists evaluate and revise grand theoretical statements about "the network society," "e-topias," or "digital ontology." As early as the 1980s, scholars argued that digital communications systems have the transformative power of previous epoch-defining technologies, with capacity to alter symbolic production (Negroponte 1995), democratic politics (Sunstein 2001), even constructions of the self (Castells 1996). By 2000, when advanced technologies had diffused broadly, it was not unusual to read statements such as this one, from Manuel Castells (2001, 1): "The Internet is the fabric of our lives. If information technology is the present-day equivalent of electricity in the industrial era, in our age the Internet could be likened to both the electrical grid and the electric engine because of its ability to distribute the power of information throughout the entire realm of human activity. . . . The Internet is the technological basis for the organizational form of the Information Age: the network." But major disagreements remain over the extent, the pace, and the character of cultural changes caused by digital technologies; and we can identify three organizing schools—*the digital revolutionaries, the cyber-skeptics*, and *the cultural evolutionists*—in the current literature on cultural production in a digital age.

Digital revolutionaries argue that new technologies have generated deep structural changes in the fields of cultural production. The most enthusiastic revolutionaries emphasize the utopian and libertarian features of decentralized and deregulated informational networks. Nicholas Negroponte (1995) was most concerned with the material transformation and distribution of cultural objects, shifting from tangible "atoms" to digital "bits." On one hand, he argued, digitization moves the source of a cultural object's value away from the channel of distribution and more squarely into the object itself. On the other hand, historically established distinctions between aesthetic genres lose their significance when symbolic objects are repackaged into digital codes. Movies, for example, "become just a special case of data broadcast" (p. 49). In a similar vein, William Mitchell (1999) and Donna Haraway (1991) have argued that digital communications technologies blur conventional divisions that long organized cultural life, blending the material and immaterial, organic and artificial, actual and virtual, and breaking down leisure, labor, and family time in ways that alter the rhythms of daily life. Digital revolutionaries need not be cyber-celebrationists or utopians. Castells (1998), for example, argued that new communications technologies have facilitated widespread cultural and political change. Yet he also expressed serious concerns about emerging and ongoing inequities in the network society.

---

*[W]e can identify three organizing schools—
the digital revolutionaries, the cyber-skeptics,
and the cultural evolutionists—in the current
literature on cultural production in a
digital age.*

Cyber-skeptics do not deny that digital technologies have helped change cultural production, but they see digitization as a mechanism through which culture industries advance larger projects, thereby threatening the integrity of creative fields or the relative autonomy of artists and intellectuals. Moreover, they believe that technology is not a primary causal force of change as much as it is an effect of investments driven by economic, political, or cultural interests. Skepticism and anxiety are common during periods when new technologies enter the matrix of cultural production. They flourished in the nineteenth century with the rise of dime novels in the United States and serials in England (Williams 1958; Starr 2004), in most nations with the emergence of commercial television (Hoggart 1957), TV journalism (Hallin 1992), and commercial fashion (Ewen 1988). Many critics of technological "advances" in cultural production work in the tradition of the Frank-

furt School (Adorno and Horkheimer 1976; Adorno 1985; Benjamin 1968), apply-
ing long-standing concerns about the commodification of aesthetics, the homogenization of popular culture, or the loss of authentic expression to the digital age.
Contemporary critics have added another layer of concern. Inspired by Foucault's
(1977) analysis of surveillance and the capillary forms of micro-power or control,
scholars such as Joseph Turow and Phil Howard (in this volume) are beginning to
show how software and interactive digital technologies help entertainers, news
companies, marketers, and political parties collect data from and about their audience, often with their consent.

Other cyber-skeptics are inspired by Pierre Bourdieu's (1993, 1996) analysis of
the "fields of cultural production," expressing concerns over the ways "intrusions"
by actors (institutions and individuals) in the economic or political fields alter conditions inside fields of literature, science, journalism, and art (see especially issue
number 134 of *Actes de la Recherche en Sciences Sociales*, which is dedicated to
digital technologies in the workplace). Commercial culture industries, these scholars argue, often use new technologies to shift control over work conditions from
those with specialized craft skills to those with managerial or technical expertise
(Saint Laurent 2000; Klinenberg 2000), thereby weakening the position and
further compromising the autonomy of cultural producers.

Cultural evolutionists share elements of Bourdieu's approach, but they emphasize the slow pace of organizational and institutional change between periods of
technological development, arguing that deeply embedded practices, routines,
and beliefs structure the incorporation of new materials into any production process. Studies of cultural production have long been a hallmark of American and
European sociology. But in the 1970s, scholars such as Paul Hirsch (1972), Richard
Peterson (1976), Peterson and David Berger (1975), and Charles Kadushin (1976)
developed an approach that closed the gap between cultural, organizational, and
occupational sociology, analyzing symbolic production through the concepts and
questions that previously guided industrial research.

While the Frankfurt School critics decried the commodification of culture, a
growing number of American sociologists studied creative industries just as they
would car manufacturing, asking about the institutional arrangements that stabi-
lize markets, define an organizational field, structure career opportunities, and
fine-tune the product. Creativity, regardless of the field, is constrained or enabled
by the conditions of production, and cultural sociologists have studied the internal
workings of diverse industries including architecture (Sarfatti-Larson 1993), country music (Peterson 1976), the news (Tuchman 1978; Fishman 1980; Gans 1979),
commercial television (Gitlin 1981), cuisine (Fine 1992), and fashion design
(Crane 1997). These industries change, but not instantly, not predictably, and not
simply because engineers introduce a new technology to the labor process. Cultural fields, and the economic, creative, and organizations forces that constitute
them, determine the uses of new technologies just as much as new technologies
shape cultural objects. In a recent review essay, Richard Peterson and N. Anand
(2004) proposed that there are six key facets of the cultural production process:

technology, law and regulation, industry structure, organizational structure, occupational careers, and the market. Citing the printing press, the pianoforte (which allowed Beethoven to express his skills), and music recording devices, the authors acknowledge that "changes in communication technology profoundly destabilize and create new opportunities in art and culture." Yet even these powerful technologies were filtered through the other five facets of cultural production, just as the Internet is today. The implication of this model is that social scientists should be cautious before directly attributing change in the culture industries to digital devices. New communications technologies offer "affordances" (to use Boczkowski's [2004] term) that enable new production practices and processes, but a broad set of contextual features determine how cultural industries change.

The conceptual toolbox developed through the sociology of cultural production provides a useful set of analytic resources for studying the social conditions that shape creative industries. Yet scholars have criticized the conventional approach of American cultural sociology for letting a focus on what is social in a cultural product displace attention to its meanings and social uses, including the ways it inspires new kinds of expression (see Zolberg 1990; Halle 1993; Heinich 2002; Mukerji and Schudson 1991); for treating cultural fields as relatively autonomous spheres, thereby marginalizing questions about power, exploitation, and the political economy of culture industries (Hesmondhalgh 2002); for failing to explain periods of revolutionary change within cultural fields; and for refusing to acknowledge the distinctive character of cultural production as a creative process, one that differs sharply from production of other commercial goods. "In practice," Peterson and Anand (2004, 326-27) explained, "the production perspective denies that there is something essentially unique about fine art, constitutional law, or theology. Rather, it emphasizes that these high-status fields can be studied like other symbol-producing institutions."

Yet the sociology of culture approach can be productively joined to other forms of analysis. In the study of digitalization, for example, we need to understand what motivated the creation and adaption of new technologies for cultural production (see Galloway in this volume), what affordances the new products offer (see Boczkowski and Ferris, Howard, Klinenberg, and Turow in this volume), and what ways consumers and producers make meaning through them (see Ito and Schull in this volume). As the uses of digital technologies blur traditional distinctions between producers and consumers, social scientists need to move the sites of their research to new arenas and to deepen understanding of the ways circulation of cultural objects (or now, electronic files) contributes to the production process. The questions of how people use new technologies for cultural work and what role these practices play in daily life are increasingly important to the study of creativity in action. So too are questions about the balance of power and control in cultural fields, which are dominated by a small number of commercial conglomerates whose reach extends nearly as far as the network itself.

The emerging conflict between states, corporations, and creative actors who aim to harness the power of digital technologies in different ways promises to be one of the most important policy disputes of the twenty-first century. The essays assembled here can only assess the embryonic stages of digitization in cultural production, but the history of other communications technologies shows that the outcome of early struggles over their use, regulation, and circulation can set the path for future development (Starr 2004). This volume of the *Annals* could not be more timely.

References

Adorno, Theodor W. 1985. On the fetish character in music and the regression of listening. In *The essential Frankfurt reader*, ed. A. Arato and Eike Gebhardt, 270-99. New York: Continuum Books.

Adorno, T. W., and Max Horkheimer. 1976. *Dialectic of enlightenment*. New York: Continuum Books.

Anand, N., and Richard Peterson. 2000. When market information constitutes fields: Sensemaking of markets in the commercial music industry. *Organization Science* 11 (3): 270-84.

Aufderheide, Patricia. 1999. *Communications policy and the public interest: The case of the 1996 telecommunications act*. New York: Guilford.

Bagdikian, Ben. 2004. *The media monopoly*. 7th ed. Boston: Beacon.

Baker, C. Edwin. 2002. *Media, markets, and democracy*. New York: Cambridge University Press.

Becker, Howard. 1982. *Art worlds*. Berkeley: University of California Press.

Benjamin, Walter. 1968. The work of art in the age of mechanical reproduction. In *Illuminations: Essays and reflections*, ed. Hannah Arendt, 217-51. New York: Schocken Books.

Boczkowski, Pablo. 2004. *Digitizing the news: Innovation in online newspapers*. Cambridge, MA: MIT Press.

Bourdieu, Pierre. 1993. *The field of cultural production*. New York: Columbia University Press.

———. 1996. *Rules of art: Structure and genesis of the literary field*. Stanford, CA: Stanford University Press.

Castells, Manuel. 1996. *The rise of the network society*. Oxford, UK: Blackwell.

———. 1997. *The power of identity*. Oxford, UK: Blackwell.

———. 1998. *The end of millennium*. Oxford, UK: Blackwell.

———. 2001. *The Internet galaxy: Reflections on the Internet, business, and society*. Oxford: Oxford University Press.

Castells, Manuel, and Peter Hall. 1994. *Technopoles of the world: The making of twenty-first century industrial complexes*. London: Routledge.

Crane, Diane. 1997. Globalization, organizational size and innovation in the French luxury fashion industry: Production of culture theory revisited. *Poetics* 24 (3): 393-414.

Ewen, Stuart. 1988. *All consuming images*. New York: Basic Books.

Fine, Gary Alan. 1992. The culture of production: Aesthetic choices and constraints in culinary work. *American Journal of Sociology* 97:1286-94.

Fishman, Mark. 1980. *Manufacturing the news*. Austin: University of Texas Press.

Foucault, Michel. 1977. *Discipline and punish*. New York: Vintage Books.

Gans, Herbert. 1979. *Deciding what's news: A study of CBS Evening News, NBC Nightly News, Newsweek, and Time*. New York: Pantheon.

Gitlin, Todd. 1981. *The whole world is watching: Mass media in the making and unmaking of the left*. Berkeley: University of California Press.

Halle, David. 1993. *Inside culture*. Chicago: University of Chicago Press.

Hallin, Daniel C. 1992. The passing of "high modernism" of American journalism. *Journal of Communication* 42 (3): 14-25.

Haraway, Donna. 1991. *Simians, cyborgs and women*. New York: Routledge.

Heinich, Nathalie. 2002. *La Sociologie de l'art*. Paris: Découverte.

Hesmondhalgh, David. 2002. *The cultural industries*. London: Sage.

Hirsch, Paul. 1972. Processing fads and fashions. *American Journal of Sociology* 77 (4): 639-59.

Hoggart, Richard. 1957. *The uses of literacy*. London: Chatto and Windus.

Jones, Alex. 2004. Bloggers are the sizzle; not the steak. *Los Angeles Times*, July 20.

Kadushin, Charles. 1976. Networks and circles in the production of culture. *American Behavioral Scientist* 19:769-84.

Klinenberg, Eric. 2000. Information et Production Numerique. *Actes de la Recherche en Sciences Sociales* 134:66-75.

Klinenberg, Eric, and Andrew Perrin. 2000. Symbolic politics in the information age. *Information, Communication and Society* 3 (1): 17-38.

Koku, Emmanuel, Nancy Nazar, and Barry Wellman. 2001. Netting scholars: Online and offline. *American Behavioral Scientist* 44 (10): 1752-74.

Larsen, Elena, and Lee Rainie. 2002. *Digital town hall: How local officials use the Internet and the civic benefits they cite from dealing with constituents online.* Washington, DC: Pew Internet and American Life Project.

Lessig, Lawrence. 2004. *Free culture: How big media uses technology and the law to lock down culture and control creativity.* New York: Penguin.

McChesney, Robert. 2004. *The problem of the media: U.S. communications politics in the 21st century.* New York: Monthly Review Press.

McCourt, Tom, and Patrick Burkart. 2003. When creators, corporations, and consumers collide: Napster and the development of on-line music distribution. *Media, Culture, and Society* 25 (3): 333-50.

McCourt, Tom, and Eric Rothenbuhler. 1997. SoundScan and the consolidation of control in the popular music industry. *Media, Culture, and Society* 19:201-18.

Mitchell, William. 1999. *E-topia.* Cambridge, MA: MIT Press.

Mukerji, Chandra, and Michael Schudson, eds. 1991. *Rethinking popular culture.* Berkeley: University of California Press.

Negroponte, Nicholas. 1995. *Being digital.* New York: Vintage Books.

Norris, Pipa. 2001. *Digital divide: Civic engagement, information poverty, and the Internet worldwide.* New York: Cambridge University Press.

Peterson, Richard. 1976. *The production of culture.* Thousand Oaks, CA: Sage.

Peterson, Richard, and N. Anand. 2004. The production of culture perspective. *Annual Review of Sociology* 30:311-44.

Peterson, Richard, and David Berger. 1975. Cycles in symbol production. *American Sociological Review* 40 (1): 158-73.

Saint Laurent, Anne-France, de. 2000. Qui fait quoi? Pratiques de l'informatique et résistance des métiers dans un quotidien regional. *Actes de la Recherche en Sciences Sociales* 134:56-61.

Sarfatti-Larson, Magali. 1993. *Behind the postmodern façade: Architectural change in late twentieth-century America.* Berkeley: University of California Press.

Sassen, Saskia. 1991. *The global city: New York, London, Tokyo.* Princeton, NJ: Princeton University Press.

Saxenian, AnnaLee. 1994. *Regional advantage: Culture and competition in Silicon Valley and Route 128.* Cambridge, MA: Harvard University Press.

Scott, Alan. 1999. The US recorded music industry: On the relation between organization, location and creativity in the cultural industry. *Environmental Planning* 31 (11): 1965-84.

Servon, Lisa. 2002. *Bridging the digital divide: Technology, community, and public policy.* Oxford, UK: Blackwell

Sunstein, Cass. 2001. *Republic.com.* Princeton, NJ: Princeton University Press.

Starr, Paul. 2004. *The creation of the media: Political origins of modern communications.* New York: Basic Books.

Tuchman, Gaye. 1978. *Making news: A study in the construction of reality.* New York: Free Press.

Vaidhyanathan, Siva. 2001. *Copyrights and copywrongs: The rise of intellectual property and how it threatens creativity.* New York: New York University Press.

———. 2004. *The anarchist in the library: How the clash between freedom and control is hacking the real world and crashing the system.* New York: Basic Books.

Williams, Raymond. 1958. *Culture and society, 1780-1950.* New York: Columbia University Press.

Zolberg, Vera. 1990. *Constructing a sociology of the arts.* Cambridge: Cambridge University Press.

Zook, Matthew. 2005. *The geography of the Internet industry.* Oxford, UK: Blackwell.

Global Networks and the Effects on Culture

By

ALEXANDER R. GALLOWAY

This analysis aims to derive general principles for understanding the information age through an examination of the global computer networks that facilitate it. Computer networks are created via shared technical standards called protocols. These protocols exhibit several key characteristics, including openness, flexibility, robustness, and voluntary adoption. While computer networks such as the Internet were originally invented to avoid specific social and political threats during the height of the cold war, today networks suffer from a host of new vulnerabilities. Computer viruses provide a case study for understanding these new vulnerabilities and the future political challenges posed by networks of all kinds.

Keywords: network; Internet; protocol; technical standards; computer virus

In recent years, social scientists of all stripes have struggled to come to terms with digital media and the distributed computer networks facilitated by them. It appears that few sectors of culture have survived this dramatic historical shift unscathed. Yet much contemporary research begins from the assumption, incorrect in my mind, that the "information society" is an adequate stand-in for the information machines that power it (Castells 1996; Lessig 2001), and thus it is possible for one to study the former while skipping the latter. At the same time, those who *do* know how information machines work (computer scientists and electrical engineers, mostly) spend little time ruminating on the larger cultural implications of such machines (Stevens 1994; Hall 2000). This article is an attempt to reverse this trend. Indeed, to understand cultural production in the digital age, one must have a firm grasp of both the digital and cultural spheres. Otherwise, one risks conclud-

Alexander R. Galloway received his Ph.D. from Duke University and is currently an assistant professor of media ecology at New York University. His first book, Protocol: How Control Exists after Decentralization, *is published by MIT Press.*

DOI: 10.1177/0002716204270066

ing things about culture that are based in misunderstandings of technological facts. Let me start, then, with an overview of some of the relevant historical transformations that have taken place in the digital age.

The Internet Protocols

The Internet is a global distributed computer network, rooted in the American academic and military culture of the 1950s and 1960s. In the late 1950s, in response to the Soviet Sputnik launch and other fears connected to the cold war, Paul Baran at the Rand Corporation created a computer network that was independent of centralized command and control and thus able to withstand a nuclear attack that targeted centralized hubs. American anxiety over Soviet technological advancement was very real after the Sputnik launches of the late 1950s. "The launching of the sputniks told us," wrote John Dunning for *The New York Times Magazine* in 1957, "that a great despotism is now armed with rockets of enormous thrust, and guidance systems that could deliver a hydrogen warhead of one or more megatons to any spot in the United States" (see also Denning 1990, 19). So in August 1964, Baran published an eleven-volume memorandum for the Rand Corporation outlining his research, documents that "were primarily written on airplanes in the 1960 to 1962 era," he recounts (Baran 1999). Katie Hafner and Matthew Lyon (1996) dispute the purely militaristic origins of the Internet, arguing instead that the Internet derived from the altruistic concerns of a few academics rather than the strategic interests of the Department of Defense. Yet they equivocate, writing on one hand that "the project had embodied the most peaceful intentions—to link computers at scientific laboratories across the country so that researchers might share computer resources. . . . The ARPAnet and its progeny, the Internet, had nothing to do with supporting or surviving war—never did" (p. 10); while on the other hand, they admit that Baran "developed an interest in the survivability of communications systems under nuclear attack" (p. 54).

Baran's network was based on a technology called "packet-switching" that allows messages to break themselves apart into small fragments. The term was coined not by Baran but by British scientist Donald Davies who, unaware of Baran's work, also invented a system for sending small packets of information over a distributed network. Both scientists are credited with the discovery; however, because of Baran's proximity to the newly emerging Advanced Research Projects Agency (ARPA) network, which would be the first to use Baran's ideas, Davies's historical influence has diminished. In packet-switching, each fragment, or packet, is able to find its own way to its destination. Once there, the packets reassemble to create the original message. In 1969, ARPA at the U.S. Department of Defense started the ARPAnet, the first network to use Baran's packet-switching technology. The ARPAnet allowed academics to share resources and transfer files. In its early years, the ARPAnet (later renamed DARPAnet) existed unnoticed by the outside world, with only a few hundred participating computers, or "hosts." All addressing for this network was maintained by a single machine located at the Stanford

Research Institute in Menlo Park, California. By 1984, the network had grown larger. Paul Mockapetris invented a new addressing scheme, this one decentralized, called the Domain Name System (DNS). The computers had changed also. By the late 1970s and early 1980s, personal computers were coming to market and appearing in homes and offices. In 1977, researchers at Berkeley released the highly influential "BSD" (Berkeley Software Distribution) flavor of the UNIX operating system, which was available to other institutions at virtually no cost. With the help of BSD, UNIX would become the most important computer operating system of the 1980s.

In the early 1980s, the suite of protocols known as TCP/IP (Transmission Control Protocol/Internet Protocol) was also developed and included with most UNIX servers. TCP/IP allowed for cheap, ubiquitous connectivity. In 1988, the Defense Department transferred control of the central "backbone" of the Internet over to the National Science Foundation, which in turn transferred control to commercial telecommunications interests in 1995. In that year, there were 24 million Internet users. Today, the Internet is a global distributed network connecting about a billion people around the world.

At the core of networked computing is the concept of *protocol*. A computer protocol is a set of recommendations and rules that outline specific technical standards. The protocols that govern much of the Internet are contained in what are called RFC (Request for Comments) documents. The expression derives from a memorandum titled "Host Software" sent by Steve Crocker on April 7, 1969, which is known today as RFC 1. Called "the primary documentation of the Internet" (Loshin 2000, xiv), these technical memoranda detail the vast majority of standards and protocols in use on the Internet today. The RFCs are published by the Internet Engineering Task Force (IETF). They are freely available and used predominantly by engineers who wish to build hardware or software that meets common specifications. The IETF is affiliated with the Internet Society (ISOC), an altruistic, technocratic organization that wishes "to assure the open development, evolution and use of the Internet for the benefit of all people throughout the world" (ISOC 2004). Other protocols are developed and maintained by other organizations. For example, many of the protocols used on the World Wide Web (a network within the Internet) are governed by the World Wide Web Consortium (W3C). This international consortium was created in October 1994 to develop common protocols such as Hypertext Markup Language (HTML) and Cascading Style Sheets. Scores of other protocols have been created for a variety of other purposes by many different professional societies and organizations.

Protocol is not a new word. Prior to its usage in computing, protocol referred to any type of correct or proper behavior within a specific system of conventions. It is an important concept in the area of social etiquette as well as in the fields of diplomacy and international relations. Etymologically it refers to a flyleaf glued to the beginning of a document, but in familiar usage the word came to mean any introductory paper summarizing the key points of a diplomatic agreement or treaty.

With the advent of digital computing, however, the term has taken on a slightly different meaning. Now, protocols refer specifically to standards governing the implementation of specific technologies. Like their diplomatic predecessors, computer protocols establish the essential points necessary to enact an agreed-upon standard of action. Like their diplomatic predecessors, computer protocols are vetted out between negotiating parties and then materialized in the real world by large populations of participants (in one case citizens and in the other computer users). Yet instead of governing social or political practices as did their diplomatic predecessors, computer protocols govern how specific *technologies* are agreed to, adopted, implemented, and ultimately used by people around the world. What was once a question of consideration and sense is now a question of logic and physics.

To help understand the concept of computer protocols, consider the analogy of the highway system. Many different combinations of roads are available to a person driving from point A to point B. However, en route one is compelled to stop at red lights, stay between the white lines, follow a reasonably direct path, and so on. These conventional rules that govern the set of possible behavior patterns within a heterogeneous system are what computer scientists call protocol. Thus, protocol is a technique for achieving voluntary regulation within a contingent environment.

These regulations always operate at the level of coding—they encode packets of information so they may be transported; they code documents so they may be effectively parsed; they code communication so local devices may effectively communicate with foreign devices. Protocols are highly formal; that is, they encapsulate information inside a technically defined wrapper, while remaining relatively indifferent to the content of information contained within. Viewed as a whole, protocol is a distributed management system that allows control to exist within a heterogeneous material milieu.

Unique Characteristics of the Internet Protocols

In this day and age, technical protocols and standards are established by a self-selected oligarchy of scientists consisting largely of electrical engineers and computer specialists. Composed of a patchwork of many professional bodies, working groups, committees, and subcommittees, this technocratic elite toils away, mostly voluntarily, in an effort to hammer out solutions to advancements in technology. Many of these scientists are university professors. Most all of them either work in industry or have some connection to it. Membership in this technocratic ruling class is open. "Anyone with something to contribute could come to the party" (Feinler 1999), wrote one early participant. But, to be sure, because of the technical sophistication needed to participate, this loose consortium of decision makers tends to fall into a relatively homogeneous social class: highly educated, altruistic, liberal-minded science professionals from modernized societies around the globe. And sometimes not so far around the globe. Of the twenty-five or so original protocol pioneers, three of them—Vint Cerf, Jon Postel, and Steve Crocker—came from a single high school in Los Angeles's San Fernando Valley (Cerf 1988). Furthermore, during his long tenure as RFC editor, Postel was the single gatekeeper through whom all protocol RFCs passed before they could be published. Hafner and Lyon (1996, 145) describe this group as "an ad-hocracy of intensely creative, sleep-deprived, idiosyncratic, well-meaning computer geniuses" (see also Malkin 1992).

There are few outsiders in this community. Here, the specialists run the show. To put it another way, while the Internet is used daily by vast swaths of diverse communities, the standards makers at the heart of this technology are a small entrenched group of techno-elite peers. The reasons for this are largely practical. "Most users are not interested in the details of Internet protocols," Cerf (personal communication 2002) observes. "They just want the system to work." Or as former IETF Chair Fred Baker (personal communication 2002) reminds us, "The average user doesn't write code. . . . If their needs are met, they don't especially care how they were met."

To keep the system working, the protocol designers built into the system several key characteristics. Inspired by Baran's original vision, the Internet protocols are designed to accommodate massive *contingency*. This characteristic is illustrated best by the TCP. TCP makes communication on the Web notably reliable: information is monitored during transport and is re-sent if lost or corrupted. The robust quality of these networks is achieved by following a general principle: "be conservative in what you do, be liberal in what you accept from others" (Postel 1981). This means that TCP hosts should "liberally" accept as much information as possible from other, foreign devices. But if any of the information is corrupted, the host, acting "conservatively," will delete the information and request a fresh copy be re-sent. As the RFC notes, the goal of TCP is "robustness in the presence of communication unreliability and availability in the presence of congestion" (ibid.). This is known in the standards community as the "robustness principle."

It is worth looking at a single standards body in detail, one that illustrates well the general characteristics I wish to highlight in the standards community at large. ANSI, the American National Standards Institute, is responsible for aggregating and coordinating the standards creation process in the United States. While it does not create any standards itself (Internet protocols or otherwise), it is a conduit for federally accredited organizations in the field that are developing technical standards. The accredited standards developers must follow certain rules designed to keep the process open and equitable for all interested parties. ANSI then verifies that the rules have been followed by the developing organization before the proposed standard is adopted. ANSI is also responsible for articulating a national standards strategy for the United States. This strategy helps ANSI advocate in the international arena on behalf of U.S. interests. ANSI is the only organization that can approve standards as American national standards.

Many of ANSI's rules for maintaining integrity and quality in the standards development process revolve around principles of openness and transparency. For this reason, they are a good case study for understanding the unique characteristics of today's network standards. ANSI writes that

- Decisions are reached through *consensus* among those affected.
- Participation is *open* to all affected interests.

- The process is *transparent*—information on the process and progress is directly available.
- The process is *flexible*, allowing the use of different methodologies to meet the needs of different technology and product sectors. (ANSI 2004)

Besides being consensus-driven, open, transparent, and flexible, ANSI standards are also voluntary, which means that no one is bound by law to adopt them. Voluntary adoption in the marketplace is the ultimate test of a standard. Standards may disappear in the advent of a new superior technology or simply with the passage of time. Voluntary standards have many advantages. By not forcing industry to implement the standard, the burden of success lies in the marketplace. And in fact, proven success in the marketplace generally predates the creation of a standard. The behavior is emergent, not imposed. (An interesting counterexample to this trend of voluntary adoption happened on January 1, 1983, when the ARPAnet instigated a mandatory rollover to the then-new protocol suite TCP/IP. If a host did not roll over, it would eventually have been dropped from the network.) Yet it is important to underscore that while most technical standards today are voluntary, this does not mean that they are haphazardly or infrequently adopted. In fact, the core standards of the Internet (TCP/IP) are some of the most universally adopted technologies in the history of mankind. Statisticians estimate that there are approximately 1 billion Internet users today, and to connect, each one must implement dozens of identical standards.

Case Study: Computer Viruses

But what are the social and cultural effects of universal network standards? The principles of flexibility and robustness have changed everything from economic supply chains (with "just in time" fulfillment) to how one goes about buying a book (with "collaborative filtering" on Web sites like Amazon.com). But to carry these ideas further, it is worth looking at a specific example: computer viruses.

While a few articles on viruses and worms appeared in the 1970s and the beginning of the 1980s, Frederick Cohen's work in the early 1980s is cited as the first sustained examination of computer viruses (see Cohen 1994; Burger 1988, 19). He approached this topic from a scientific viewpoint, measuring infection rates, classifying different types of viruses, and so on.

> The record for the smallest virus is a Unix "sh" command script. In the command interpreter of Unix, you can write a virus that takes only about 8 characters. So, once you are logged into a Unix system, you can type a 8 character command, and before too long, the virus will spread. That's quite small, but it turns out that with 8 characters, the virus can't do anything but reproduce. To get a virus that does interesting damage, you need around 25 or 30 characters. If you want a virus that evolves, replicates, and does damage, you need about 4 or 5 lines. (Cohen 1994, 38)

Cohen first presented his ideas on computer viruses to a seminar in 1983. His paper "Computer Viruses—Theory and Experiments" was published in 1984, and his Ph.D. dissertation titled "Computer Viruses" (University of Southern California) was published in 1986. Cohen defines a computer virus as "a program that can 'infect' other programs by modifying them to include a, possibly evolved, version of itself" (Cohen 1994, 2). Other experts agree: "a virus is a self-replicating code segment which must be attached to a host executable" (Polk et al. 1995, 4). Variants in the field of malicious code include worms and Trojan horses. A worm, like a virus, is a self-replicating program but one that requires no host to propagate. A Trojan horse is a program that appears to be doing something useful but also executes some piece of undesirable code hidden to the user.

At the core of networked computing is the concept of protocol. *A computer protocol is a set of recommendations and rules that outline specific technical standards.*

In the 1960s in places like Bell Labs, Xerox PARC, and MIT, scientists were known to play a game called Core War (Dewdney 1984a, 22). In this game, two self-replicating programs were released into a system. The programs battled over system resources and eventually one side came out on top. Whoever could write the best program would win. These engineers were not virus writers; nor were they terrorists or criminals. Just the opposite, they prized creativity, technical innovation, and exploration. Core War was a fun way to generate such intellectual activity. The practice existed for several years unnoticed. "In college, before video games, we would amuse ourselves by posing programming exercises," said Ken Thompson, codeveloper of the UNIX operating system, in 1983. "One of the favorites was to write the shortest self-reproducing program" (Thompson 1990, 98). The engineer A. K. Dewdney (1984b, 14) recounts an early story about a self-duplicating program called Creeper that infested the computer system and had to be brought under control by another program designed to neutralize it, Reaper. Dewdney brought to life this battle scenario using his own gaming language called Redcode.

At 5:01:59 p.m. on November 2, 1988, Robert Morris, a twenty-three-year-old graduate student at Cornell University and son of a prominent computer security engineer at the National Computer Security Center (a division of the National Security Agency), released an e-mail worm into the ARPAnet (Rochlis and Eichin 1990, 202). The precise time of day comes from analyzing the computer logs at Cornell University. Others suspect that the attack originated from a remote login at an MIT computer. This self-replicating program entered approximately sixty thousand computers in the course of a few hours, infecting between twenty-five hundred and six thousand of them (Cohen 1994, 49). And while it is notoriously difficult to calculate such figures, some speculations put the damage caused by Morris's worm at more than $10 million, a figure calculated by summing the number of hours of labor required to repair infected machines, the cost of hardware replacement (if any), and the cost of lost productivity due to downed machines.

Computer viruses thrive in environments that have low levels of diversity. Wherever a technology has a monopoly, you will find viruses.

While the media cited Morris's worm as "the largest assault ever on the nation's computers," the program was largely considered a sort of massive blunder, a chain reaction that spiraled out of control through negligence (*The New York Times*, November 4, 1988, A1). Computer viruses thrive in environments that have low levels of diversity. Wherever a technology has a monopoly, you will find viruses. They take advantage of technical standardization to propagate through the network. Consider the following analogy: what if nine out of ten people carried identical genes? In such a world, disease would spread far and wide with ease. For if a genetic vulnerability was discovered in one victim, the next victim and the next would automatically share the same vulnerability. Disease would have little difficulty jumping from host to host, quickly infecting large sections of the population.

Now imagine if 90 percent of computers were identical. This is roughly how the world of computers looks today. Nine out of ten computers today carry identical genetic code, known by a slightly more familiar name: Microsoft Windows. Microsoft's 90 percent market share creates what scientists call a monoculture. In biology, a monoculture exists whenever a single crop or organism takes over an entire ecology. The same thing exists today in the computerized realm. We are living in a computer monoculture. The monoculture is why computer viruses and e-mail worms exist. Computer viruses are able to propagate far and wide in computer networks by leveraging a single vulnerability from computer to computer. In the summer of 2003, the "Blaster" e-mail worm infected more than four hundred thousand computers in a short period of time. By contrast, it took eight months for SARS to infect eight thousand people. Biodiversity is a natural barrier to contagion. And diversity within the human species helped keep SARS from spreading further. Likewise, the computer monoculture fueled epidemics like Blaster.

If diversity existed in the computer sector, viruses would die out overnight. Linux or Macintosh machines are disproportionately saved from the digital plague. The reason lies not in superior security systems (both platforms are vulnerable to digital exploits); it lies in the fact that neither is a monoculture. They occupy the 10 percent fringe. Viruses that originate on Windows machines have a difficult time jumping to other species of computer, leaving Linux or Macintosh users uninfected (though they may still feel the effects of e-mail worms without becoming infected themselves).

As the example of computer viruses illustrates, the various internal characteristics of the Internet can be leveraged in powerful ways by malicious code. Because the Internet is so highly standardized, viruses can propagate quickly by exploiting technical vulnerabilities. Because the Internet is globally interconnected, a single virus will likely have massive repercussions. Because the Internet is so robust, viruses can route around problems and stoppages. And because the Internet is so decentralized, it is virtually impossible to kill viruses once they are released.

Epilogue: The Political Challenges Posed by Networks

I have tried to illustrate how some of the core features of digital networks exert influence over culture and society. Let me return to the original sentiments of networking pioneer Paul Baran. Here, he mentions explicitly how the Internet was invented to avoid certain vulnerabilities of nuclear attack:

> The weakest spot in assuring a second strike capability was in the lack of reliable communications. At the time we didn't know how to build a communication system that could survive even collateral damage by enemy weapons. Rand determined through computer simulations that the AT&T Long Lines telephone system, that carried essentially all the Nation's military communications, would be cut apart by relatively minor physical damage. While essentially all of the links and the nodes of the telephone system would survive, a few critical points of this very highly centralized analog telephone system would be destroyed by collateral damage alone by missiles directed at air bases and collapse like a house of card. (Baran 1999)

In Baran's original vision, the organizational design of the Internet involved a high degree of redundancy, such that destruction of a part of the network would not threaten the viability of the network as a whole. After World War II, strategists called for moving industrial targets outside urban cores in a direct response to fears of nuclear attack. Peter Galison (2001, 20) calls this dispersion the "constant vigilance against the re-creation of new centers." These are the same centers that Baran derided as an "Achilles' heel" and that he longed to purge from the telecommunications network. "City by city, country by country, the bomb helped drive dispersion" (ibid., 25), Galison continues, highlighting the power of the A-bomb to drive the push toward distribution in urban planning. Whereas the destruction of a fleet of Abrams tanks would certainly impinge upon army battlefield maneuvers, the destruction of a rack of Cisco routers would do little to slow down broader network communications. Internet traffic would simply find a new route, thus circumventing the downed machines. *New Yorker* writer Peter Boyer (2002, 61) reports that DARPA is in fact rethinking this opposition by designing a distributed tank, "a tank whose principal components, such as guns and sensors, are mounted on separate vehicles that would be controlled remotely by a soldier in yet another command vehicle." This is what the military calls Future Combat Systems (FCS), an initiative developed by DARPA for the U.S. Army. It is described as "flexible" and "network-centric." Thus, the Internet can survive attacks not because it is stronger than the opposition, but precisely because it is weaker. The Internet has a different diagram than a nuclear attack does; *it is in a different shape*. And that new shape happens to be immune to the older.

[T]he current global crisis is one between centralized, hierarchical powers and distributed, horizontal networks.

All the words used to describe the World Trade Center after the attacks of September 11, 2001, revealed its design vulnerabilities vis-à-vis terrorists: it was a tower, a center, an icon, a pillar, a hub. Conversely, terrorists are always described with a different vocabulary: they are cellular, networked, modular, and nimble. Groups like al-Qaeda specifically promote a modular, distributed structure based on small, autonomous groups. They write that new recruits "should not know one another" and that training sessions should be limited to "7-10 individuals." They describe their security strategies as "creative" and "flexible" (al-Qaeda 2002, 50, 62).

This is indicative of two conflicting diagrams. The first diagram is based on the strategic massing of power and control, while the second diagram is based on the distribution of power into small, autonomous enclaves. "The architecture of the World Trade Center owed more to the centralized layout of Versailles than the dispersed architecture of the Internet," wrote Jon Ippolito (2001, A27) after the attacks. "New York's resilience derives from the interconnections it fosters among its vibrant and heterogeneous inhabitants. It is in decentralized structures that promote such communal networks, rather than in reinforced steel, that we will find the architecture of survival." The war against terrorism resembles the war in Vietnam or the war against drugs—conflicts between a central power and an elusive network. It does not resemble the Gulf War, or World War II, or other conflicts between states.

"As an environment for military conflict," *The New York Times* reported, "Afghanistan is virtually impervious to American power" (Taubman 2001). (In addition to the stymied U.S. attempt to rout al-Qaeda after September 11, the failed Soviet occupation in the years following the 1978 coup is a perfect example of grossly mismatched organizational designs.) Being "impervious" to American power today is no small feat. Destruction of a network is an all-or-nothing game. One must destroy all nodes, not simply take out a few key hubs. But the opposite is not true. A network needs only to destroy a single hub within a hierarchical power to score a dramatic triumph. Thus, Baran's advice to the American military in 1964 was to become network-like. And once it did, the nuclear threat was no longer a catastrophic threat to communications and mobility (but remains, of course, a catastrophic threat to human life, material resources, and so on). The category shift that defines the difference between state power and guerilla force shows that through a new diagram, guerillas, terrorists, and the like can gain a foothold against their opposition. But as Ippolito (2001) points out, this should be our category shift too, for antiterror survival strategies will arise not from a renewed massing of power on the American side, but precisely from a distributed (or to use his less precise term, decentralized) diagram. Heterogeneity, distribution, and communalism are all features of this new diagrammatic solution.

In short, the current global crisis is one between centralized, hierarchical powers and distributed, horizontal networks. John Arquilla and David Ronfeldt (2001), two researchers at the Rand Corporation who have written extensively on the hierarchy-network conflict, offer a few propositions for thinking about future policy:

- Hierarchies have a difficult time fighting networks.
- It takes networks to fight networks.
- Whoever masters the network form first and best will gain major advantages. (p. 15)

In recent decades, the primary conflict between organizational designs has been between hierarchies and networks, an asymmetrical war. However, in the future the world is likely to experience a general shift downward into a new bilateral organizational conflict—networks fighting networks.

"Bureaucracy lies at the root of our military weakness," wrote advocates of military reform in the mid-1980s. "The bureaucratic model is inherently contradictory to the nature of war, and no military that is a bureaucracy can produce military excellence" (Hart and Lind 1986, 240, 249). The dilemma, then, is that while hierarchy and centralization are almost certainly politically tainted due to their historical association with fascism and other abuses, networks are both bad and good. Drug cartels, terror groups, black hat hacker crews, and other denizens of the underworld all take advantage of networked organizational designs because they offer effective mobility and disguise. But more and more, one witnesses the advent of networked organizational design in corporate management techniques, manufacturing supply chains, advertisement campaigns, and other novelties of the global economy, as well as all the familiar grassroots activist groups who have long used network structures to their advantage. In a sense, networks have been vilified simply because the terrorists, pirates, and anarchists made them notorious, not because of any negative quality of the organizational diagram itself. In fact, liberatory movements have been capitalizing on network design protocols for decades if not centuries. The goal, then, is not to destroy technology in some neo-Luddite delusion, but to push it into a state of hypertrophy, further than it is meant to go. Then, in its injured, sore, and unguarded condition, technology may be sculpted anew into something better, something in closer agreement with the real wants and desires of its users.

To end, I offer a few instructions for those interested in the effects of global computer networks on cultural production. First is the principle of openness. As the success of the Internet protocols or the Linux operating system illustrates, open technologies have scored major victories over proprietary technologies in recent decades. Value comes less from the protectionist hoarding of social and cultural assets and more from the open deployment of those assets. Leverage the swelling mass of social momentum; lead with a carrot, not a stick. Second, build social institutions that can "route around" problems, just like the core protocols do. Design high degrees of flexibility into social systems. Remove centralized hubs and bottlenecks. Do not just match a problem with a suitable solution; make the problem irrelevant. Third, a warning: following the robustness principle, network technology will tend to standardize rather than diversify. This means that cultural producers will become more and more encumbered by technologies that exploit standardized systems, such as spam, e-mail worms, and computer viruses. So while many of the previous cold war vulnerabilities are gone, a new set of vulnerabilities exist. Finally, those interested in innovative cultural production must understand the *political* import of networks. They are no longer solely the tool of grassroots groups and guerrillas. The "powers that be" have finally come to understand networks too, and what was previously liberating about networks may very well not be liberating in the future.

References

RFC (Request for Comments) documents are archived in several locations online and are accessible via a normal Web search.

al-Qaeda. 2002. *The al-Qaeda documents.* Vol. 1. Alexandria, VA: Tempest.

American National Standards Institute (ANSI). 2004. National standards strategy for the United States. http://www.ansi.org (accessed July 21, 2004).

Arquilla, John, and David Ronfeldt. 2001. *Networks and netwars: The future of terror, crime, and militancy.* Santa Monica, CA: Rand.

Baran, Paul. 1964. *On distributed communications.* Santa Monica, CA: Rand.

———. 1999. Electrical engineer, an oral history conducted in 1999 by David Hochfelder, IEEE History Center, Rutgers University, New Brunswick, NJ. http://www.ieee.org/organizations/history_center/oral_histories/transcripts/baran.html.

Boyer, Peter. 2002. A different war. *The New Yorker,* July 1.

Burger, Ralf. 1988. *Computer viruses.* Grand Rapids, MI: Abacus.

Castells, Manuel. 1996. *The rise of the network society.* Oxford, UK: Blackwell.

Cerf, Vinton. 1988. I remember IANA. RFC 2468.

Cohen, Frederick. 1984. Computer viruses—Theory and experiments. In *Proceedings of the 7th National Computer Security Conference*, 240-63. Gaithersburg, MD: NCSC.

———. 1986. Computer viruses. Ph.D. diss., University of Southern California, Los Angeles.

———. 1994. *A short course on computer viruses*. New York: John Wiley.

Denning, Peter, ed. 1990. *Computers under attack: Intruders, worms, and viruses*. New York: ACM.

Dewdney, A. K. 1984a. Computer recreations. *Scientific American* 251 (September): 22.

———. 1984b. In the game called Core War hostile programs engage in a battle of bits. *Scientific American* 250 (May): 14.

Dunning, John. 1957. If we are to catch up in science. *The New York Times Magazine*, November 10.

Feinler, Jake. 1999. 30 years of RFCs. RFC 2555.

Galison, Peter. 2001. War against the center. *Grey Room* 4:6-33.

Hafner, Katie, and Matthew Lyon. 1996. *Where wizards stay up late: The origins of the Internet*. New York: Touchstone.

Hall, Eric. 2000. *Internet protocols: The definitive guide*. Sebastopol, CA: O'Reilly.

Hart, Gary, and William Lind. 1986. *America can win*. Bethesda, MD: Adler & Adler.

Internet Society (ISOC). 2004. Internet Society mission statement. http://www.isoc.org/isoc/mission/ (accessed July 21, 2004).

Ippolito, Jon. 2001. Don't blame the Internet. *Washington Post*, September 29, A27.

Lessig, Lawrence. 2001. *The future of ideas: The fate of the commons in a connected world*. New York: Random House

Loshin, Pete. 2000. *Big book of FYI RFCs*. San Francisco: Morgan Kaufmann.

Malkin, Gary. 1992. Who's who in the Internet: Biographies of IAB, IESG and IRSG members. RFC 1336. FYI 9.

Polk, W. Timothy, Lawrence E. Bassham, Lisa J. Carnahan, and John P. Wack. 1995. *Anti-virus tools and techniques for computer systems*. Park Ridge, NJ: Noyes Data Corporation.

Postel, Jon, ed. 1981. Transmission Control Protocol. RFC 793.

Rochlis, Jon A., and Mark W. Eichin. 1990. With microscope and tweezers: The worm from MIT's perspective. In *Computers under attack: Intruders, worms, and viruses*, ed. Peter Denning. New York: ACM.

Stevens, W. Richard. 1994. *TCP/IP illustrated*. Vol. 1. New York: Addison Wesley.

Taubman, Philip. 2001. An imbalance of power: Afghanistan's deceptive strength. *The New York Times*, September 20, sec. A, col. 1, p. 30.

Thompson, Ken. 1990. Reflections on trusting trust. In *Computers under attack: Intruders, worms, and viruses*, ed. Peter Denning. New York: ACM.

Multiple Media, Convergent Processes, and Divergent Products: Organizational Innovation in Digital Media Production at a European Firm

By
PABLO J. BOCZKOWSKI
and
JOSÉ A. FERRIS

This article addresses the intersection of two underexplored themes in studies of cultural production in traditional and digital media: the role of technology in news work and the processes that shape media convergence. The authors analyze organizational innovation in digital media production at GMS, a European firm that operates print and broadcast outlets in several specialized news markets. Between 1994 and 2003, GMS went from a phase of digital media experimentation undertaken by teams located within each existing newsroom, to the creation of a separate unit handling the online content of all print and broadcast newsrooms, to the ongoing integration of news production into a single newsroom per specialized market that generates different products for the various outlets in each market. This analysis illuminates how adopting online technologies has involved shifts in the locus of content creation in a path of increasing convergence in production processes but continued divergence of media products.

Keywords: cultural production; news production; new media; digital media; newspapers; media industry

Т his article addresses the intersection of two underexplored themes in studies of cultural production in traditional and digital media: the role of technology in news work and the processes that shape media convergence. On one hand, research about print and broadcast media has demonstrated that understanding media products requires paying attention to the organization of their production processes. However, work in this domain of inquiry has largely

Pablo J. Boczkowski is Cecil and Ida Green Career Development Assistant Professor of Organization Studies at MIT Sloan School of Management. He studies how the construction and use of new media technologies affect work practices, communication processes, and interaction with consumers, focusing on organizations and occupations that have traditionally been associated with print media. His first book, Digitizing the News: Innovation in Online Newspapers *(MIT Press, 2004), analyzes how American daily newspapers developed electronic publishing ventures in the 1980s and 1990s. In addition to continuing research on content creation in*

DOI: 10.1177/0002716204270067

neglected the role of technology in these processes. On the other hand, analyses of new media have suggested that the digitization of information has led to erasing the boundaries that separate print, television, radio, and online technologies. Accounts of this phenomenon, however, have mostly focused on the products of media convergence—analyzing their symbolic forms and cultural and policy implications—with less attention devoted to the processes that shape the creation of these products. To explore both themes and their relationships, this article adopts traditional media scholarship's focus on the production process to look at digital media and digital media scholarship's emphasis on technology to examine production dynamics. It sheds new light on these themes by analyzing organizational innovation in digital media production at GMS, a European firm that operates print and broadcast outlets in several specialized news markets. Between 1994 and 2003, the firm went from a phase of digital media experimentation undertaken by teams located within each existing newsroom, to the creation of a separate unit handling the online content of all print and broadcast newsrooms, to the ongoing integration of content production into a single newsroom per specialized market that generates different products for the various outlets in each market.

The analysis challenges two tenets of scholarship about cultural production in traditional and digital media: the implicit "one newsroom–one medium" assumption of most sociology of news production and the dominant idea of product homogenization in the discourse of media convergence. First, the analysis elicits the dynamics of situations in which multiple newsrooms collaborated to produce content for their respective media and others in which one newsroom produced content for multiple media, thus turning the one newsroom–one medium assumption into an alternative whose existence has to be explained instead of assumed. Second, organizational factors partly account for a trend toward a convergence in production processes at GMS that was coupled with sustained divergence in the resulting products, thus underscoring the need to examine the organization of production to understand the shape of convergent media products at different times and places. Finally, the various combinations of newsrooms and media, and pro-

online news organizations, he recently began studying issues of information intermediation and professional work through an examination of the transformations in librarianship that have taken place in relation to libraries' construction and use of new media technologies.

José A. Ferris (BA, Communications, Universidad de Navarra, 1989; MBA, MIT Sloan School of Management, 2004) has eleven years of experience in the media industry. He has worked both on the editorial side (as a reporter, editor, and foreign correspondent, among other positions, for financial publications) and on the business side (as a manager and executive of newspapers both in his native Spain as well as in South America). He has also participated in Internet-related ventures developed by the newspapers he has worked for.

NOTE: We would like to thank the people at GMS for providing a most conducive environment for this research. We would also like to acknowledge the valuable feedback received from Joellen Easton, Eric Klinenberg, Frederick Turner, an anonymous reviewer, and attendees to a session at the 2004 annual meeting of the International Communication Association, where an earlier version of this article was presented. Correspondence concerning this article should be addressed to the first author.

cesses and products, were often associated with decisions affecting not a single publication, Web site, television or radio station, but GMS as a whole or several of its units simultaneously, thus highlighting the explanatory power of a level of analysis—that of the multimedia firm—that has not received much attention in studies of cultural production in traditional and digital media.

Cultural Production in Print and Broadcast Media

Scholars who have "gone inside" print and broadcast media have shed light on the role of interpersonal, institutional, moral, and political factors shaping the news (Epstein 1973; Ettema and Glasser 1998; Gans 1980; Kaniss 1991; Roshco 1975; Tuchman 1978). A fundamental contribution of this tradition of inquiry has been that understanding the organization of production is critical to making sense of the news as a cultural product. In Gieber's (1964, 180) celebrated phrase, "News is what newspaper men make it." A similar spirit permeates Gitlin's (1994, 13) study of organizational decision making in prime-time television: "I could not hope to understand why network television was what it was unless I understood who put the images on the small screen and for what reasons."

Despite the many important contributions of this tradition of inquiry, it has had two limitations that have become particularly salient to making sense of the contemporary media landscape. The first one is a pervasive, though often unstated, one newsroom–one medium assumption. That is, studies have usually focused on the operations of a single newsroom that produces content for a single medium such as a print newspaper or a radio station. Although this assumption was quite realistic up to three decades ago, the trends toward consolidation, diversification, and alliances that have marked the media industry in recent times (Bagdikian 1983; Compaine and Gomery 2000) have frequently meant that content produced by a single newsroom is delivered across multiple media or that personnel from more than one newsroom jointly produce content subsequently disseminated in multiple media. To maintain this assumption as a given runs the risk of proceeding with outdated images of the work involved in content production as well as preventing the creation of analytical resources suitable for dealing with the dynamics that characterize the situations of multiple newsrooms–multiple media or one newsroom–multiple media.

The second shortcoming has been the lack of attention given to the role of technology in news production: "media sociologies . . . have lagged the technical . . . evolution of the news worker's milieu" (Sumpter 2000, 335). This shortcoming has been particularly limiting when it comes to understanding the contemporary media landscape in light of the computerization of newsrooms since the 1970s (Marvin 1980; Picard and Brody 1997; Smith 1980; Weaver and Wilhoit 1986). According to Schudson (2000, 182), "There has been little academic attention to the concrete consequences of the technological transformation of news production." One exception has been a recent study by one of the current authors (Boczkowski 2004) about the development of online newspapers in the United States. Among other conclusions, this study has shown that understanding the technological dimension of news production is critical to making sense of editorial dynamics: "materiality matters in online newsrooms . . . technical considerations affect who gets to tell the story, what kinds of stories are told, how they are told, and to what public they are addressed" (Boczkowski 2004, 177).

Cultural Production in Digital Media

In contrast with studies of print and broadcast media, scholarship about digital media has stressed the role of technology in the production of culture. One of the most widely circulated ideas in this regard has been that of "media convergence": the notion that because of the capabilities of digital technologies, content and services previously offered through various media will in the future be conveyed to a single artifact, usually a networked computer. This notion gained currency in the 1990s, as it became the dominant idea to making sense of transformations in cultural practices and artifacts associated with the popularization of the Internet and the World Wide Web (Baldwin, McVoy, and Steinfield 1996; Chandler and Cortada 2000; Greenstein and Khanna 1997; Manovich 2001; Poster 2001). To Owen (1999, 16), "The prophecy of convergence is this: television sets, telephones, and computers—and the networks that bind them—are or will become the same. The internet will be all."

In light of its popularity, it is not surprising that convergence has also permeated discourse about print and broadcast media's appropriation of online technologies (Black 2001; Elberse 1998; Owen 1999; Schiller 1999). According to Hall (2001, 6), "Online journalism . . . is also the industry that is experiencing the full and unmediated impact of converging media forms." Scholars have analyzed the implications of convergence for both the production and consumption of news. Concerning production matters, Pavlik (2001, 108) has suggested that "converging computing and telecommunication technologies are rapidly rewriting the traditional assumptions of newsroom organization and structure." Regarding news consumption, Lin and Jeffries (1998, 350) have argued that "it will be crucial to assess audience-multimedia technology relationships in light of the audience's entire communication and media environment, including electronic and print media infrastructures."

Of particular relevance to the purpose of this article, two features that have marked most of such discourse are a focus on convergence as a product and an emphasis on how these digital products tend to erase the differences among analog media such as print and broadcast. Perhaps nobody has expressed the product focus—with the parallel black boxing of the production process—as forcefully as Negroponte (1996, 18): "When all media is digital . . . bits commingle effortlessly." Concerning the homogenization of convergent media products, Yoffie (1997, 2) has stressed that convergence means the "unification of functions—the coming together of previously distinct products that employ digital technologies"; and Seib (2001, 6) has suggested that "in journalism, [convergence] means a growing similarity in news presentation through various media."

One of the most widely circulated ideas . . . has been that of "media convergence": the notion that because of the capabilities of digital technologies, content and services previously offered through various media will in the future be conveyed to a single artifact, usually a networked computer.

Some studies have begun to shed light on the limitations of looking at convergence as an end state of media homogenization (Benkler 1998; Deuze 2004; Gordon 2003; Higgins 2000; Jenkins 2001; Preston and Kerr 2001; Zavoina and Reichert 2000). In his study of online newspapers, Boczkowski (2004, 17) has argued that these newspapers have unfolded "in an ongoing process in which different combinations of initial conditions and local contingencies have led to divergent trajectories." Thus, looking at product homogenization has made less visible the social contingencies that shape the process of producing convergent products—hence ignoring the main legacy of social studies of news making in print and broadcast media, and that these contingencies partly account for the variation that so far has existed in these products.

Site and Method

GMS[1] was born in January 1990 from the merger of five publishing and related companies controlled by the same owners in the same European country. It began as a print publisher and added broadcast and online media in the past ten years. GMS has never had a financial loss and is the leader in most of the markets in which it operates. In 2002 it had the following media:

- Sports information division: *Goal*, a daily with an average daily circulation of 490,000; Goal.com, with a monthly average of 154 million visitors; and Radio Goal.

- Business information division: *Invertis*, a daily with an average daily circulation of 65,000; Invertis.com, with a monthly average of 18 million visitors; Invertis TV, available through a satellite service with 3 million subscribers; and *Business Report*, a weekly magazine with an average weekly circulation of 30,000.
- "Others" information division: *Dona*, a women's monthly magazine with an average monthly circulation of 159,000; Beautylady.com, with a monthly average of 4 million visitors; *Doctors Daily*, a free medical newspaper with an average daily circulation of 50,000; Doctors Daily.com, with a monthly average of 2 million visitors; and *Studio*, a free weekly educational magazine with an average weekly circulation of 75,000.

The second author visited GMS in the summer of 2003. Among other data collection strategies, he conducted thirty-five open-ended, hour-long interviews. These interviews—together with follow-up exchanges with key actors by phone and electronic mail conducted during the second half of 2003—constitute the main source of data for this article. Approximately half of the interviewees were editorial personnel, some working for the online media and some for the traditional media, and proportionally distributed according to the weight of the various information divisions: eight journalists from the Sports division, six from the Business division, and four from the Others division. The approximately other half of interviewees included GMS-wide personnel in areas of top management, advertising, and information systems support. The overall sample provided an array of views and experiences about organizational innovation in relation to digital media at GMS between 1994 and 2003.

Organizational Innovation at GMS

In this section, we briefly describe the innovations in organizational strategies and structures for digital media production adopted at GMS between 1994 and 2003. In this ten-year period, digital media went from being a secondary function to becoming the primary strategic focus, to being integrated into the other media. Several organizational structures were created at these various stages.

The first steps and the creation of the Electronic Extensions Department, 1994-99

Most people at GMS first learned about the Internet and digital media upon reading stories about technological developments in the United States that appeared in the company's financial publications in the early 1990s. Maurice Moore, at that time editor of *Business Report* and with a long-time personal interest in new media technology, played a key part in this process by regularly assigning his reporters to write Internet-related stories and sending reporters to visit media organizations pursuing interesting digital media efforts. It is thus not surprising that when Moore was appointed president of GMS, reporting to the chief executive officer and the executive chairman in June 1995, he was also put in charge of online publishing initiatives:

The top executives and the founders of GMS had no idea in 1995 of what the Internet was about. They knew that behind the Internet there might be something interesting for the company, and they were smart enough to let me do what I really thought was good for the company. (Maurice Moore, personal communication, June 6, 2003)

At the end of 1995, the Electronic Extensions Department was created to centralize developments in the broadly defined area of digital media. This included tasks such as analysis of initiatives pursued by competitors; design and implementation of technical solutions for GMS online publications; and production of CD-ROMs with information, mainly company rankings, prepared by GMS's print newspapers. The new department's name indicates that it was seen as a secondary function, an "extension" to the core print business. Despite this secondary role, the creation of the department meant a growing trend toward the allocation of financial, human, and symbolic resources to digital media at GMS.

To lead the Electronic Extensions Department, Moore appointed Stan Krueger, a rising-star journalist at *Business Report*, where he had also been Moore's deputy for a few years. Because of his good reputation at GMS, Krueger's appointment was a signal of the importance that Moore assigned to digital media. To staff the department, Moore initially asked the editors of print publications to relieve one or two members of their newsrooms of some of their regular duties and make them responsible for producing the online editions of their respective publications. The personnel assigned to create and maintain online publications were located in the traditional newsrooms but reported to the head of the Electronic Extensions Department. In most cases, the defining criterion for choosing these initial online staffers was their possession of higher than average knowledge of computers. As time went by, new employees were hired for the Electronic Extensions Department. GMS has a long-established summer internship program for college students in journalism and communications majors, from which it recruits the top performers for full-time positions in the newsroom. The new hires for the Electronic Extensions Department came from this pool. The decision to assign a summer intern either to a traditional newsroom or to the Electronic Extensions Department resulted from asking a person whether they had some knowledge of the Internet, hypertext markup language, or computers. Those who answered yes were sent to the new department.

Being asked to work on an online edition was frequently not a highly regarded assignment by many in the print newsroom. To Mathew Johnson, who later became deputy director of the Digital Media Department, "Editors of the newspapers did not feel at that time that the Web pages were part of the newspapers" (personal communication, June 3, 2003). The Electronic Extensions personnel experienced a somewhat secondary status, relative to that of their traditional media counterparts, throughout this period. For instance, according to Krueger, "In 1997, only Moore paid attention to us; the rest of the top management ignored us. . . . The editors of the papers also ignored us, and many reporters thought the department members were computer experts with no idea of journalism" (personal communication, June 2, 2003).

GMS publications launched their first Web pages in 1996. The main goal of these pages was to experiment with new technologies and to do something similar to what the world's leading publications were doing in the area of online publishing. There was no overall strategy for this experimentation or for how it might affect the print business. As with most early online newspapers, these first Web pages reproduced the print papers' content. They also increasingly added online-only features, however, such as the live written narration of a soccer match on Goal.com and the offering of interactive stock market charts on Invertis.com. As with the people who created them, the digital products were also seen as secondary to the print products, something that was evident, for instance, in the treatment of scoops. "It is absolutely clear that if Goal.com gets a good scoop, we will keep that information so as to be released by *Goal*, on the paper, not on Goal.com," states Adrian Spiegel, editor of *Goal* and former editor of Goal.com. "We may publish that scoop immediately on the Web only if we have enough evidence that the scoop may be obtained by other competitors," adds Spiegel (personal communication, June 3, 2003).

To summarize, during this period, digital media production was undertaken by specialized units located within the traditional newsrooms but reporting to the new Electronic Extensions Department and generated products that reproduced content originally created for the traditional publications while increasingly adding Internet-only information and services such as updates during the day and database applications. This resulted from a firmwide strategy and structure of innovation championed by a powerful actor without much involvement or interest from the rest of the top management and in which all things digital enjoyed a lower status than their print counterparts.

The rise of the Internet Department, 1999-2000

As the end of the 1990s approached, GMS executives were busy preparing to take the company public. In 1999, GMS retained the services of a management consulting firm to help formulate the company strategy in relation to this process. Among other things, this firm recommended the creation of an Internet department that "had to turn into a smaller company inside a larger company, and that the whole [GMS] had to orbit around the Internet department" (Stan Krueger, personal communication, June 6, 2003). As people at the company put it, 1999 was the year that digital media changed from an "ugly duck" to a "white swan." In light of the extraordinarily high valuation that Internet-related stocks had at the time, turning GMS into an Internet company was a notion appealing to its top executives. All of a sudden, the Internet became the icon of digital media and the center of attention: "In 1997 or 1998, nobody gave a dime for the Internet, while in 1999 and 2000 all the dimes in GMS were ready to be invested in the Internet" (Maurice Moore, personal communication, June 6, 2003). In 1999, GMS created the Internet department and appointed Stan Krueger to lead it.

The creation of the Internet department took place at a time of feverish activity in the media industry. The Internet and the World Wide Web seemed poised to transform the media landscape, and traditional media companies such as GMS found themselves in a position to develop their own new ventures as well as partner with newly founded new media ventures. Andrea Verst was hired by *Invertis* as a summer intern in 1996, then joined its online newsroom and two years later moved to the Internet Department with the task of developing new business opportunities. She comments on this experience in the following terms: "In 1999 and 2000 there were several general portals and Web pages of different industries that wanted content. . . . We were the best positioned to offer content, and many companies approached us. I had to deal with hundreds of them" (personal communication, June 4, 2003).

This burst of activity changed the tone and routines even at a mature and traditional company such as GMS. For example, the Internet Department operated without any budget during its entire lifecycle, a practice previously unimaginable at GMS. According to Maurice Moore, "It was impossible to have [a budget] because the circumstances and the pace changed so quickly that it was physically impossible to have a reliable budget. We worked under these circumstances during a year and a half" (personal communication, June 6, 2003).

The Internet Department was charged with the mission of overseeing all the content of its online publications; developing and implementing new tools to support these publications; pursuing new opportunities in nonprint businesses; and, in general, infusing the whole company with a new media ethos. To this end, the department was staffed with one professional for every function—that is, an advertising sales manager with his or her team, a controller, a marketing vice president, and so on. In addition, it also placed one person in each one of GMS's other departments whose main duty was to "inoculate the Internet virus into the traditional organization or department" (Stan Krueger, personal communication, June 2, 2003).

In addition to these new functions, the Internet Department centralized the online newsrooms of traditional publications and placed these newsrooms in a new building, together with the rest of the new department's employees. This physical separation was quite controversial, increased the disdain of many experienced journalists toward online publishing, and triggered conflict across the "traditional media/digital media" border. At that time, says Krueger, "I was responsible for both the content and the management of everything displayed on Web pages, and many editors did not like to see me managing 'their' content" (personal communication, June 2, 2003).

The creation of the Internet Department, with its broad and ambitious goal, meant the development of many new positions at GMS. In the case of new positions in the online newsrooms, the hiring criteria adopted to fill them continued to privilege technical over editorial competence, which deepened the differences between traditional and digital media personnel. For instance, Phil Mastrein, an experienced financial journalist who had worked many years for *Invertis* and was appointed editor of Invertis.com in December 1999, recalls that

> there were four newly hired people for Invertis.com and in two months one of them had already quit because he thought that the job was too demanding. The truth was that he was

annoyed by the fact that I called him at home at 10:00 in the evening and asked him to go to a press conference the following morning, something quite normal in a newspaper. He had no passion for journalism, but he had sent his resume by e-mail and knew a lot of Dreamweaver programming. (Personal communication, June 10, 2003)

The Internet Department generated online publications that drew from content originally created for their traditional media counterparts but continued adding increasing amounts of information and services that took advantage of the technological capabilities of the World Wide Web. For instance, journalists at *Goal* have often complained about the little space they have to write stories in light of the importance that pictures have in a sports newspaper. As time went by, several of them began writing a shorter story for the print publication and a longer version for its online counterpart. According to Adrian Spiegel, "Many journalists realized that the Internet was an endless medium in which their texts could be displayed with no limits, allowing them to give longer versions of their stories to the readers" (personal communication, June 3, 2003). Also, the archival and search capabilities of digital technologies led to the development of publicly available digital repositories of information at GMS's online publications. Jason Mortimer, editor of *Doctors Daily* since its launch in 1992, argues that on DoctorsDaily.com, users can find "papers published by the best medical magazines on every type of disease or human organ . . . [as well as] the medical legislation that has recently been passed. We are like a doctors' library of medical and legal texts" (personal communication, June 4, 2003).

In sum, the Internet Department emerged as an outcome of a GMS-wide strategy partly related to the diffusion and popularization of digital media in society but also to the preexisting decision to take the company public. This strategy raised the status of digital media at GMS, but differences between "old" and "new" media personnel remained. The Internet Department further centralized the process of digital media production than had its predecessor, and the resulting products continued drawing from content originally created for traditional media while adding a growing quantity of online-only information and services.

The Digital Media Department and the beginning of newsroom integration, 2000-2003

In March 2000, with the Nasdaq stock market falling dramatically and many Internet companies going out of business, people at GMS began to question the "new economy" thinking behind the role assigned to the Internet Department in the previous year. At that time, GMS was continuing to prepare for its debut in the stock market, and its top executives decided to retain the services of another management consulting firm to reanalyze the strategy and structure of the company. The outcome of this new analysis was a decision to reorient the company's strategic focus toward its core content areas and to restructure the editorial units accordingly. That is, the main idea was to reorient GMS from a media company—defined either by its print publications, as in the 1994 to 1999 period, or its Web sites, as in the 1999 to 2000 period—to a content company. According to Moore, "We know how to produce information, that's our core business. If a customer wants information through the Internet, we will send it via Internet; but our core business is providing content, not technology" (personal communication, June 6, 2003). This strategic reorientation also dovetailed with a slow process of asset diversification that had begun in the late 1990s, when top executives at the company realized that *Invertis* and *Goal* were well-positioned brands that could be extended to other media such as TV and radio, as happened with the launch of Invertis TV in 1998 and Radio Goal in 2001.

Being asked to work on an online edition [of a GMS newspaper] was frequently not a highly regarded assignment by many in the print newsroom.

A new structure was put in place when the company went public in October 2000. It grouped all GMS's editorial units in three information divisions: Sports, Business, and Others. Maurice Moore was appointed executive member of the GMS board of directors, with direct responsibilities related to corporate development and the editorial content of the company's media. The executive vice presidents of the three information divisions reported to him, together with other business units of the company.

As part of this company-wide reorientation and restructuring, the Internet Department was renamed the Digital Media Department—Stan Krueger remained as its head—and various changes affected its daily operations. To begin, the online newsrooms went back to each traditional media newsroom, and the traditional newsroom editors were put back in charge of their online contents. Another change was the suppression of the role of the Internet leader in the traditional departments. For instance, the traditional marketing department eliminated the role of the Internet leader, but GMS Digital Media continued to have its traditional new media marketing leader. Furthermore, the era of "no budget, let us invest without constraints" was over, and the company resumed investing selectively according to "old economy" criteria.

After that restructuring, the Digital Media Department became a unit supporting GMS online publications through the creation and implementation of new tools and developing new business opportunities to sell content and services linking GMS core capabilities with platforms including not only the Web but also cellular phones and portable digital assistants. For instance, in 2003, GMS Digital Media launched new services such as the display of pictures initially taken for *Goal* on consumers' cellular phones and the transmission of breaking news alarms to computers, cellular phones, and portable digital assistants. In addition, the online publications expanded the array of Internet-only offerings, which made sensible the launch of a fee-based Premium Service on Invertis.com in April 2002. It gave subscribers access to the full version of every story published in *Invertis* plus updates during the day, stock and mutual funds quotes and charts, and access to searchable archives of past stories, among other things. The presentation of the information on the Web site also differed from that in the print paper. According to Phil Mastrein,

> We saw that the Invertis.com audience wanted to see at a glance—as soon as they opened our page—the performance of the stocks and market indexes that they are interested in. So we readapted our Web page to offer these features. We also saw that the comments of one of the stock markets analysts had to be put on the first page. . . . Time and trial and error have given us knowledge in how to deal with this newborn medium [the World Wide Web]. (Personal communication, June 11, 2003)

The period between the end of 2000 and 2002 was a difficult financial time for GMS and the media industry in general, not only because of the downturn in the stock markets, but also because of the dramatic fall in advertisement spending. *Invertis* saw a decline in sales and advertisement, and GMS as a whole had layoffs for the first time in its history. Partly because of the overstaffing of online newsrooms in the then-recent era of no budgetary restrictions, and partly because of the deflated expectations about the short-term commercial future of online publishing, the layoffs affected digital media personnel more than their peers on the print side. For instance, the number of people working in the newsroom of Invertis.com in mid-2003 was less than half of those in mid-2000. According to Moore,

> At the end of 2002, we went through a process of self-criticism as a result of the situation of *Invertis*. We wondered about the way we were doing things, about the past results, and especially about the lack of predisposition to cooperate among the business media that we have. (Personal communication, June 6, 2003)

What resulted from this process of self-examination was a major structural change, bound to strongly influence the content production process: the integration of the newsrooms of different media in the same content areas. The idea is that a given reporter, who may be specialized in track and field, for instance, may find a story and transmit it at noon through the radio, write one version for Goal.com during the afternoon, and then rewrite that story, from another perspective, for the following day's newspaper. On top of that, all these versions of the same story may be available on Goal.com, which may also work as a content repository. Online newsrooms as separate entities cease to exist as an outcome of this latest restructuring because all newsrooms within an information division converge into a single entity divided by beats and areas of specialization. For example, if there are two reporters specialized in real estate at *Invertis*, and one in each of the other newsrooms of the business information division—Invertis.com, Invertis TV, and *Business Report*— all these five reporters will be working together for the four business information media. Therefore, a reporter who was just reporting for the online version begins to also report in front of a camera for Invertis TV and writing both for *Invertis* and for *Business Report*.

As data for this study were collected, the process of newsroom integration was only starting. But signs of organizational transformation were already under way. For a while, the editors of *Goal*, Goal.com, and Radio Goal have had lunch every Monday to talk about joint projects and other developments that may be beneficial for the *Goal* brand as a whole, no matter if they affect the newspaper, the Web, or the radio. According to Adrian Spiegel, editor of *Goal*, "We see what we can do in the paper to increase the audience of the radio and of the Web page, while they do the same to increase the newspaper's circulation. We are all in the same boat" (personal communication, June 11, 2003). Furthermore, the newsrooms of *Invertis*, Invertis.com, Invertis TV, and *Business Report* were relocated together in the same floor in September 2003. Previously, only *Invertis* and Invertis.com shared the same floor. In the new location, editors and heads of the departments sit next to each other, while reporters are grouped according to the area of their specialization.

To sum up, negative financial conditions affecting the stock market in general and the media industry in particular triggered a strategic reorientation around content areas and structural innovations such as the creation of the Digital Media Department and the integration of newsrooms. The production process of digital and traditional media showed signs of convergence, with a single newsroom per information division in charge of the content provided by the multiple media operated within each division. This convergence in production processes was associated with a divergence in the resulting products, as was evident in the continued growth of distinctive digital content and services, among other indicators.

Discussion

The story of organizational innovation in digital media production at GMS challenges two pervasive notions of traditional and digital media scholarship: the one newsroom–one medium assumption and the trend toward product homogenization in media convergence. Because the relationships between newsrooms and media, and processes and products, were tied to dynamics that either pertained to GMS as a whole or crossed the boundaries of several of its units, this study makes a third analytical contribution by showing the explanatory value of focusing on the level of analysis of the multimedia firm—often overlooked in studies of cultural production in traditional and digital media.

Most studies of cultural production in traditional media have focused on the workings of a single newsroom and looked at their output for a single medium. Even the studies that have adopted a comparative approach, such as Gans's (1980) classic *Deciding What's News*, have implicitly held the notion of one newsroom–one medium. A notable exception is Klinenberg's (2000) study of production processes at a large, multimedia American news organization. Although not explicitly conceptualizing the one newsroom–one medium assumption, Klinenberg's contribution is important because it portrays internewsroom, intracompany dynamics that have become critical in contemporary settings. Our analysis of GMS builds upon this contribution to begin conceptualizing the limitations of this assumption.

During the ten-year period examined in this article, the organizational structure changed from a publication's single newsroom with distinct units producing content for traditional and digital media, to a separate digital newsroom producing content for all the traditional media, to a single newsroom per information division producing content for multiple media. Throughout this period, the production processes, and resulting products, of one newsroom were partly shaped by dynamics of other newsrooms or units. For instance, the work and output of online staffers was partly affected by what their traditional counterparts published. Although less frequent, the case of scoops generated by print personnel, but that ended up being broken on the online publication first and then rewritten for the print publication the following day, illustrates traditional newsroom dynamics influenced by those of the online newsroom. The recently launched process of newsroom integration promises to question even more the one newsroom–one medium assumption, because in this case, a single newsroom will produce different content for multiple media. This analysis does not suggest that we should abandon the notion that we can focus on a single newsroom to account for its production in one medium but that it should turn from a given into an option in the analysis of cultural production in media organizations. It also suggests the need to update our images of cultural production in the technically intensive and organizationally complex contemporary media settings and to develop conceptual resources able to make sense of dynamics that mark technical and cross-boundary practices in such settings.

Studies of cultural production in digital media have often emphasized the product homogenization that results, or will result, from media convergence. However, the story of GMS's adoption of digital media also presents a more complicated picture in this regard. In the ten years examined for this article, digital media at GMS moved from being a secondary endeavor at the periphery of the company's content production process, to turning into the very axis around which this production should rotate, to becoming integrated with the print and broadcast units into a single system of production. The trend seems to be toward a normalization of digital media and a convergence of production processes across all media. But this trend has been accompanied by a divergence in the products of traditional and digital media, as can be seen mostly in the format of these products—data limitations have prevented us from undertaking a systematic content analysis of these products over this ten-year period. This divergence results from technical and organizational practices that have shaped the process of producing the various media products. First, actors have taken advantage of the distinctive technological capabilities of digital media to create information and services different from those of the print publications, such as writing longer versions of stories, providing updates during the day, developing interactive applications, and offering access to archived material. Second, the differences in background, expertise, and orientation between the personnel in traditional and digital units have contributed to product divergence because joint work has not been a straightforward enterprise and because traditional staffers have been more interested in editorial matters whereas their digital counterparts have been more focused on technological issues. Whether there will be a shift toward product homogenization in the future remains to be seen. This study, however, underscores the need to reconsider technology-driven ideas such as product homogenization in media convergence and the value of examining the organization of production to make sense of the resulting products.

Finally, this study illustrates the explanatory power of extending the level of analysis of scholarship about production dynamics in media organizations. The most common approach of this scholarship has been to focus on the production processes of a single medium such as a newspaper, a radio station, or a Web site. In the case of Web sites that have traditional counterparts, scholars have sometimes looked at the relationships between the two. What has been much less common is a focus on the multimedia firm level of analysis and its relationships to the production dynamics of specific units and the resulting products. Building upon the insights provided by some recent exceptions such as Gilbert (2002) and Klinenberg (2000), the case presented in this article shows that there is much to be gained by exploring dynamics that cross these levels of analysis: for instance, factors such as the decision to take GMS public and the financial performance of *Invertis* directly affected the resources, orientation, and structure of the work undertaken by the digital media personnel. We do not have any systematic evidence indicating that this type of factors is common to other media organizations. The growth of ownership concentration in the media industry in past decades, however, suggests that looking at these dynamics that cross levels of analysis should be part of the agenda of researchers studying contemporary settings that are not independent or do not significantly depend on interorganizational alliances. In this sense, we hope that this article constitutes a useful step toward broadening the analytical scope of studies of cultural production in media organizations in this age of digital media.

Note

1. The names of the company, media, and interviewees quoted in this article have been changed.

References

Bagdikian, B. 1983. *The media monopoly*. Boston: Beacon.

Baldwin, T., S. McVoy, and C. Steinfield. 1996. *Convergence*. Thousand Oaks, CA: Sage.

Benkler, Y. 1998. Communications infrastructure and the distribution of control over content. *Telecommunications Policy* 22:183-96.

Black, D. 2001. Internet radio: A case study in medium specificity. *Media, Culture & Society* 23:397-408.

Boczkowski, P. 2004. *Digitizing the news: Innovation in online newspapers.* Cambridge, MA: MIT Press.

Chandler, A., Jr., and J. Cortada. 2000. The information age: Continuities and differences. In *A nation transformed by information: How information has shaped the United States from colonial times to the present,* ed. A. Chandler Jr. and J. Cortada, 281-99. New York: Oxford University Press.

Compaine, B., and D. Gomery, eds. 2000. *Who owns the media? Competition and concentration in the mass media industry.* Mahwah, NJ: Lawrence Erlbaum.

Deuze, M. 2004. What is multimedia journalism? *Journalism Studies* 5:139-52.

Elberse, A. 1998. Consumer acceptance of interactive news in the Netherlands. *Press/Politics* 3 (4): 62-83.

Epstein, E. 1973. *News from nowhere.* New York: Random House.

Ettema, J., and T. Glasser. 1998. *Custodians of conscience.* New York: Columbia University Press.

Gans, H. 1980. *Deciding what's news.* New York: Vintage.

Gieber, W. 1964. News is what newspapermen make it. In *People, society, and mass communication,* ed. L. Dexter and D. White, 173-82. New York: Free Press.

Gilbert, C. 2002. Can competing frames co-exist? The paradox of threatened response. Harvard Business School Working Paper 02-056, Cambridge, MA.

Gitlin, T. 1994. *Inside prime time.* London: Routledge.

Gordon, R. 2003. The meanings and implications of convergence. In *Digital journalism: Emerging media and the changing horizons of journalism,* ed. K. Kawamoto. Lanham, MD: Rowman & Littlefield.

Greenstein, S., and T. Khanna. 1997. What does industry convergence mean? In *Competing in the age of digital convergence,* ed. D. Yoffie, 201-26. Boston: Harvard Business School Press.

Hall, J. 2001. *Online journalism: A critical primer.* London: Pluto.

Higgins, M. 2000. Divergent messages in a converging world. *The Information Society* 16:49-63.

Jenkins, H. 2001. Convergence? I diverge. *Technology Review,* June, p. 93.

Kaniss, P. 1991. *Making local news.* Chicago: University of Chicago Press.

Klinenberg, E. 2000. Information et Production Numerique. *Actes de la Recherche en Sciences Sociales* 134:66-75.

Lin, C., and L. Jeffries. 1998. Factors influencing the adoption of multimedia cable technology. *Journalism & Mass Communication Quarterly* 75:341-52.

Manovich, L. 2001. *The language of new media.* Cambridge, MA: MIT Press.

Marvin, C. 1980. Delivering the news of the future. *Journal of Communication* 30:10-20.

Negroponte, N. 1996. *Being digital.* New York: Vintage.

Owen, B. 1999. *The Internet challenge to television.* Cambridge, MA: Harvard University Press.

Pavlik, J. 2001. *Journalism and new media.* New York: Columbia University Press.

Picard, R., and J. Brody. 1997. *The newspaper publishing industry.* Boston: Allyn & Bacon.

Poster, M. 2001. *What's the matter with the Internet?* Minneapolis: University of Minnesota Press.

Preston, P., and A. Kerr. 2001. Digital media, nation-states and local cultures: The case of multimedia "content" production. *Media, Culture & Society* 23:109-31.

Roshco, B. 1975. *Newsmaking.* Chicago: University of Chicago Press.

Schiller, D. 1999. *Digital capitalism: Networking the global market system.* Cambridge, MA: MIT Press.

Schudson, M. 2000. The sociology of news production revisited (again). In *Mass media and society,* 2nd ed., ed. J. Curran and M. Gurevitch, 175-200. London: Arnold.

Seib, P. 2001. *Going live: Getting the news right in a real-time, online world.* Lanham, MD: Rowman & Littlefield.

Smith, A. 1980. *Goodbye Gutenberg.* New York: Oxford University Press.

Sumpter, R. 2000. Daily newspaper editors' audience construction routines: A case study. *Critical Studies in Media Communication* 17:334-46.

Tuchman, G. 1978. *Making news.* New York: Free Press.

Weaver, D., and G. C. Wilhoit. 1986. *The American journalist.* Bloomington: Indiana University Press.

Yoffie, D. 1997. Introduction: CHESS and competing in the age of digital convergence. In *Competing in the age of digital convergence,* ed. D. Yoffie, 1-35. Boston: Harvard Business School Press.

Zavoina, S., and T. Reichert. 2000. Media convergence/management change: The evolving workflow for visual journalists. *Journal of Media Economics* 13:1143-51.

Convergence: News Production in a Digital Age

A paradox of contemporary sociology is that the discipline has largely abandoned the empirical study of journalistic organizations and news institutions at the moment when the media has gained visibility in political, economic, and cultural spheres; when other academic fields have embraced the study of media and society; and when leading sociological theorists have broken from the disciplinary cannon to argue that the media are key actors in modern life. This article examines the point of journalistic production in one major news organization and shows how reporters and editors manage constraints of time, space, and market pressure under regimes of convergence news making. It considers the implications of these conditions for the particular forms of intellectual and cultural labor that journalists produce, drawing connections between the political economy of the journalistic field, the organizational structure of multimedia firms, new communications technologies, and the qualities of content created by media workers.

Keywords: convergence; news media; newsroom; journalism; sociology of media; local news

By
ERIC KLINENBERG

A paradox of contemporary sociology is that the discipline has largely abandoned the empirical study of journalistic organizations and news institutions at the moment when the media has gained visibility in political, economic, and cultural spheres; when other academic fields have embraced the study of media and society; and when leading sociological theorists— including Bourdieu (1998), Habermas (1989), Castells (1996), and Luhmann (2000)—have broken from the disciplinary cannon to argue that the media are key actors in modern life. Herbert Gans (1972) called attention to this

Eric Klinenberg is an assistant professor of sociology at New York University. His first book, Heat Wave: A Social Autopsy of Disaster in Chicago *(University of Chicago Press), won five scholarly book prizes and is currently being adapted for the screen and the stage. Klinenberg has published articles in journals including* Ethnography *and* Theory and Society, *and he writes often for magazines and newspapers such as* Le Monde Diplomatique, The Washington Post, *and the* London Review of Books. *His next book, on local media in a digital age, will be published by Henry Holt.*

DOI: 10.1177/0002716204270346

"famine in media research" in a review article in the *American Journal of Sociology*. Yet—with the notable exceptions of a few landmark studies conducted in the 1970s (Tuchman 1978; Gans 1979; Fishman 1980)—in the past thirty years American sociologists have largely stayed out of newsrooms and ignored the conditions of journalistic production. Although a few studies are emerging of digital technologies in newsrooms (see especially Boczkowski 2004), and of labor issues for journalists (see Majoribanks 2000), the media scholar Timothy Cook (1998, x) noted that "it is as if a virtual moratorium were placed on further studies" of newsrooms. The sociology of news organizations is all but dead.

Ironically, studies of media are flourishing elsewhere in the academy. Today, most major universities have developed schools, departments, and programs dedicated to media and communications. Political scientists consider the news organization a political institution (or "fourth estate"), and most government agencies employ public relations specialists to manage their representations in the public sphere. Economists attribute fluctuations in the market to reports and opinions broadcast in the specialized business media, and financial analysts pay close attention to the way media pundits cover various industries and companies. Anthropologists have discovered the centrality of media as a source of imagination, migration, and the articulation of identity, and they are observing sites of production, reception, and circulation in diverse settings (Appadurai 1996; Ginsburg, Abu-Lughod, and Larkin 2002). Recent sociological accounts of news have been either historical, most notably the work of Michael Schudson (1978, 1995) and Paul Starr (2004); cultural, as in debates over the various public spheres (Calhoun 1993; Jacobs 2000); political, such as "media effects" studies; or theoretical. Todd Gitlin (2002), for example, argued that contemporary experience is "supersaturated" with a torrent of images and information so pervasive that most people take it for granted. Similarly, Manuel Castells (1996, 333) claimed that the media have reconstituted time and space, fundamentally altering the symbolic substratum of social life. Variants of these claims are surely familiar to anyone familiar with social scientific and humanities research today.

If, indeed, there is consensus that media products are central to the operations of different fields of action, it is surprising that sociologists have stopped examining how organizations responsible for producing the news and information work. Research in other disciplines often emphasizes the importance of sociological studies of news institutions, only to cite work that is several decades old and no longer reliable to explain how newsrooms work. Lacking current research, critics are left to guess about the strategies, practices, and interests that shape major news corporations; determine the content of news products; and produce the "symbolic power" (Bourdieu 1994) of publicly defining, delimiting, and framing key issues and events. Communications scholars, for example, often rely on anecdotal evidence for their assessments of how changes in the media industry have affected conditions of news production. Within sociology, social problems scholars typically do careful work to *show that* journalists selectively frame public issues; yet they rarely follow up by going inside newsrooms and asking reporters and editors how they constructed their stories, instead *speculating about why* the coverage takes certain forms.[1]

There has been no shortage of activity and change within media institutions and the journalistic field since the 1970s. The past thirty years has been a revolutionary period in the news media, which have experienced

- the advent of cable television, the beginning of a twenty-four-hour news cycle, and the steady decline of newspaper readership levels (though not a decline in newspaper profitability);
- the introduction of advanced communications technologies, such as satellites, the Internet, desktop publishing, and, most important, computers, which were rarely used in the newsrooms of the 1970s;
- the demise of family-owned news organizations with special interests in supporting journalistic principles with lower revenues and the emergence of chain papers and multimedia production companies;
- the rise of conglomerate media giants that use synergistic production and distribution strategies (in which different branches of the company share and cross-promote each others' resources and services);
- the related destruction of legendary divisions between managerial and editorial operations, the mythical church and state of the journalistic field;
- the birth of new forms and formats, such as the television news magazine, dramatized news footage, and product-driven news sections;
- the deregulation of media markets, and specifically of restrictions on ownership of multiple media outlets in the same city; and
- a crisis of legitimacy for journalists, who often complain that new conditions of production undermine their capacity to meet their own standards, struggle with the emergence of a polarized labor force including a celebrity class of journalistic elites, and consistently rank at the bottom of opinion polls rating the popularity of various professions (Gans 2003).

These transformations are pervasive: in 1945, for example, roughly 80 percent of American daily papers were independently owned. By 2000, about 80 percent were owned and operated by publicly traded chains, and major media corporations were actively building lines of vertical and horizontal integration to link everything from news production to entertainment to advertising in-house (Dugger 2000). Yet in the United States, little ethnographic work penetrates these organizations to describe or explain how they work.

This article examines the point of journalistic production in one major news organization and shows how reporters and editors manage constraints of time, space, and market pressure under regimes of convergence news making. I describe how news organizations, like firms in other American industries during the recent phase of "flexible accumulation," have downsized their staffs while imposing new demands that workers become skilled at multitasking with new technologies. Digital systems for reporting, writing, file sharing, and printing facilitate this flexibility. I consider the implications of these conditions for the particular forms of intellectual and cultural labor that journalists produce, drawing connections between the political economy of the journalistic field, the organizational structure of multimedia firms, new communications technologies, and the qualities of content created by news workers.

This article grows out of a multiyear ethnographic project based on case studies of news organizations that began as print media but now use advanced technologies to produce and distribute content across platforms. Here, I draw upon field-work to show how changes in the journalistic field, particularly the rise of new technologies and the corporate integration of news companies, have led to a double fragmentation: first, for newsmakers, whose daily work has been interrupted and rearranged by additional responsibilities and new pressures of time and space; second, for news audiences, whom marketers have segmented into narrow units and who are encouraged to forge symbolic or imagined communities on the basis of market concerns. This article focuses on one particular but also particularly important case: Metro News, an emerging second-tier media corporation that is broadly considered an industry model organization for integrating different forms of media work.[2] Recently Metro News won *Fortune* magazine's survey for "most admired news company" several years in a row, the industry's leading publications routinely feature it as an exemplary case, and international firms visit often for tours of the facility. In the late 1990s I spent three weeks inside the Metro News newsroom, where I observed journalists and editors in action as they worked on stories, conducted formal editorial meetings, and searched for news. I also conducted and taped interviews with twenty-five reporters, editors, and managers. When I began the project, the news editor not only allowed me to sit in on meetings and interrupt his busy reporters. He also let me occupy an unused office in the corner of the main news floor, and I could bring reporters back into my private room and give them space to speak openly about their work.

Convergence and the New Media Market

Metro News has been a major player in the American politics and society since the mid-nineteenth century. For the first fifty years of its life, the Metro News company devoted its energy to local news and politics, and at the turn of the twentieth century, its editor gained attention by arguing that the mission of an urban paper is to acculturate and integrate new immigrants to local as well as American national culture. In the next decades, the company grew with the times, establishing a new paper in New York after World War I, a local radio station in the 1920s, and an affiliated television station in 1948. Still, the core of the company was its main paper, so when readership began to decline in the 1970s, Metro News, like most other newspaper companies, had to refashion its mission. Its new managers decided that a great newspaper could not survive unless it was embedded in a great news and entertainment network. This is the moment of rebirth for the Metro News and for other media organizations. Unfortunately, the classic sociological studies of news work were conducted just before this renaissance.

From 1975 until today, major media companies such as Metro News have evolved through four key development strategies: First, *taking companies out of private hands* (usually ending the control of wealthy families who held long ties to the news profession), *raising capital with public stock offerings* (Metro News, for example, went public in the early 1980s), and *reforming the corporate mission* to meet the bottom-line demands of stockholders. Second, and related, is *bringing in new corporate managers to streamline production systems in the newsroom* and to reduce labor costs. Third, *making massive investments in digital communications technologies* and remaking the corporate infrastructure. Fourth, *establishing lines of horizontal integration in the company*, which meant acquiring or merging with other content providers and distributors, such as television stations, Internet companies, and magazines, and linking the marketing as well as the news divisions across subsidiary firms. Metro News began aggressively purchasing new papers and local TV stations in the 1970s, and today its holdings include more than a dozen city newspapers, with major dailies in the largest urban markets. It owns a national television superstation, a share of another national network, and more than two dozen local TV stations. Finally, it operates a fleet of radio stations in leading markets, a book publisher, several television production companies, massive digital media investments, a professional sports franchise, and local cable television news stations that broadcast local news around the clock.

[I]n 1945 . . . roughly 80 percent of American daily papers were independently owned. By 2000, about 80 percent were owned and operated by publicly traded chains . . .

For the company, ownership of such diverse operations is the key to a *synergistic* mode of production (Auletta 1998), whereby each media outlet uses the products of the others to enhance its offerings and, to use the language of the industry, to *cross-promote its brands*. On the business side, synergy allows big news companies to integrate their advertising sales work and create special packages for clients; this gives them a major competitive advantage over smaller media companies and also increases the efficiency of their marketing projects. At the organizational level, the Metro News's acquisitions of newspapers in California, New York, and Florida allow the corporation to cut and streamline its slate of domestic and international bureaus. Local reporters in Los Angeles, Chicago, or New York City are both city and national correspondents because their work is used by different papers. Similarly, one foreign bureau can provide news and photography for several papers at once. And freelancers—who are increasingly popular with news companies—can broker deals with a corporate network rather than a single outlet. Digital communications infrastructures are crucial for this level of convergence since they allow for immediate circulation of content and distribute information in easily editable formats.

But this is only the beginning of synergy. Metro News also uses each branch of its operation to produce content for several media at once, and it has turned its company into a flexible producer. Within any single metropolitan news agency, the main newsroom is increasingly likely to contain a television studio, Internet production facilities, radio equipment, sophisticated graphics machines, and hundreds of computer terminals for print journalists. There are separate staffs for the different media, but workers in the various departments have frequent contact with each other, in part because they all produce material for many platforms.

Just what these cultural workers produce is the subject of major debate inside Metro News and the profession more broadly. Reporters and professional observers complain that the corporate management has classified their product as "content," a category that suits any story, image, or other form of intellectual property, rather than journalism (see Auletta 1998). According to journalists and editors, the craft distinctions between different genres of news work that historically organized the field are beginning to blur. Media managers argue that their staff should be able to tell stories across platforms, and many reporters are increasingly worried about bottom-line-driven assaults on their vocational techniques and professional values. Although the news media was born as a commercial medium and has always been deeply entangled with corporate, profit-driven interests, insiders fear that the logic of the market has penetrated to unprecedented depths of the modern newsroom (Underwood 1993; Downie and Kaiser 2001). In response, journalists are making use of the language of the professions, mobilizing the image of the professional journalist who is independent, specially trained, skeptical, and objective to defend their status from incursions by the market and new players in the field.

The New Newsroom

The organizational transformation of Metro News has produced major changes in the physical and social space of its offices. Reporters and editors can see powerful signs of their industry's transformation in their work spaces, which have been completely redesigned so that journalists can move freely between print, television, radio, and Internet outlets and meet the demands of the new media environment. The most striking difference in the newsroom is that in 1999 the company placed a television news studio at the physical and symbolic center of the office, directly in front of the editor's door, so that the editorial staff orbits around the studio. This is, of course, hardly an innocent move since journalists have fierce internal battles about the ways that television news culture—with its emphasis on video, sound bites, and soft features—threatens the integrity of other reporting practices.

For much of the newspaper staff, the emergence of television as the centerpiece of the organization signals the rise of a different journalistic mission, one determined by the production values of TV news. But then there is another, more seductive side of television: everyone, including print reporters, recognizes the power of TV to reach a massive audience, and for reporters, television represents a route to celebrity, wealth, and influence. In fact, one adviser to the company told me that the introduction of television into the newsroom had been "the biggest non-story of the year. It turns out," he explained, "that print reporters want to be on TV just as much as everyone else."

Perhaps the deepest source of the journalists' frustration is their perception that the new environment has forced them to take on additional responsibilities in the same work period, which has particularly severe consequences for cultural production that requires serious, independent thinking. Of course, there is nothing new about either deadlines or news cycles. Modern journalists have always worked against the clock to meet their rigid production and distribution schedules, and news stories are necessarily written in haste. During the 1970s, national television news programs were broadcast once a day, in the early evening, which gave the production team a clear twenty-four-hour span to cover "breaking news." Most major newspapers were published in the early morning or afternoon, and with the contemporary printing technologies, reporters had to file their stories several hours in advance.

The time cycle for news making in the age of digital production is radically different: the regular news cycle has spun into an erratic and unending pattern that I characterize as a *news cyclone*. The advent of twenty-four-hour television news and the rapid emergence of instant Internet news sites have eliminated the temporal borders in the news day, creating an informational environment in which there is always breaking news to produce, consume, and—for reporters and their subjects—react against. In the new media world, a Metro News writer says, "There's a writing process that's just *constant, constant, constant* . . . in everything we're doing we're dealing with the clock. *Bang. Bang. Bang. Bang. Bang.* And that clock just goes on."

Synergy and Digital Systems

So, just how has Metro News managed to meet the new time pressures and to increase the efficiency and productivity of its already busy staff? This is the deeper story of synergy, and it is also the place where digital technologies enter the picture. In the new media newsroom, journalists have to become *flexible laborers*, reskilled to meet demands from several media at once. And as companies break down the division of news labor, reporters experience a time compression that they make sense of through the language of stress and pressure. As one reporter explains,

> Metro News is a multimedia company. . . . Increasingly, there are pressures to put reporters who are covering stories on television, and there are other demands that you have as a reporter for other ways of covering stories. Let me be specific. There have been pressures to participate in cyberspace . . . they put your stuff on cyberspace and they ask you to do other things, provide links, [create] other kinds of information. There's [also] an emphasis

in journalism now, much more than ever, on graphics. So some of the time that you're writing the story has to be spent with the graphics team talking to them about what we're doing, so that their graphics can add to what we're doing and not simply repeat. But also you are providing some reporting information for graphics, which is a whole new layer. [All of this] requires conversations with other people in the newsroom, and that requires time taken away from just the story. . . . [After describing other responsibilities involved in television and internet she concludes:] Very recently . . . one of the things that they decided to try was having reporters write conceptual headlines for their stories. . . . I think to some people it's like, just another thing to do. You know, we've already got graphics, we've already got ties to photo, sometimes we have to appear on TV and do cyberspace. *And now we're going to have to make suggestions for headlines too?*

For Metro News, such coordinated news-making activities keep labor costs down and increase the output and efficiency of the production process. For reporters, though, the new regime creates real professional challenges: the more they work with different media, for example, the more they realize that content does not move easily from one medium to the next, and therefore they must develop techniques for translating work across platforms. It is no surprise, then, that the new journalism textbooks and curricular programs emphasize developing news skills that work in several media. Many veteran journalists worry that if television becomes the most valuable and important medium for major news companies, then being telegenic will become the most important journalistic skill and a criterion for entry-level reporting jobs. What is more immediately worrisome for journalists is that the new responsibilities also reduce the editorial staff's time to research, report, and even to think about their work. Time matters in special ways for cultural producers since incursions into the working schedule undermine one's ability to perform a craft (see Bourdieu 2000). The greatest fear among print journalists is that the production routines for daily television news will become normative in their medium as well. In a discussion with me, one reporter explained that

some people are very concerned about the redesign of our newsroom and how our TV station is going to have a presence on the desk. Digital is going to be on the desk. And on the other hand, I think that it's all to the good and that the more we get integrated and familiar with these other areas, the more likely we will be in the future to be prepared for whatever happens in the future, rather than be isolated and out of print.
EK: Are you asked to take any other responsibilities?
So far I haven't been. I mean, I was asked one time to lead a chat room on ethnic issues by our digital folks. But there are a lot of other people who are constantly being asked to get on TV and talk about their stories. I just haven't really done that. I was on the television news for a project I did on National earlier this year on the elections. . . . So I haven't really been affected by that push. But I know of folks in Washington . . . I think they have pretty heavy TV duties in Washington, a lot of live stories on what they're covering. And that takes up a lot of their time. They have to write the scripts. OK, so they write their news stories and then they write their scripts and they don't get paid for that and it takes a lot of time. And I don't know if that's going to be coming for us as well.
    I guess my only concern is that right now we have for many years been the source for TV news. You know, they read us and then they go out and do their stories. So if having news television in here means that we'll get to do . . . I mean I would rather do my story for both mediums than have somebody scarf up my story and do it, and kind of steal it from me after I did all the work. So there's sort of two ways to look at it.

Editors have related concerns: they have to sustain a certain level of journalistic quality to maintain the company's reputation. Indeed, it is important to have Pulitzer Prize–winning investigations, and in the past several years, the Metro News has had many. But it achieves this system by introducing a new system of stratification inside the newsroom, with elite reporters given ample time to do large projects and a large staff of second-tier journalists responsible for much of the daily workload. This hierarchical arrangement is similar to those emerging in other cultural fields, including the academy.

The time cycle for news making in the age of digital production . . . has spun into an erratic and unending pattern that I characterize as a news cyclone.

In their most extreme forms, concerns about efficiency can push journalists to forgo traditional kinds of reporting and to rely, instead, on the most easily accessible information: news that is available online. In recent years, several leading professional news publications have run stories about the industry's most dangerous computer virus, whose symptoms include staying at the desk and using material from the Web for reporting that is faster and easier than work in the streets. There are several well-known cases in which journalists relying on Web-based information used faulty statistics as the basis for published stories. Reporters, particularly when they are working against the clock, are susceptible to Internet misinformation. Online reporting practices are unlikely to displace traditional reporting techniques, as some of the most concerned critics worry. But media organizations are learning that the same digital systems that improve journalists' ability to do research in the office can also have perverse effects.

The responsibility to produce content that can be used across platforms also places a different kind of pressure on editors and business managers. For them, directing a multimedia company requires ensuring that a sufficient level of content meets the needs of each medium, and this means that reporters assigned to key beats or stories have to produce even if they want more time to explore. According to one reporter, "Being productive means you're gathering information that is short order. . . . Everything, all the incentives, come down to producing for tomorrow." One effect of this imperialism of the immediate is that Metro News, long renowned for serious and time-consuming investigative reports, has reduced the number of investigative stories. Between 1980 and 1995, the newspaper cut the number of investigative stories by 48 percent. One reporter explains his view of the change as follows: "The whole idea of giving reporters time and space to explore just doesn't seem like an efficient way to do business." The core city reporting staff no longer has enough time to penetrate into the deep pockets of urban life and come up with surprising stories. Crime, local scandals, entertainment, all the events that are easy to cover have become more prominent in the city news. As one city editor told me,

> The best way to blanket the city, and the most efficient way to blanket the city, is to cover the [big] institutions [with beats]. So, it's hard to justify, from a resource standpoint, a more burdensome way of getting information, which is out on the streets. It's not efficient at all. There are no press releases, no spokespeople, and if there are, there is a bunch of spokespeople [saying different things]. And to sort through that and weave through that and get a clear picture is just time-consuming and it's harder to devote the resources to doing that.

Target Marketing and Media Segmentation

One of the most economically significant characteristics of digital news systems is that they have enabled media organizations to push the principles of target marketing to new levels, to make specialized information and entertainment products that appeal to narrow groups of consumers but that can be sold by one advertising staff (see Turow 1998). Competition within the American media market has fragmented the mass audience on which network television stations and major newspapers built their fortunes. According to one major media executive, "People want to know what their neighbors are up to. People want to know what's going on in their block. People want information that touches their lives" (quoted in Lieberman 1998). Today the strategy of most news companies is to locate and target affluent audiences. For many city papers, the major impact of new digital technologies (especially publishing technologies) is that they enable companies to target coverage to the suburban areas that contain most of the affluent readers whom advertisers want to reach. Using digital technologies, Metro News has expanded its system of zoned newspaper production and distribution so that it prints not only a special section for each of the zoned regions in the metropolitan area but occasionally different front pages, with special headlines, photos, and stories, as well. One reporter expressed her frustration with this system of target marketing:

> Something might go on page one in the city and then something else will go in the suburbs in the suburban papers. . . . Oftentimes, we have stories that have been like page one in *USA Today* or the *Wall Street Journal*, but could only get read by people in one zone. So nobody saw the story if they lived in the suburbs, until they read it two weeks later on the front page of the *USA Today*, or until they saw it on TV because TV picked it up. So that's really frustrating from the point of view of the reporter who thinks they've got a nicely written story, to not get play because the editors think that won't be of interest to people in Dixon County. And then my argument to that is well these white people in Dixon County will be mighty interested when these Mexican people get pushed out and soon they'll be

on their door-step. (Laughs,) And he said, well we can change the lead. "In a move that made white residents of Dixon County uneasy . . . "

Yet there is an important exception to the rise of target-marketed news: it is not available to people who live in poor neighborhoods or suburbs and lack a strong base of desirable professionals for advertisers to target. As a former *Chicago Tribune* editor explains, "By reducing circulation efforts among low-income, minority readers, newspapers actually improve the overall demographic profile of their audiences, which they then use to justify raising advertising rates" (Squires 1993).

The Internet, rather than television or print, offers the most exciting possibilities for creating new forms of journalism with advanced technology and convergence production. The Internet is the ideal medium for deepening coverage with interactive links to video, text, and graphics, and the spatial constraints are relatively loose online. (In theory, of course, Internet reporting need not be bound by any spatial constraints. But many editors still try to sharpen their stories so that they conform to conventional narrative forms from print media.) Yet by 2003, few news organizations had developed a business model that generated profits for news Web sites, and particularly after the collapse of the dot-com industry, news companies were reluctant to invest significant resources in the most innovative kinds of online media production. A former editor who developed the new media offerings in one major Florida newspaper told me that

> in most companies, the real convergence action involves putting print reporters on television, and that's just not the way to make convergence work. One thing is that it doesn't take advantage of the medium. There's nothing journalistically or technologically interesting about putting a print reporter on TV—it's just uses personnel in a more flexible way, getting more out of them. The real innovations in convergence journalism are going to come on the web, or eventually on interactive television, where you can produce new kinds of content. Now the problem is that no one knows how to make a web-based business model that works for journalism. So although the internet is the best place to combine text, video, graphics, and interactivity—all the things that make multimedia production exciting— there's not much corporate interest in doing it because it's not really profitable, and it's not clear that it will be. And you can't get support for innovative news production if there's not a business model that works.

Some participants in convergence projects argue that other, less visible journalistic benefits come from convergence production. Sharing resources and staff helps both television and newspaper companies expand the scope of their reporting, allowing them to cover stories that they would otherwise miss. A study by the Project for Excellence in Journalism found that convergence production systems can help improve the quality of television news since TV staffs are comparably small and print reporters bring depth to their offerings. But several newspaper reporters complain that the stories and sources from television tend to focus on crime and violence issues since those are major topics on local TV news.[3] Many print journalists believe that the greatest influence of television news practices on newspapers is to promote this visual information at the expense of textual depth, and they are anxious that the norms and forms of television will take over the paper.

Conclusion: Newsrooms in an
Age of Digital Production

From the late nineteenth century, when American urban newspapers announced their project of integrating and acculturating new immigrants to local and national culture, journalists and social scientists have argued that news organizations "not only serve but create their communities" by providing raw materials for collective social and political life (Fuller 1996, 228). In recent years, cultural critics and sociologists have grown so interested in global circuits of information and the possibilities for cosmopolitan uses of news that they have scarcely recognized how media companies use the Internet and other advanced communication technologies to alter their local coverage.[4] According to the *Columbia Journalism Review*, from 1985 to 1995, space for international news fell in each of the major American weekly news magazines: from 24 to 14 percent at *Time*, from 22 to 12 percent at *Newsweek*, and from 20 to 12 percent at *U.S. News and World Report*. Network television news programs, which devoted 45 percent of their broadcasts to foreign affairs in the 1970s, gave 13.5 percent of their time to international news in 1995 (Hickey 1998). According to Downie and Kaiser (2001), after September 11, the American news media exhibited an increased interest in foreign affairs and heightened international coverage. Yet one year later, in the new Afterward to the paperback edition of the same book (2002), they reported that soon after the disaster most news organizations returned to their pre–September 11 patterns of coverage. The optimism about the future of foreign reporting they expressed in the first edition seems unwarranted (also see Alterman 2003, 263-64).

When news organizations do cover national and international events, editors and managers encourage journalists to "localize" the stories, that is, to illustrate why news far from home is relevant to the local community. One prominent media consultant told me that "if you want to write a story about the war in Kabul, you're better off tying it to the Kabul House restaurant in town." In theory, news audiences can use advanced communications technologies to obtain enormous amounts of information about the world. In practice, as advertisers and news executives know, most people use the news to gain a world of information about their personal interests, their hometown, and themselves. Target marketing and convergence production techniques have helped to create informational islands of communities whose segregation in physical space is increasingly joined and reinforced by the differentiation of specialized news products. As Cass Sunstein (2001) argued, new media and digital technologies have played important roles in this segmenting process.

The consequences of the emergent journalistic and managerial practices described here are already visible. Convergence news companies expect their journalistic staff to be flexible and fast, and both editors and corporate managers are already revaluing their workers, considering multimedia skills in their story assignments as well as in hiring and retention decisions. Many journalists and media critics complain that the additional labor demands and the work speedup required for convergence have undermined the conditions of news production, mainly by reducing the time available to report, research, write, and reflect on stories. Convergence companies contest these claims, pointing to various awards won by staff in television, print, and the Internet as evidence that multimedia production enriches their offerings and improves their staff. Journalists respond by pointing to an emerging stratification of the labor force, in which major companies support a small elite corps of reporters who are able to conduct serious investigations and long-term projects, and the remaining majority who have more responsibilities than ever. Yet it is notoriously difficult to reliably appraise the overall quality of reporting across fields and themes. Instead of attempting a normative evaluation of whether the new conditions of production are good or bad for journalism, I conclude by explaining how convergence regimes and corporate managerial strategies affect various qualities of news content and features of news work.

[The newsroom has] been completely redesigned so that journalists can move freely between print, television, radio, and Internet outlets and meet the demands of the new media environment.

The penetration of market principles and marketing projects into the editorial divisions of news organizations is one of the most dramatic changes in the journalistic field, and there is no question the mythical walls separating the editorial and advertising are mostly down. When Gans (1979) studied news organizations in the 1960s and 1970s, he found that editors would occasionally grant access to political officials and listen to their input for various stories and issues, but—as a matter of journalistic principle—not to advertisers or corporations. In the late 1990s, Times Mirror CEO and *Los Angeles Times* publisher Mark Willes generated professional outrage by announcing that advertisers should play a key role in shaping journalistic content. In the early 2000s, editorial meetings with advertisers and the internal marketing staff are routine, and the editors I met unabashedly reported that they worked hard to produce more marketable and profitable products. At the *Chicago Tribune*, architects integrated the famously separate elevator banks for management and journalists, symbolically eliminating the historical markers of journalism's sacred and profane sides. In 2003, managers at the *Dallas Morning News* even began handing out $100 bills to reporters who memorized the company's five business goals and could recite them on demand (Celeste 2003).

It is important to note that news companies have long been driven by bottom-line considerations and that media moguls from William Randolph Hearst to Rupert Murdoch have built enormous fortunes through aggressive capitalist management. Yet in recent years, several high-ranking editors, including James Squires from the *Chicago Tribune*, James Fallows from *U.S. News and World Report*, and Leonard Downie Jr. and Robert Kaiser from *The Washington Post*, have argued that corporate managers and advertisers are now active participants in editorial decision making and that their interests now structure the form and content of news to an unprecedented degree (Squires 1993; Downie and Kaiser 2001).

The most notable examples of advertisers taking part in editorial decision making include the case of the *Los Angeles Times* sponsoring the Staples Center, sharing revenue on a 168-page magazine produced by the editorial staff and inserted into the Sunday paper in 1999; the new special sections determined by advertising and dedicated to mutual funds, communications and computer technologies, and home and gardening in most major newspapers; and the rise of service-oriented "news you can use," human interest, health, and entertainment reporting and of news beats such as "malls," "shopping," and "car culture" (Underwood 1993). Contemporary news organizations conduct extensive and expensive research to learn what kinds of content consumers want, too, and they have made important qualitative changes in their offerings to meet market demand. Several new media forms express the strength of market logic in the newsrooms: television newsmagazines, dramatized television news footage and musical scores for news, newspaper "advertorials," niche tabloids for young urban consumers (such as Chicago's *Red Streak* and *Red Eye*, produced by the *Sun-Times* and the Tribune Company, respectively), and Internet reports with ads linked to stories on related products and services. Newspapers' increasing emphasis on color graphics, weather packages, business reporting, and cross-promotional packages are part of the same trend.

The market pressures transforming the journalistic field have changed other fields as well, including the academy, the medical profession, and publishing. Identifying these shifts in the media as features of broader political economic forces in contemporary societies, as many critics do, is a necessary but insufficient part of sociological analysis. The internal dynamics of any given field always absorb and refract the exogenous forces that enter and alter it, and fieldwork inside media organizations and the industry's social space helps to specify how change happens in this particular sphere. One surprising feature of the journalistic field is that news organizations harness advanced communications technology to speed up and extend the work process for reporters and to enhance their local offerings to suburban markets.

The most exciting innovations in journalistic forms, particularly those involving multimedia packages disseminated through the Internet, have received little support from news organizations because they are not profitable. Moreover, the celebrated genres of the American journalistic craft, particularly investigative reporting, long-term projects, and penetrating urban affairs work, have lost corporate support in all but the most elite publications because of their inefficiencies and the costs of production. One editor of a midsized newspaper told a *Columbia Journalism Review* editor, "If a story needs real investment of time and money, we don't do it anymore"; and a television newsman reports, "Instead of racing out of the newsroom with a camera crew when an important story breaks, we're more likely now to stay at our desks and work the phones, rewrite the wire copy, hire a local crew and a free-lance producer to get pictures at the scene, then dig out some file footage, maps, or still photos for the anchor to talk in front of, or maybe buy some coverage from a video news service like Reuters, AP, or World Television News" (quoted in Hickey 1998).

Digital technologies have changed journalistic production in newsrooms, but not according to journalists' preferences. When conglomerates and publicly traded companies took over news organizations and entered the journalistic field, they imported corporate managerial techniques and developed new strategies to increase the productivity, efficiency, and profitability of news businesses (Squires 1993; Underwood 1993; Dugger 2000; Downie and Kaiser 2001). Media executives and managerial-minded editors not only downsized their journalistic staffs, they also invented new regimes of convergence production to expand their offerings across media (Auletta 1998). They designed applications of digital technologies to facilitate the process of multimedia work and increase their capacity to repackage articles from one newspaper to another or one platform to another (Harper 1998; Pavlik 2001) and invested lightly in innovations to basic journalistic forms, offering little support for multimedia offerings that take full advantage of the Internet's affordances. Digital systems in major news companies remain in embryonic stages of development, and it is difficult to predict how they will develop. But the political economy, cultural conventions, and regulatory restrictions governing the news industry will play powerful roles in determining how advanced communications technologies enter the matrix of journalistic production, just as they did before the digital age.

Notes

1. A notable exception is Gilens (1999), who showed that major American news magazines vastly overrepresented African Americans in photographs of poor people, particularly the "undeserving" or unsympathetic poor. He then conducted interviews with photography editors to ask why they used these images and if they recognized their own patterns of representation.

2. Metro News is a pseudonym.

3. Downie and Kaiser (2001, 170) reported, "An exhaustive 1999 study of 590 local newscasts on fifty-nine stations in nineteen cities . . . found that nine of every ten local stories on those newscasts came 'from either the police scanner or scheduled events.' Fewer than one in ten stories came from the reporter's own initiatives."

4. Many scholars invoke Arjun Appadurai's (1996) language of "scapes" and "flows" to portray a floating world of hypermobility, fast action, and congenital rootlessness. Yet in *Modernity at Large*, Appadurai was centrally concerned with "the place of locality" amidst global flows. His theoretical writing called attention to the various cultural processes and institutions that shape local subjects and local knowledge, to the ways that situated communities operate as both *contexts* and *producers of contexts* in contemporary life. Appadurai recounted many familiar techniques for the spatial production of locality, "the building of houses, the organi-

zation of paths and passages, the making and remaking of fields and gardens" (p. 180). Yet he paid little attention to how local news organizations contribute to this process.

References

Alterman, Eric. 2003. *What liberal media? The truth about* bias *and the news*. New York: Basic Books.

Appadurai, Arjun. 1996. *Modernity at large: Cultural dimensions of globalization*. Minneapolis: University of Minnesota Press.

Auletta, Ken. 1998. Synergy city. *American Journalism Review*, May. http://www.ajr.org/article_printable.asp?id=2446/.

Boczkowski, Pablo. 2004. *Digitizing the news: Innovation in online newspapers*. Cambridge, MA: MIT Press.

Bourdieu, Pierre. 1994. *Language and symbolic power*. Cambridge, MA: Harvard University Press.

———. 1998. *On television*. New York: New Press.

———. 2000. *Pascalian meditations*. Stanford, CA: Stanford University Press.

Calhoun, Craig, ed. 1993. *Habermas and the public sphere*. Cambridge, MA: MIT Press.

Castells, Manuel. 1996. *The rise of the network society*. Oxford, UK: Blackwell.

Celeste, Eric. 2003. Snooze alarm. *Dallas Observer*, February 13.

Cook, Timothy. 1998. *Governing with the news: The news media as a political institution*. Chicago: University of Chicago Press.

Downie, Leonard, Jr., and Robert Kaiser. 2001. *The news about the news: American journalism in peril*. New York: Knopf.

———. 2002. *The news about the news: American journalism in peril*. New York: Vintage.

Dugger, Ronnie. 2000. The corporate domination of journalism. In *The business of journalism*, ed. William Serrin, 27-56. New York: New Press.

Fishman, Mark. 1980. *Manufacturing the news*. Austin: University of Texas Press.

Fuller, Jack. 1996. *News values: Ideas for the information age*. Chicago: University of Chicago Press.

Gans, Herbert. 1972. The famine in American mass-communications research: Comments on Hirsch, Tuchman, and Gecas. *American Journal of Sociology* 77:697-705.

———. 1979. *Deciding what's news: A study of CBS Evening News, NBC Nightly News, Newsweek, and Time*. New York: Pantheon.

———. 2003. *Democracy and the news*. New York: Oxford University Press.

Gilens, Martin. 1999. *Why Americans hate welfare: Race, media, and the politics of antipoverty policy*. Chicago: University of Chicago Press.

Ginsburg, Faye, Lila Abu-Lughod, and Brian Larkin, eds. 2002. *Media worlds: Anthropology on new terrain*. Berkeley: University of California Press.

Gitlin, Todd. 2002. *Media unlimited: How the torrent of images and sounds overwhelms our lives*. New York: Metropolitan Books.

Habermas, Jurgen. 1989. *The structural transformation of the public sphere*. Cambridge, MA: MIT Press.

Harper, Christopher. 1998. *And that's the way it will be: News and information in a digital world*. New York: New York University Press.

Hickey, Neil. 1998. Money lust: How pressure for profit is perverting journalism. *Columbia Journalism Review*, July/August. http://archives.cjr.org/year/98/4/moneylust.asp/.

Jacobs, Ronald. 2000. *Race, media, and the crisis of civil society*. Cambridge: Cambridge University Press.

Lieberman, David. 1998. The rise and rise of 24-hour local news. *Columbia Journalism Review*, November/December. http://archives.cjr.org/year/98/6/tvnews.asp/.

Luhmann, Niklas. 2000. *The reality of the mass media*. Stanford, CA: Stanford University Press.

Majoribanks, Tim. 2000. *News corporation, technology, and the workplace*. Cambridge: Cambridge University Press.

Pavlik, John. 2001. *Journalism and new media*. New York: Columbia University Press.

Schudson, Michael. 1978. *Discovering the news: A social history of American newspapers*. New York: Basic Books.

———. 1995. *The power of news*. Cambridge, MA: Harvard University Press.

Squires, James. 1993. *Read all about it: The corporate takeover of America's newspapers*. New York: Random House.

Starr, Paul. 2004. *The creation of the media: Political origins of modern communications*. New York: Basic Books.

Sunstein, Cass. 2001. *Republic.com*. Princeton, NJ: Princeton University Press.

Tuchman, Gaye. 1978. *Making news: A study in the construction of reality*. New York: Free Press.

Turow, Joseph. 1998. *Breaking up America: Advertisers and the new media world*. Chicago: University of Chicago Press.

Underwood, Doug. 1993. *When MBAs rule the newsroom*. New York: Columbia University Press.

Digital Gambling: The Coincidence of Desire and Design

By
NATASHA DOW SCHULL

Drawing on ethnographic research conducted in Las Vegas among game developers and machine gamblers, I correlate a set of digitally enhanced game features with phenomenological aspects of gamblers' experience, demonstrating the intimate connection between extreme states of subjective absorption in play and design elements that manipulate space and time to accelerate the extraction of money from players. The case of the digital gambling interface exemplifies the tendency of modern capitalism to bring space, time, and money into intensified relation and sheds light on the question of what might or might not be distinctive about the rationalities and libidinal investments of the "digital age."

Keywords: technology; ethnography; gambling; culture; digital age; capitalism; modernity

What I want to do is get into my playing rhythm, stay there longer and just play.
—Maria

The three-reel mechanical slot machine that served as a blueprint for gaming technology since the 1890s was transformed by electromechanical technology in 1963 with the introduction of the hopper, an internal payout device adapted from bank coin counters. The advent of video games in the 1970s led to the replacement of reels and levers with screens and buttons. In the 1980s, the digital microprocessor (a computer chip with memory) was incorporated into the slot machine as a means of regulating the

Natasha Dow Schull received her doctorate in anthropology from the University of California, Berkeley. At present she holds a Robert Wood Johnson postdoctoral position in the Health and Society Scholars program at Columbia University, based jointly at the Institute for Social and Economic Research and Policy and the Mailman School of Public Health. She is completing a book manuscript on the predicaments of technology and dependency in Las Vegas.

NOTE: I would like to thank Aaron Nathan for the stimulating feedback he provided throughout the writing of this article and Peter Bearman for his attentive comments on the final draft.

DOI: 10.1177/0002716204270435

hopper and other functions. The most critical component of the microprocessor for gambling machines is the random number generator, or RNG, which runs through number combinations at high speed until the play button is pressed, whereupon it generates a number combination, compares this number to a statistically determined table of payout rates, and instructs the hopper to deliver a win or not. Some in the industry call the RNG the "really new god."

In recent decades, the gaming industry—formerly known as the gambling industry—has established itself as an engine for experimentation and innovation with emergent digital capabilities, producing military-grade surveillance networks, sophisticated systems of accounting, and sleek gaming machinery. In this article, I focus on the design and play of digital gambling platforms to illuminate the distinctive rationalities and libidinal investments of the "digital age." Drawing on ethnographic research conducted in Las Vegas among game developers and machine gamblers, I correlate a set of digitally enhanced game features with phenomenological aspects of gamblers' experience, demonstrating the intimate connection between extreme states of subjective absorption in play and design elements that manipulate space and time to accelerate the extraction of money from players. The case of the digital gambling interface exemplifies the tendency of modern capitalism to bring space, time, and money into intensified relation and sheds light on the question of what might or might not be unique about the digital age.

Digital Game Design

> Technology provides managers unprecedented means for orchestrating resources, due to emerging capabilities in communications, connectivity, and interoperability.
> —Cummings and Brewer (1994, 69)

The publications of gaming industry analyst Leslie Cummings on techniques of casino management echo those of Frederick W. Taylor written earlier in the century on the scientific management of the workplace (Taylor 1911). Cummings's (1997) objective was to "harness technology for continuous productivity improvements" (p. 64). She explained,

> While the term productivity often refers to measures such as output per worker . . ., *gaming productivity* refers to wagering action (play) per patron per interval. *Expediting* refers to advancing and facilitating gaming action so that players can be more productive because their play is faster, extends for a longer interval, and/or involves more dollars placed at risk (wagered) per period than otherwise would be expected. (p. 63)

Technology used well, Cummings (1997, 65) suggested, accelerates "the constant cycling of player action toward large numbers of wagers in order to place the gaming operation at the greatest win advantage relative to players." As in Taylor's writings, *time* is a critical site of technological intervention: "pruning dead time or unproductive motions from various phases of play is a particular focus for getting more play into each time interval" (ibid., 76). The aim of compressing a greater number of spending gestures into smaller units of time echoes Karl Marx's (1867/1960) insight that "moments are the element of profit," along with Michel Foucault's (1979, 152-54) apt characterization of modern disciplinary logic: "it is a question of extracting, from time, ever more available moments and, from each moment, ever more useful forces." A key instance of "productivity enhancement" by game developers is the switch from pull-handle to push-button machines, allowing for rapid play. "You can rest your hand on the button," said Neil Nicastro, president of Chicago-based gaming company WMS Industries; "You don't ever have to move your hand" (Video Vice 2000). "The effective difference in expediting play," Cummings (1997, 76) noted, "is dramatic. Averaging play at a rate of five games per minute pulling a handle would result in 300 games an hour. If instead the player uses the push-button, the number of games can double this rate of play, from 300 to 600 games each hour." In fact, experienced gamblers play up to 900 hands an hour. The newest of machines feature touch screens that further reduce the time it takes to play.

---

*The aim is not only to speed up play
but to extend its duration.*

The "cashless machine" with embedded bill acceptor promotes gaming productivity by enabling players to insert large bills into machines and acquire credits rather than feeding coins in one at a time. "Is the coin dead?" wonders a journalist in an industry trade magazine, observing that money is disappearing from the casino environment and being replaced by "virtual cashless play." Not only can the automatic translation of inserted money into credits disguise the true value of cash and increase the likelihood of recycled wins, it can also compensate for the potential errors of the human body: "If you have a machine that takes five or six nickels, that's time a player is spending to put in the coins and make sure they register. Sometimes they put them in too fast or drop them, and that relates to dollars for the casino. Because of that, the credit system or cashless slot makes sense" (*Casino Gaming Magazine* 1985, 14). The digital function of credit-play hooks up to a predigital, Taylorist logic of temporal discipline.

The objective to accelerate gaming productivity moves in tandem with an objective to maximize what gaming industry representatives call "time on device." The aim is not only to speed up play but to extend its duration. One way designers encourage longer play is by ensuring that players—who typically spend hours seated—are physically comfortable. The Gasser design firm boasts "meticulous attention to the height of seats in relation to gaming tables and slot machine handles," creating special seats to "eliminate hard, sharp edges coming in contact with the main arteries of the legs, which causes circulation to be cut and the legs to fall asleep" (Legato 1987, 15). The flow of gamblers' circulation is linked to the flow of their time and cash into the casino's machines, and a careful ergonomics crystallizes around this linkage. VLC Gaming reduces player fatigue with screens that slant at 38 degrees and game controls positioned within easy reach "because they can't slouch in their seats, they don't get tired as easily," a company representative told me at a trade show.

Wedded to these ergonomic, morphological strategies are a set of digital strategies to increase time on device. The assembly of digitally driven black boxes, pads, and insertion panels that cover the surface of today's gambling device embody the aim to keep players seated for as long as possible: "You want a situation where the customer can get anything they want when they sit down at your machine" (Rutherford 1996, 83). Single machines are programmed with a *convergence* of gaming opportunities" such that players can "explore, browse, and experiment with selections from a library of game variations in the same box, while never leaving their seats" (Cummings 1997, 71). Some machines incorporate bingo ticket printers so that patrons playing machines in between bingo games do not waste time getting up to buy tickets. Others carry embedded television monitors: "These emerging systems can permit players to view television shows or to enjoy closed circuit special events and personal messaging while they continue their gaming activities on the same machine. Players then do not need to exit the play area" (ibid., 73). The goal is to control channels of incoming information to limit its interruptive potential. To this end, the digital repertoire of contemporary machines goes as far as to include noise cancellation technology to remove "destructive interference" coming from the outside world (Kranes 2000, 33).

Strategies to mute incoming signals and thereby prolong play are coupled with strategies to multiply the channels by which players can output signals of their desires. Computerized menus allow players to key orders into a pad of coded choices, directly transmitting specific wants (for nickels, quarters, dollar chips, a gin and tonic, alka seltzer, a mechanic) to employees in the proximity who wear "vibrating call devices":

> In the past, services for guests on the casino floor became available *ad hoc* as roving attendants circulated around their assigned gaming areas to provide beverages, change, game machine maintenance, and so on. Today, rather than wait for a service person to happen by, increasingly, players can initiate service requests directly by transmitting a signal through the gaming system on which they are playing. (Cummings 1997, 68)

Player desires are communicated and expedited through increasingly selective codes and vibrations, along increasingly refined digital circuits of control and feedback.[1]

Mobile automated teller machines, wireless handheld units, and portable credit card advance systems function to quicken and simplify the transfer of financial resources. "PersonalBanker," an online account to which customers can make deposits using cash, chips, check, or markers, can be accessed directly by using a pin number on the machine's keypad: "Players can now transfer funds directly from a checking account to credit on a gambling machine. Future gambling machines will allow customers to bypass the $300-a-day limit on an ATM card, while others will allow access to credit cards without a Personal Identification Number (PIN)" (Video Vice 2000). Advanced systems of coding and identification speed up access to credit precisely by circumventing codes and identification numbers.

Perhaps most fundamental to the gaming industry's program of "continuous productivity" are "inducements within game machine hardware and software" (Cummings and Brewer 1994, 66) that exploit the psychological principles of learning outlined by B. F. Skinner in his theory of operant conditioning. Digitized games intensify the highly effective "variable intermittent ratio reinforcement schedule," in which players never know *how much* they are going to get or *when*. Exposure to frequent near misses and small wins sustains betting, as does the option of credit play, whereby winnings can be regambled immediately as opposed to stopping with money in hand. A high event frequency or number of opportunities to gamble in a given time period allows rapid replay, resulting in a "loss period [that] is brief, with little time given over to financial considerations" (Griffiths 1999, 268).

In recent years, game developers have further reinforced the learning schedule of games by adding numerous payout lines, along with options to bet a vast number of coins to take the greatest advantage of winning combinations. Playing one hand on these machines is equivalent to playing multiple machines simultaneously. "Multiline multipliers," as they are called in Australia,[2] distribute play over as many as nine zigzagging lines (see Figures 1 and 2). Although five coins is the maximum bet per play on standard three-reel slots, when distributed over nine lines the maximum bet becomes forty-five coins (on some machines the number reaches ninety). Multicoin machines condense a tremendous amount of hit frequencies into one unit of time, turning a five cent game into a $2.25 game per unit of time, or even $5.00. "A nickel game isn't a nickel game when you're betting 90 nickels at a time," said a representative of the Williams company. These games elevate players' investment without their realizing it. "The perception," Randy Adams of Anchor Gaming told me, "is that you're winning all the time, when you're really not—you're putting 25 in and winning 15 back, 45 in and 30 back, over and over." Nathan Leland of Silicon Gaming put it this way: "Positive reinforcement hides loss."

A score of visual and auditory design elements—crisp, high-resolution graphics and enhanced animation as well as "hi-fi" sound—compose a "second-order conditioning" that adds to the reinforcement of play. Audio engineers work to simulate the sound of cascading coins: "We basically mixed several recordings of quarters falling on a metal tray and then fattened up the sound with the sound of falling dollars" (quoted in Rivlin 2004, 45). International Gaming Technology (IGT) encodes each of its games with an average of four hundred unique "sound events" to accompany different outcomes; these sounds are not meant to be noticed but to serve as

FIGURE 1
ASTRONOMICAL FORTUNE

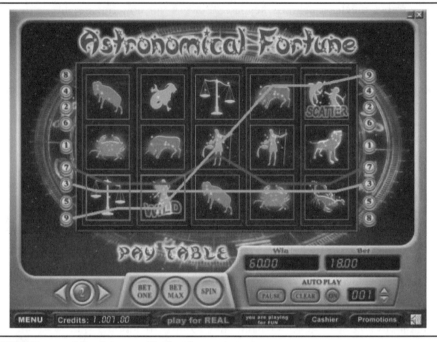

SOURCE: www.24hr-slots.com. Used with permission.

an encouraging background accompaniment to play (ibid., 47). Adams: "The idea is to create a sense of winning by pulsing all the human senses with sounds and animated symbols and paylines flashing, nonaversive visual and auditory cues."

As game designers have learned how to "teach" gamblers to stay at machines, they have developed an equally nuanced sense of how to modulate technology to accommodate gamblers' play flow, or "zoning rhythm," as Leland calls it. His company added a dynamic play rate to their video poker machines when they became too slow for experienced players: "The screen shows animated video hands that deal the cards. If you play slow, it deals slow. When you go so fast [imitates rapid pressing on buttons], the game detects it and *adapts*. Even then, some players were annoyed that it was too slow, and we had to speed it up. If a player goes fast enough, the cards pop up without any animation." The dynamic rate feature resets when there is a pause in play, readying itself to conform to the next player's speed. Unlike the factory machines of the mechanical age, with whose uniform rhythms the worker was required to coordinate his own movements, digital machines adapt themselves to the unique speed of each player.

On a broader scale, digitization enables engineers to mathematically adjust games' payout tables or reward schedules to select for specific player profiles within a diverse market. Through the delicate demographic operation of "matching math with markets, player types with schedule types," it becomes possible to

FIGURE 2
LUCKY SEVENS

SOURCE: www.24hr-slots.com. Used with permission.

solicit "distinct audiences of risk-takers": lower-denomination players seeking frequent small wins respond to certain pay schedules; higher-denomination players seeking big wins respond to others. Marcus Prater at Bally Gaming remarks, "Different types of humans manifest themselves through different machines, different math." Technological procedures of differentiation, he suggests, draw out human differentiation; at the same time, human diversity solicits technological diversity. IGT, for instance, features a staggering number of variations on the theme of video poker, each targeting a different player profile (see Table 1).[3]

Designers' desire to create a "total machine" that could respond to the singular preferences desires of every player comes across in a comment made by an employee of Joe Kaminkow, head of machine design at IGT: "[Joe] wants a machine that pays a ton of small pays, lots of medium-sized pays and a huge jackpot. In other words, he wants us to do the impossible" (quoted in Rivlin 2004, 81). One gaming entrepreneur with whom I spoke had a patent in formulation for what amounts to a personalized reward machinery of the sort Kaminkow imagines. It runs through "progressives"—banks of machines linked to an ever-escalating jackpot (that gamblers augment with their play), displayed on a large digital meter suspended over the machines like a money clock. My informant had found a way to change the payout rate on machines depending on the read of this meter; if it rises

TABLE 1

VERSIONS OF VIDEO POKER MADE BY ONE COMPANY (www.igt.com)

Austin Powers™ Poker	Matrix Poker®
Big Split Poker™	Multi-Hand BlackJack™ Video Poker
Chase the Royal™ Draw Poker	Multi-Strike Poker™
Double Down Stud® Poker	Play It Again Poker™
Double Pay™ Poker	Spin Poker™
Fast Action Draw Poker™	Super Times Pay™ Video Poker
Fifty Play Draw Poker™	Ten Play™ Draw Poker
Five Aces Poker™	Three Card Draw Poker™
Flex Play Poker™	Trade Up Poker™
Game King 4.3 Poker™	Triple Play™ Draw Poker
Game King 5.1 Poker™	Triple Play™ Five Play™ Draw Poker
Hold 'Em Challenge™ Video Poker	Triple Play™ Five Play™ Ten Play™ Poker
Hundred Play Draw Poker™	White Hot Aces™ Poker

to $100,000, he knows he will be able to lower the payout rate and still draw people to play. Although his technology is not yet able to tailor itself to the gaming patterns of particular players by selectively altering payout to retain their play, its innovation is to operationalize the recognition that motivations change in relation to a game's stakes and that more money can be extracted if payout rates are manipulated accordingly. Essentially, this technology will enable games to perform a function that many players already believe they do: alter payouts depending on play.[4] "Technology is catching up to the gambler's paranoia," the patent entrepreneur told me.

For the gaming industry, gambling machines function not only as individual play boxes but as "electronic surveillance devices" (*Casino Gaming Magazine* 1990, 6) whose internal monitors track a player's game preferences, wins and losses, number of coins played per game, number of games played per minute, number of minutes or hours of play, number of visits to the casino, number of drinks consumed, and more.[5] Individual machines perform these recording functions within a larger network of units controlled by a central computer. Originally engineered to track player behavior inside just one casino, digital tracking technologies embedded in games now track behavior across diverse consumer spaces by linking machines in taverns, supermarkets, pharmacies, and convenience stores. Not only the casino but the "local community" (Cummings 1997, 68) is turned into a laboratory for the collection of "live data."[6]

Machines are taking over the gambling scene. In Nevada, 45 percent of gaming property floor space was dedicated to coin-operated gambling in 1980; at present, gambling machines occupy 77 percent (State of Nevada Gaming Control Board 2004). In a dramatic turnaround from 25 years ago, machine revenue today generates more than twice the combined revenue of all other types of games (ibid.).[7] In areas of Las Vegas where local residents tend to play (North Las Vegas and Boulder Strip, for instance), machines garner as high as 89 percent of revenue. The spread of gambling technologies through the physical landscape of Las Vegas (and beyond) is accompanied by less measurable but no less consequential shifts in the internal, subjective landscape of those who play them.

Phenomenology of the Zone

The only thing that exists is the screen in front of you. You go into the screen, it just pulls you in.

—Isabella

Interaction with the digitally enhanced features of new game platforms renders a more continuous playing experience than do "live games" or older-model slot machines, efficiently sustaining a dissociated subjective state that gamblers call the "zone," in which conventional spatial, bodily, monetary, and temporal parameters are suspended. The zone depends on a set of interlinked phenomenal elements, each of which correlates with the digital properties of gambling machines presented above: *being alone, not being interrupted, speed, choice, tempo*.

Machine gamblers typically express their preference for machine play over live games in terms of a desire to be *alone*, to exit social space. Maria told me, "I couldn't stand to have anybody within my . . . zone. I wanted to isolate, just get lost." Rocky said, "I didn't want to have a human interface." Strategizing to prevent human exchange, Isabella would "pick machines with empty spots on either side and play a little on each of the two outer machines to keep them busy." Archie places coin cups upside-down on adjacent machines to give the impression that they are in use.

[Recent gambling machines'] internal monitors track a player's game preferences, wins and losses, number of coins played per game, number of games played per minute, number of minutes or hours of play, number of visits to the casino, number of drinks consumed, and more.

The unequivocal desire to be alone that gamblers express is linked to a demand for *noninterruption*. When someone talks to Diane, she cashes out and moves to another machine: "I resent someone breaking my trance. Don't ask me if I want anything, don't talk to me, don't congratulate me. It's me and my machine. I want to hang a *DO NOT DISTURB* sign on my back." Sharon devised measures to stave off interruptions and thereby guard the continuity of her play: "I'd gravitate toward the corners, where no one could bother me. I'd get all my quarters at once because

I didn't want change girls coming up to me. I'd bring a liter of diet coke because I didn't want cocktail waitresses bugging me. I'd buy a pack of cigarettes before I went in. I'd sometimes put my foot up on one side and that was the final barrier: *LEAVE ME ALONE.*"

Newer model gaming platforms accommodate players' demand for isolation by protecting them against the intrusion of incoming signals; they support continuous, uninterrupted play with features such as bill acceptors and credit functions that do not require stopping to insert coins at every hand. Such features ensure the possibility for *speed*—another aspect of play fundamental to the zone. Diane: "In live games, people take too long to decide what they're doing, they interrupt the flow—the *go go go*—and I can't stand it, I have to get up and go to a machine." Maria: "The faster I played, the better. You probably couldn't even see the cards, that's how fast I'd go [her eyes widen and glaze over in front of an imaginary screen, index finger punching rapidly]." A game designer told me, "The really hardcore players analyze the cards so quick I don't have time to even see what's up there, and I designed those games."

Speed, to a greater degree than aloneness and noninterruption, is a condition of the zone over which gamblers feel a sense of control. Digitized features like the dynamic play rate promote a sense of "autonomy" whereby "players can *interact with* and *control* some game aspects" (Cummings 1997, 74). The ability to modulate play—adjust volume, speed of play, choose cards and bet amounts—is understood by game developers to increase psychological and financial investment. Bonus games that pop up when players reach certain credit levels often present themselves as skill based (for example, a bowling ball whose trajectory appears to be controlled by a joystick) when in fact they are entirely programmed, promoting what game developers call an "illusion of control."

New games further cultivate this sense of autonomy through the digitally facilitated *choices* that distinguish them from traditional slots: "Slots are on a whole other pecking order—cherries, bars, etcetera. You don't have to think. With video poker you get to choose the cards, you have *input*," said Patsy. Julie: "I didn't like the old slot machines—there's no challenge, no decisions to make, and you can't pick how many credits to bet." Maria: "With the old machines, you rely on whatever comes up; with games like video poker, you can make *choices*—that may have been the thing that hooked me." At the same time that speed of play suspends gamblers in sort of holding pattern, a constant stream of choice "holds" attention and assists social withdrawal. Shelly: "The machines don't require the kind of attention that live games do, where you have to be sharp, aware, take other people into account. You can play the machines when you're totally numb and exhausted because they require just enough of your attention that you can't really think about anything else." In the zone, attention is thoroughly absorbed by a steady repetition of choosing operations; choice and speed play off one another in the sense that decisions are made to the beat of a *tempo* set between person and machine. Gamblers describe themselves as playing the machine like a musical instrument. When player and instrument are "in sync," they attain a sort of perfection—"hitting the harmonic," as Randall says, or being "in tune": "If the play is not in tune, then I start to get anxious because it means I will not be able to sit and play for a while, get into the zone, stay there."

Game features that promote continuous productivity collude with the gambler's wish to enter a zone that effectively suspends the social, bodily, temporal, and monetary parameters of existence. Isabella recounts the loss of her body as a point of perspective in mappable space (see Jameson 1991):

> There's a show that comes on after *Star Trek*, it's all in high tech—an illusional bad guy tries to design computer programs to suck people into his web, where they become his drones. That's what gambling on the machines correlates to. On TV they express it by *pulling*—the bodies actually disappear and go into the screen, and then they go through the games of the computer. The computer gambling was like that: I wasn't totally present, I was gone. My body was there, outside the machine, but at the same time I was inside the machine, inside the game, in that king and queen turning over . . .

Marx (1867/1960, 604) wrote that a capitalist mode of production turns the "laborer into a fragment of a man, degrades him to the level of a machine." Digital capabilities take these fragmenting tendencies a step further: the machine player (who is, arguably, a contemporary proxy for the factory laborer) is not merely socially isolated and made into a fragment of a man but is removed from the palpable dimensions of his own body.

Julie describes how machines facilitate exit from the register of *money:* "You have no concept of value anymore. If you put in a twenty dollar bill, it's no longer a twenty dollar bill—it has no value in that sense. It's like a token, it excludes money value completely." In the economy of the zone, money loses its charge as a material means of acquisition and exchange and is converted into the currency of play, a supraeconomic means of suspension from conventional circuits of exchange: "You're not playing for money; you're playing for credit. Credit so you can sit there longer, which is the goal. It's not about *winning*; it's about *continuing to play*. Bill acceptors free players from conscious awareness of money and allow them to enter into a space of credit in which money, as such, disappears.

Winning—too much, too soon, or too often—can itself precipitate stoppage in play flow and disturb the economy of suspension. Sharon would rather "spend two hours losing a jackpot" than cash it out, as this would mean exiting the zone to wait for the machine to drop her winnings, or, in the event that its hopper is low, for attendants to come pay her off. Maria told me, "What I want to do is get into my playing rhythm, stay there longer and just play." Players emphasize the importance of a balance or equilibrium between wins and losses to maintain a plateau of credit and ward off interruption: "If it's a moderate day—*win, lose, win, lose*—you keep the same pace. But if you win big at first, it can prevent you from getting in the zone and staying there." Machines that allow players to calibrate the number of credits they bet offer them some control over the rhythm of loss and gain, as Shelly describes: "If I only had 20 credits left, I'd play one at a time [instead of playing maximum credits, 5 at a time] to stretch it out and keeping playing." Julie's technique is different—instead of slowing her pace and reducing coin input to regain credit, she takes advantage of features that allow her to modulate her speed: "The pace picks up, you speed up, your fingers move so fast. As you have less and less money, as the credit gets lower and lower, you get faster and faster. You're trying to speed up and get into the zone where you can just play and be away." Interacting with these games, players experience the ebb and flow of money as a function of their own movement.

Gamblers' exits from the constraints of body and money are inextricably linked to an exit from *time*. They often recount their bodily abandonment in hours—"for 15, 16, 17 hours I sat there." "Clock time," as Archie calls it, "disappears." Shelly told me, "One night I went in around eight o'clock and figured I'd play until maybe midnight or so because I had to go to work the next day; the next thing I knew the sun was coming up." Gamblers' experience of duration—the subjective sense of temporal flow—is not so much eliminated as it is altered in the zone, where it condenses, expands, and stretches according to an idiosyncratic course of play. Digital game features like the "dynamic play rate" promote a sense of release from the measured pace of chronometric time. Randall comments that speed makes him feel he is "bending time." Racing in his dragster (in which he achieved speeds of up to two hundred miles per hour), on his motorcycle, and on the video poker machine, he goes "into a different time frame, like in slow motion. It's a whole other time zone." Time, like money, becomes a manipulable playing currency rather than a determinative order.

The relationship between game features and the flow of player experience is characterized by an increasing *fittedness*. Design strategies for rendering "continuous productivity" match gamblers' desire for the insulating continuity of the zone and vice versa. In the game-fitted phenomenal world of the zone, human and machine seem to *merge*, as Randall describes: "I get to the point where I no longer realize that my hand is touching the machine, I don't feel it there. I feel connected to the machine when I play, like it's an extension of me, as if physically you couldn't separate me from the machine." Beyond the physical merging of human and machine is a more abstract merging of intention and response, desire and game, as Patsy narrates: "My eyes feel like they're lining up the bars on the screen, I see them turning, and then *stop*, like it's under my influence." Josie: "It's like you go around in the numbers, and *you* decide where to stop." Lola speaks in terms of a communicative vibration: "There's times I feel this vibration between what I *want* and what *happens*."

The digitally facilitated immediacy of machine response to player desire absorbs and neutralizes that desire and, in so doing, solicits further desire.[8] As I elaborate below, player desire likewise absorbs the very technology whose response it anticipates and, in so doing, solicits further technological intervention. As the gap between desire and design grows smaller, the two appear to coincide.

Endgame: AutoPlay

Fun is the common denominator—people want entertainment.
—Randy Adams, director of machine design at Anchor Gaming

At the start of his interview with me, Gardner Grout of Silicon Gaming stated that the goal of his company was "to make the most entertaining slot machines." Toward the end of the interview, he contradicted himself: "One thing that we didn't get at the beginning is that people don't really want to be entertained. That's the big problem. Hardcore players are not interested in entertainment, or bonuses. In fact, bonuses interrupt them. They want to be totally absorbed." Players who find innovative digital contrivances bothersome or interruptive challenge engineers and their philosophies of entertainment. Game developers respond, somewhat disappointedly, by muting the very features that define the cutting edge of digital game design, as Gardner describes: "We spent a lot of time designing bonus features with animations that came up when you won a prize, but some people just want to keep *playing*. So, we put shorter animations, and added more sound and music as a sort of background reward that you could continue to play over if you wanted to just keep going." As it turns out, at a certain point in the career of the digital game it became necessary to background the digital itself. The intensification of digital capabilities leads not only to an exit from embodied space and chronometric time, the dematerialization of money, and the cancellation of desire by way of its immediate fulfillment, but to the falling away of the material technology itself.

Gamblers' exits from the constraints of body and money are inextricably linked to an exit from time.

Julie explains, "With old slot machines I'm not a part of the game, I'm just a part of the machine." I ask her, "And you're not part of the machine when you play new games?" She responds, "The machine isn't even really there. . . . It's important in the beginning because you *see* it—I only play the ones with the blue screen. But as you play the machine becomes less and less important; it starts out the machine and then it's the *game*." Once players are absorbed in the game, the technological, aesthetic features that draw them in stop mattering. Sharon describes playing video poker:

> In the end, I wouldn't even look at the cards. I'd just put bills in, get a bunch of credits, and press the buttons in rapid succession. *Deal—Draw—Play Max; Deal—Draw—Play Max*. I'd just watch the credit meter go up and down. You reach an extreme point where you don't even delude yourself that you're in control of anything but strapping yourself into a machine and staying there until you lose. All that stuff that may attract you in the beginning—the choice, the decisions, the skill—is stripped away.

Certain poker machines in Australia feature an AutoPlay option that formalizes the method of play Sharon describes above. Players insert money, wait for credits to register, then simply press the AutoPlay button and let the game play itself (see Figure 2). The elements of skill and choice, said by game developers to distinguish new from old games, slip back into the raw chance of the traditional or "predigital" slot machine—except that now players do not even pull the handle themselves; instead they merely watch as the credit meter goes up and down. Although the AutoPlay feature does not formally exist in North American–licensed machines, some players manage to reproduce it. As Stacey Friedman of Silicon Gaming observed, "In South Carolina, they would load up credits on poker machines, push the play button down and jam a toothpick in there."

One designer had this to say about AutoPlay: "It's just *pure gambling*—all chance, no skill. Basically that's what all gambling comes down to: putting things in a box that says *yes* or *no*." His description of the "pure" gambling operation likens it to the operation of the binary digital computer itself, in which all events are represented as two possible outcomes—zero or one, yes or no. After the body folds into the machine and the machine folds into the game, what is left is the abstract, digital procedure of the game itself. In AutoPlay there is no feedback, no vision of the game's output, no perception; AutoPlay marks the point at which the varied, complex forms of interactivity and productivity that have become the trademark of the "digital age" loop into recursive forms of disengagement. Players cease to be desiring subjects betting against the RNG to win; instead, they coincide with the digital procedure of the RNG and the statistical program it implements, such that they themselves come to occupy the position of the "really new god."

After the body folds into the machine and the machine folds into the game, what is left is the abstract, digital procedure of the game itself.

Walter Benjamin (1968) has argued that "the countless movements of switching, inserting, pressing" that punctuate modern life and its technologies (intimately connected as they are with the autonomization and standard timing of industrial labor) alter the structure of human experience. "Thus technology has subjected the human sensorium to a complex kind of training," he wrote of traffic signals. In modernity, "the shock experience has become the norm" (p. 162). Perhaps today we have moved from shock to the zone, a state of absorption characterized by flow and continuity. The zone exemplifies traits of "postmodernity" as a number of cultural critics have outlined them: The zone is characterized by play rather than purpose, chance rather than design, absence and immersion rather than presence and perspective, the collapse of time and space (or "time-space compression"), the "waning of affect," the free-floating circulation of credit in market exchange (Jameson 1991; Harvey 1989a, 1989b).

Yet the design tactics of game developers suggest that digital gambling technologies continue to exemplify the aims of modern discipline; the zone, no matter how "free-floating," remains in continuous relation with the material artifact of the gambling machine and its instrumental program of value extraction. Digital gambling machines, like their predecessors (and, indeed, like much of the technology at work in capitalist economies), aim to harness space and time to financially generative ends (Jameson 1991; Harvey 1989a, 1989b; Bell 1973). In this sense, they are contemporary vehicles for the principle of general equivalence—the exchangeability or convertibility across time, body, labor, money, and commodities (Marx 1867/1960). The material I have presented suggests that technologies of the "digital age" are distinct not because they depart from this principle but because they radicalize it, accelerating the convertibility of time, body, labor, and money in the interest of profit, until all those categories vanish, as in AutoPlay.

Digital games' acceleration or intensification of equivalence across bodily, temporal, and monetary registers may be the logical extension of a modern technological ethos but at the same time marks a qualitative shift in social and existential experience. Strategies of modern discipline such as fragmentation, regimentation, and discontinuity are not abandoned; instead they are sped up to a point where they function on a register of interactivity, adaptability, choice, modulation, flow, and continuity (Deleuze 1992); shock is absorbed. Levers, pulleys, clocks, and cameras are integrated with a computerized substrate of ever more complex configuration, promising players the *perpetuum mobile* of the zone and ensuring "continuous productivity."

Notes

1. Exemplifying the automatic self-regulation built into the control apparatus of cybernetic systems, gambling machines signal technicians without human prompting, programmed as they are with "maintenance tickler schedules for routine tune-ups and self diagnostics" (Cummings 1997, 76).

2. Australia, which has the highest gambling machine per capita ratio of any nation, is consistently cited by game developers for the combinatory complexity of its gambling technologies and for its residents' fluency with this complexity. Marcus Prater of Bally Gaming: "The Australian market is more evolved than ours. The mechanical reel spinner disappeared from the gaming landscape and they were left with video, pinball, and other arcade games with bonuses and diversity—they grew up with it and seem to understand all of the unbelievably complicated winning combinations. When there are nine lines zigzagging everywhere it's hard to know why you're winning—I'm in the business and I don't even know. It's a more mature market, kind of like the locals market here in Vegas where players go to casinos three times a week and understand the pay schedules. Maybe that's where the States are headed."

3. For all the talk of shifts to multiline reel games with themed bonus features, in fact video poker remains the staple game of the gaming industry. It is likely that the lack of industry buzz around video poker is linked to the game's relative closure to technological innovation. At one time, as a developer at International Gaming Technology (IGT) put it, "Video poker and its illusion of control inverted the whole equation of gambling machines." Since then, however, there has been virtually no change in the basic structure of the game. Vallejo

explains, "With a game like video poker, there's a finite mathematical universe, and only so many elaborations you can squeeze out of it—it's not so flexible statistically." Prater: "You can redistribute pay in all the pay tables, but by now every formula possible of video poker pay distribution has been done. You don't have many options left except to add more levels of play, multideck machines like double and triple play." Video poker's restricted potential for evolution notwithstanding, the game is a continuing success. "It's a perfect game," says Grout. "You can't really improve on it; all the elements are there." Its configuration of elements solicits a broad spectrum of hit-frequency inclinations—it can be played on a low hit frequency (where the aim is jackpot) and on a high hit frequency (where the aim is on the "lower end" of the pay scale).

4. Technology companies usually offer Nevada casinos the choice of five different payback percentages on video slot machines, ranging from 88 to 97 percent, corresponding to state regulations. If a casino requests a 94 percentage payback rate on a game, the game's chip will be set accordingly. If a casino wishes to change that percentage, it will have to buy and insert a new chip. "From a labor standpoint," Prater points out, "the idea that casinos are always changing their chips is ludicrous—it's expensive and impractical." On video poker, payback percentage depends on the choices one makes; at optimal play strategy, it is possible to win a 96 percent or higher payback (which falls to 34 percent if one does not know the rules of the game).

5. Norman Klein (2002, 24) wrote, "The slot machine is a symbol of the globalized electronic economy. It stands for cybernetic controls across many markets at once. New computerized digital tracking services perform like a cyborg for the house: tracking players, slots, tables, revenue sources, demographics, doing the taxes, providing up to the minute WIN reporting, player photos, electronic signature identification, messages for players on screens . . . . For the trackers on the casino floor, there are portable hand-held tracking devices; for their bosses, multiple casino access. This is indeed a software chimera, the tail of a serpent attached to the head of a lion."

6. Dr. Craig Fields, vice chairman and technological savant of Alliance Gaming Corporation where he is in charge of refining linkages between games, across casinos, is former director of the Pentagon Defense Advanced Research Projects Agency (DARPA), which funded the research that resulted in the creation of the Internet. "Fields quit DARPA when he concluded that the greatest users of high technology were not to be found in the military but in the entertainment industry" (Rutherford 1996, 81).

7. Nevada's annual gaming revenue was $9.4 billion in 2002 (American Gaming Association 2004; see www.americangaming.org), with slot win accounting for approximately $6.3 billion of that amount (State of Nevada Gaming Control Board 2004). Nationally, the gross annual revenue for all forms of gaming that year was $68.7 billion—more than consumers spent on movies, recorded music, theme parks, spectator sports, cruise ships, and video games combined. This figure is a striking jump from 1990 when the total was $26.6 billion (American Gaming Organization 2004; see www.americangaming.org).

8. This tightened loop of desire and response accounts for the addictiveness of gambling machines. As one researcher of gambling addiction noted, "The hard writing that nature gave us didn't anticipate electronic gaming devices . . . because the video form is faster than the mechanical form, they hold the potential to behave in the fashion of psychostimulants like cocaine or amphetamines" (Howard Shaffer, quoted in Rivlin 2004, 74).

References

Bell, Daniel. 1973. *The coming of post-industrial society: A venture in social forecasting*. New York: Basic Books.

Benjamin, Walter. 1968. On some motifs in Baudelaire. In *Illuminations*, ed. and with Introduction by Hannah Arendt, trans. Harry Zohn. New York: Schocken Books.

Casino Gaming Magazine. 1985. Cashless slot machines: The industry's view. August, pp. 11-16.

———. 1990. Player tracking. . . . It's a service business. April, pp. 6-7.

Cummings, Leslie E. 1997. A typology of technology applications to expedite gaming productivity. *Gaming Research and Review Journal* 4 (1): 63-79.

Cummings, Leslie E., and Kathleen P. Brewer. 1994. An evolutionary view of the critical functions of slot machine technology. *Gaming Research and Review Journal* 1 (2):67-78.

Deleuze, Gilles. 1992. Postscript on the societies of control. *October* 59 (Winter): 3-7.

Foucault, Michel. 1979. *Discipline and punish: The birth of the prison*. New York: Vintage Books.

Griffiths, Mark. 1999. Gambling technologies: Prospects for problem gambling. *Journal of Gambling Studies* 15 (3): 265-83.

Harvey, David. 1989a. *The condition of postmodernity: An inquiry into the origins of cultural change*. Oxford, UK: Blackwell.

———. 1989b. *The urban experience*. Baltimore: Johns Hopkins University Press.

Jameson, Frederic. 1991. *Postmodernism, or, the cultural logic of late capitalism*. Durham, NC: Duke University Press.

Klein, Norman M. 2002. Scripting Las Vegas: Nor naifs, junking up, and the new strip. In *The grit beneath the glitter: Tales from the real Las Vegas*, ed. H. K. R. M. Davis. Berkeley: University of California Press.

Kranes, David. 2000. The sound of music: Is your slot floor a deafening experience? *Casino Executive*. 6 (5): 32-33.

Legato, Frank. 1987. Right down to the finest detail. *Casino Gaming*, October.

Marx, Karl. 1867/1960. *Capital*. Vol. I. New York: Vintage Books.

Rivlin, Gary. 2004. Bet on it: The tug of the newfangled slot machine. *The New York Times Sunday Magazine*, May 11.

Rutherford, James. 1996. Creative alliance. *Casino Journal*. 9 (3): 80-85.

State of Nevada Gaming Control Board. 2004. *Calendar year 2003 analysis; monthly revenue report; square footage report*. Las Vegas: State of Nevada.

Taylor, Frederick W. 1911. *The principles of scientific management*. New York: Harper and Brothers.

Video Vice. 2000. August 3. http://alabamafamily.org/gambling/videovice/videovice99.htm/.

Mobilizing Fun in the Production and Consumption of Children's Software

This article describes the relation between the production, distribution, and consumption of children's software, focusing on how genres of "entertainment" and "education" structure everyday practice; institutions; and our understandings of childhood, play, and learning. Starting with a description of how the vernaculars of popular visual culture and entertainment found their way into children's educational software and how related products are marketed, the article then turns to examples of play with children's software that are drawn from ethnographic fieldwork. The cultural opposition between entertainment and education is a compelling dichotomy—a pair of material, semiotic, technical genres—that manifests in a range of institutionalized relations. After first describing a theoretical commitment to discursive analysis, this article presents the production and marketing context that structures the entertainment genre in children's software and then looks at instance of play in the after-school computer clubs that mobilize entertainment and fun as social resources.

Keywords: children's software; children's media; interactive media; play; computer games; software industry

By
MIZUKO ITO

From the late 1970s to the end of the 1990s, a new set of cultural, economic, technological, and social relations emerged in the United States, centered on the possibilities of using computer technology to create entertaining

Mizuko Ito is a cultural anthropologist of technology use, focusing on children's and youth's changing relationships to media and communications. Her current research is on Japanese technoculture, and she is coeditor of Personal, Portable, Pedestrian: Mobile Phones in Japanese Life. *She is a research scientist at the Annenberg Center for Communication and a teaching fellow at the Anthropology Department at the University of Southern California. Her Web page is http://www.itofisher.com/mito.*

NOTE: The ethnographic research for this article was conducted as part of a project funded by the Mellon Russell Sage Foundation and benefited from being part of the broader Fifth Dimension research effort. Writing was funded in part by a Spencer Dissertation Fellowship and the Annenberg Center for Communication at the

DOI: 10.1177/0002716204270191

learning experiences for young children. Released in 1977, the Apple II, a tool of hobbyists and a handful of enterprising educators, was just beginning to demonstrate the power of personal computing and programming for the masses. A homebrew industry of programmers had been laying the foundations for a new consumer software industry by sending their products, floppy disks packaged in ziplock bags, to their networks of retailers and consumers. The video game industry hit public consciousness with the phenomenal success of *Space Invaders* in 1978, demonstrating the economic and addictive potential of a new genre of interactive entertainment. Hand in hand with these technological developments, small groups of educational researchers across the country were beginning to experiment with personal computers as a tool for creating interactive, child-driven, entertaining, and open-ended learning environments that differed from the top-down didacticism of traditional classroom instruction. The trend toward a more pleasure-oriented, child-centered, and less hierarchical approach to education and child rearing found material form in technologies that allowed greater user control and input than traditional classroom media. Across a set of diverse contexts in the United States, educators and socially responsible technologists were incubating a shared cultural imaginary that centered on the possibilities of new interactive computer technology to transform learning and engagement.

The case of commercial children's software provides a window into a dynamic field of negotiation that characterizes contemporary disputes over children's culture, education, and technology. This article presents material from a more extended analysis of the production, distribution, and consumption of children's software (Ito 2003). The focus here is on analyzing the relations between the cultural and social categories of "entertainment" and "education" and examining how they structure everyday practice; institutions; and our understandings of childhood, play, and learning. I present material on how the vernaculars of popular visual culture and entertainment found their way into children's educational software, how related products are marketed, and how these vernaculars are mobilized in the micropolitics of children's engagements with computers and adults. The examples of play with children's software are drawn from ethnographic fieldwork at Fifth Dimension After School Clubs (5thD) (Cole 1997; Vasquez, Pease-Alvarez, and Shannon 1994), a setting that mobilizes as well as complicates conventional cultural oppositions between entertainment and education, play and learning. The opposition between entertainment and education is a compelling dichotomy—a pair of material, semiotic, technical genres—that manifests in a wide range of institutionalized relations. In line with other articles in this collection, I argue that the socially

University of Southern California. This article is excerpted from a dissertation for Stanford University's Department of Anthropology titled *Engineering Play*, which benefited from readings and comments by Eric Klinenberg, Carol Delaney, Joan Fujimura, Shelley Goldman, James Greeno, Purnima Mankekar, Ray McDermott, Susan Newman, Lucy Suchman, and Sylvia Yanagisako. The description of the history of the children's software industry was drawn from interviews with software developers. I would, in particular, like to acknowledge the help and insight of Gary Carlson, Colette Michaud, Robert Mohl, and Margo Nanny, all pioneering software designers from the early years of educational multimedia.

transformative promise of new technologies is elusive in everyday practice; existing institutional configurations, social alliances, and cultural categories weigh heavily in ongoing contestations over how new technologies will be designed, deployed, and used. After presenting a historical and conceptual framework, this article presents the production and marketing context that structures the entertainment genre in children's software and then looks at instance of play in the 5thD that mobilize entertainment and fun as social resources.

Engineering Play

Research on children's media has documented the relation between changing technologies of cultural production, new children-oriented consumer markets, and shifting notions of childhood and intergenerational relations. Current discourses and industries surrounding computers and children can be located in this broader history in the engineering of children's pleasures and play. A child-centered popular culture has been growing in momentum ever since the establishment of children's fiction and comic books, and it has expanded into more genres of toys and mass media. Television was a turning point in creating a direct marketing channel between cultural producers and children. Stephen Kline (1993, 165) described how television opened up a new line of communication with children, making marketing to even young children possible. He described the Mickey Mouse Club as a turning point in the development of a distinct children's consumer culture by focusing on a children's subculture formed by television (pp. 166-67). Although this child-centered cultural production was initially still attentive to parental concerns, it has gradually blossomed into a more explicitly antiauthoritarian kids' subculture that pushes back at adult-identified values.

In *Sold Separately*, Ellen Seiter (1995) contrasted the educational or developmental orientation of toy ads in *Parenting* magazine with the ecstatic and utopian world of commercials aimed at children. She described how "commercials seek to establish children's snacks and toys as belonging to a public children's culture, by removing them from the adult-dominated sphere and presenting these products as at odds with that world" (p. 117). "Anti-authoritarianism is translated into images of buffoonish fathers and ridiculed, humiliated teachers. The sense of family democracy is translated into a world where kids rule, where peer culture is all. Permissiveness becomes instant gratification: the avid pursuit of personal pleasure, the immediate taste thrill, the party in the bag" (pp. 117-18). In a similar vein, Brian Sutton-Smith (1997) suggested that the dominant discourse among adults is one of play as progress or play as fulfilling developmental and learning goals. In contrast, he sees children as exhibiting a quite different orientation, with play used often as a form of resistance to adult culture and displaying a fascination with irrational fantasy that he calls phantasmagoria, characterized by pain, gore, sexuality, and violence. Ever since comic books, and culminating in video games, lowbrow and peer-focused children's culture has been defined as visually rather than textually oriented, relying on fast-paced fantasy and spectacle over realism, subtlety, and reflection. Media industries capitalize on the discursive regime that produces play as a site of authentic childhood agency, in particular, mobilizing phantasmagoria as a site of regressive, illicit, and oppositional power.

Adult critique of "trashy" children's entertainment has been a persistent companion to this growth of children's visual culture. Borrowing from Foucault (1978), one could consider these adult efforts to manage children's play as less a repressive regime that silences dark fantasies than an incitement to discourse that gives voice and form to categories of "unnatural" and regressive as well as "natural," wholesome, and productive play. In other words, the educational and entertainment dimensions of contemporary childhood are twinned cultural constructions, engineered through a range of socially, culturally, and technologically contingent discourses and practices. In contrast to a pervasive idea that children are naturally ludic, particularly in relation to computers, I describe how pleasure and fun are discursively constructed in the production of children's software and, in turn, are mobilized in certain types of practices and local micropolitics between children and adults in an educational reform setting. A growing discursive, technological, and capitalist apparatus is producing the "discovery" of natural and authentic children's play and imagination. When looking at children's engagement with spectacle (Debord 1995), there is a level at which it is "just" entertainment, myopic and inconsequential engagement with spectacular forms. But at another level, these are politically, socially, and culturally productive acts. This is not simply a matter of giving voice to children's inner fantasies but of creating relationships with media technologies, capitalist networks, and discourses of childhood, a celebration of childhood imagination in the hands of commerce and state regulation as much as children.

Digital technologies have appeared in these cultural politics holding out the enlightened promise of transforming "passive media consumption" into "active media engagement" and learning. Children's apparent affinity to computers has also contributed to hopes that the "digital generation" would overcome the toxic political economies of media industries pedaling products to passive child consumers (Buckingham 2000). Despite the appeal of the discourse of digital revolution, in practice, the distinctions between passive and active, top-down and democratic, entertainment and educational media are not so clear cut. As new tools for cultural engagement and everyday meaning production, interactive technologies lead not to singular effects but to a multitude of uses and appropriations, only some of which conform to adult hopes for progressive educational play. The more malleable format of digital media technologies has meant that cultural "content" is substantively created not only through social negotiations over design and marketing but also in the ongoing micropolitics of children, software, and adults manifesting certain aspects of the software in their everyday practice. I turn now to the production context of entertainment idioms in children's software and then go on to describe related instances of play.

Multimedia, Entertainment, and the Children's Software Industry

The late 1980s and early 1990s saw the dawn of multimedia, enabled by the spread of personal computers in the home and the advent of CD-ROM technology. CD-ROMs, with their superior storage capacity and ease of use (in contrast to having to install data from multiple floppy disks onto a hard drive), meant that high-resolution graphics, animation, and sounds could be accessed easily by a personal computer. Until the late 1980s, Apple IIs and MS-DOS computers provided the platforms for educational software. After the release of Microsoft Windows in 1983 and the Macintosh in 1984, the tide began to turn toward more graphically intensive personal computing.

In 1989, the *Visual Almanac*, a product of the Apple Multimedia Lab, was introduced at the MacWorld tradeshow as a limited-release product to be donated to educators. Using videodisc, a Macintosh, and Hypercard, the *Visual Almanac* heralded a new era of multimedia children's software that would soon shift from videodisc to CD-ROM. Tying together the graphical capabilities of video and the interactive qualities of the personal computer, the *Visual Almanac* was the first demonstration of the polished graphical quality in children's software that has come to be associated with CD-ROMs. Voyager was the company best known for making the transition from videodisc to CD-ROM, publishing the first commercial CD-ROM in 1989 and going on to publish children's titles derived from the *Visual Almanac*. Broderbund was another pioneering corporation in producing multimedia children's titles, creating the new genre of multimedia picture book with their *Living Books* series.

Multimedia united the lowbrow appeal of popular visual culture with the highbrow promise of the personal computer and the educational ideal of child-centered learning. Early developers shared an educational reform orientation, seeking to enrich children's learning as well as to liberate it from the dry, serious, and often alienating cultural idioms of the classroom. Children's "natural" affinity to new technology and visual culture became tools toward these ends. While the more educationally oriented and minimalist platform of the Apple II gave birth to The Learning Company and Davidson & Associates, founded by former teachers, the 1990s saw a gradual shift toward an entertainment orientation in children's products as large entertainment and software industries entered the market. Graphics and visual appeal became central to software design with sophisticated PCs, a larger market, and growing budgets. As a commercial market, these new ventures were not under the same constraints as classroom software and were given more freedom to develop content that appealed directly to children. The shift was from a pedagogical perspective that sought to elevate and educate children to an entertainment orientation that sought to give voice and shape to children's pleasures. Gaming companies like Broderbund were beginning to see children's software as an area where they could create graphically exciting and entertaining but family-friendly products. Maxis's *SimCity* became a hit product that spanned the entertainment and education markets, although it was not originally intended as an educational title. Edutainment was an expanding site of negotiation and struggle between the interests of educators, entertainers, programmers, artists, and businesspeople, with the visual culture of entertainment gaining an increasingly strong voice.

Since the late 1990s, children's software overall has been characterized by visually polished multimedia titles that can compete with entertainment media in terms of production value. The market for children's software is being polarized between curricular products that are based on a pastiche of school-coded content and "wholesome entertainment" titles that are marketed as an alternative to video gaming, providing fun and excitement without the violent content and mind-numbing repetitiveness of action games. At either of these poles, a certain level of graphical appeal is a basic requirement, but the two kinds of products rely on different selling points, educational- or entertainment-focused. Elsewhere, I have reviewed curricular titles and how children engage with them (Ito 2003). Here, I focus on titles for young children that are more entertainment-oriented.

The ads for the more entertainment-oriented titles portray children as ecstatic and pleasure seeking rather than reflective and brainy and childhood as imaginative, pure, and joyous. The ethos is parent friendly but child centered, a formula established by children's media companies ever since the Mickey Mouse Club aired on television. Rather than playing on achievement anxiety as curriculum-oriented software does, ads for these kinds of titles play on parents' desires to indulge their children's pleasures and the growing pressure on parents to be in tune with their children and keep them happy and entertained. The happiness of a child has become as much a marker of good parenting as achievement and effective discipline.

Humongous Entertainment puts the child's pleasure close up, front, and center. "This is the review we value most," declares the ad copy above a large photograph of a beaming child (see Figure 1). Humongous's adventure game *Putt-Putt Joins the Circus* does not make specific curricular claims other than promising an engaging and prosocial orientation. It lists "problem solving, kindness, teamwork, friendship" as its educational content items. The ad mobilizes discourses from the established genre of film reviews by describing how "critics rave" over the software title. The bottom of the ad lists quotes from various reviews in software magazines. The last quote from *PC Magazine* is particularly telling. "Nobody understands kids like Humongous Entertainment." The company is positioned as a channel to your children and their pleasures, the authentic voice of childhood.

Figure 2 features the adorably caped hero, Sam, and describes the software as "an interactive animated adventure." The back of the box does list educational content but in a small box that is visually de-centered from the portions describing the excitement and adventure that the title promises. The list of "critical thinking, problem-solving skills, memory skills, mental mapping and spatial relations skills" does not make any curricular claims and stresses the "creative and flexible" nature

FIGURE 1
ADVERTISEMENT FOR *PUTT-PUTT*

of the software and "the power of a child's imagination." "Feature-film quality animation" and "original music" are central selling points for the title. It can compete

FIGURE 2
BOX ART FOR *PAJAMA SAM 2*

with television and videos for your child's attention, and it still has some educational value. The "natural" imaginations and creativity of children achieve full expression through the mediation of sophisticated media technologies and an immense apparatus of image production.

"Prepare to get blown away!!" screams the copy above a wide-eyed boy, dangling off the edge of his PC in cliff-hanging mode in another ad. "The action in Disney's CD-ROM games is so awesome, your kids are gonna freak (and that's a good thing). So hold on tight and check out the action this holiday!" As far as wild fantasy goes, these products are relatively tame, based on the usual Disney formulas of fast-paced adventure and gore-free violence. Yet the pitch is to market the action and "freaky" aspects of the software as its primary appeal. Although still addressing the parent, the ad copy makes use of children's language, hailing the hip parent, in touch with children's culture and desires. The boy is dressed in baggy skate-punk shorts and trendy sneakers and has spiked hair with blond highlights. In this ad, the vernaculars of children's peer and popular cultures are mobilized to enlist the progressive parent and position Disney as the voice of children.

These more entertainment-oriented titles use the same visual elements as curricular titles such as *Reader Rabbit* and *Jump Start*. Both edutainment and entertainment titles share the same stylistic genre, and many titles are not clearly categorized as one or the other. They occupy the same shelves at retailers and are oriented to a similar demographic of middle- and upper-middle-class families but are keyed somewhat toward the more progressive and permissive parent. What distinguishes entertainment as a genre is the orientation toward a more indulgent and repetitious play orientation in contrast to a competitive and linear progress orientation. Edutainment titles, particularly those that make curricular claims, are generally linear and make much of achieving certain levels and scores. By contrast, entertainment software and elements are exploratory, often repetitive, and generally open ended. With this latter genre, what gets packaged and marketed is not achievement but fun, exploration, and imagination. These titles are also distinguished from the action entertainment titles marketed primarily toward teens and adults. In contrast to the darker hues and often frightening characters adorning the boxes of these titles, entertainment software for younger children is clearly coded as a separate market with brighter colors and smiling, wide-eyed characters like *Pajama Sam*. The packaging and marketing of these titles gives clues as to the underlying cultural logics animating the software. I turn now to the contexts of play to explore how these logics unfold in practice.

The Consumption Setting: Software and Activity in the 5thD

My research on play with children's software was conducted as part of a three-year, collaborative ethnographic evaluation examining the 5thD reform effort, in which researchers analyzed field notes and videotape from three 5thD clubs. The 5thD is an activity system where elementary-aged children and undergraduates from a local university come together to play with educational software in an after-school setting. The clubs are located at community institutions such as Boys' and Girls' Clubs, schools, or libraries and vary considerably depending on the local context and institution. What is common across the settings is a commitment to a collaborative and child-centered approach to learning, the nonhierarchical mixing of participants of different ages, and the use of personal computers running software designed for children.

When I was completing my fieldwork at the 5thD at the end of the 1990s, CD-ROM games and a more entertainment-oriented genre of products were making their appearance at the clubs. Mainstream licenses such as Lego, Barbie, and Disney were yet to arrive at the children's software scene, so I was not able to see titles such as these in my play settings. We were just beginning to see the emergence of licensing arrangement and tie-ins with television and other media and more and more titles with CD-ROM quality production value. One of the early titles that relied on entertainment vernaculars and tie-ins with other media (such as television and books) was the *Magic School Bus* series of CD-ROMs. One title in this series, *The Magic School Bus Explores the Human Body (MSBHB)* was in frequent use in the 5thD during my period of observation. This software was considered graphically cutting edge at the time, with beautiful animations and sophisticated use of sound. It is based on a scenario of traveling through the human body in a tiny school bus. The player can visit twelve parts of the body, such as the liver, lungs, esophagus, stomach, or intestines. The teacher, Ms. Frizzle, and her magic bus invert the power dynamics of the traditional classroom. The kids often appear as the more levelheaded and calmer characters, struggling to keep up with their charismatic leader. Like the entertainment industry content creators, Ms. Frizzle stands in for the liberated adult that is in touch with her uninhibited, playful, inner child. Rather than being presented in the linear and progressive logic of classroom curriculum, kids learn about subjects like the human body, space, and geology through a chaotic and dizzying set of encounters where the characters in the story careen from one scene to another.

Among the games that I observed in the 5thD, *MSBHB* most clearly represented the shift toward entertainment idioms in children's software, but many other titles also incorporated elements of entertainment-oriented visual culture. *SimCity 2000*, introduced early on in the research, is a cognitively challenging authoring tool, embedded in a graphically stunning multimedia package. The goal of the game is to create and administer a virtual city that grows and evolves based on player inputs. Another multimedia title that captured the attentions of children at the 5thD was *DinoPark Tycoon*, which allowed players to similarly create and administer a virtual dinosaur theme park. In what follows, I present examples of play with these three pieces of software, examining engagement with visual, auditory, and interactional special effects and the ways in which entertainment idioms were mobilized as relational and political resources in the 5thD.

Spectacle and Special Effect

Visual effects

The tapes of kids' game play with graphically advanced games is continuously punctuated by their notice of on-screen eye candy, an occasional "cool" or "oooh," that testifies to their appreciation of visual aesthetics of one kind or another. One undergraduate describes a boy playing *SimCity 2000* for the first time. "Every time he placed a building on the screen, he exclaimed 'Cool!' because the graphics were very complex and vivid." With a game like *MSBHB*, attention-grabbing graphics are central to the game's appeal since the game relies on an exploratory mode of interaction rather than one guided by a strong narrative story line or competitive goal orientation. The animations that form the transitions between the different parts of the body often draw appreciative "EEEW"s from both undergraduate and kid viewers as they watch the tiny bus drop into a puddle of stomach goo or fly down a sticky esophagus. "This is the fun part. This is fun. Watch," insists one kid as he initiates the opening animation. An undergraduate describes how a girl was "really excited" about showing her one small animation in *MSBHB*.

The screen in which one designs a face to go on the driver's license in *MSBHB* invites many minutes of scrolling through the different options for facial features and discussion of what is a cool or uncool feature. When multiple kids are engaging with the game, there will invariably be extended discussion about and exploration of different visual features in the driver's license. For example, when two boys are working together on a game, they argue about each facial feature, such as the eyes and eyewear or skin color. Features such as the driver's license, animations in the different scenes, or different controls in the cockpit provide an ongoing stream of visual effects that are often irrelevant to the educational content of the game but provide eye-catching distractions that keep the kids engaged. *MSBHB* incorporates visually spectacular features that are ends in themselves for game consumers, regardless of the relevance for the central play action. With *MSBHB*, undergraduate tutors constantly struggle to get kids to engage with the academic content of the game rather than these visual features. The tension between the spectacular features of the game and the educational goal of learning about the functions of the human body manifest as a tension between adult and child agendas of play.

Although *SimCity 2000* did not have the same appeal to the grotesque as *MSBHB*, it also invited pleasure in the visually spectacular and a similar set of social negotiations between adult learning goals and spectacular pleasures.

1. Jimmy (J): I want to do a highway. (Selects highway tool.) How do I do a highway? Okay. (Moves cursor around.) I'll do a highway right here.
2. Holly (H): Right there? I think you should have it . . . hmm . . . trying to think where a good place for it . . .
3. J: Right here? Here? (Moves cursor around.) Here? (Looks at H.)
4. H: Sure. What is that place there, residential?

5. J: (Budget window comes up and Jimmy dismisses it.) Yeah. I'm going to bulldoze a skyrise here. (Selects bulldozer tool and destroys building.) OK. (Looks at H.) Ummm! OK, wait, OK. Should I do it right here?

6. H: Sure, that might work . . . that way. Mmmm. You can have it . . .

7. J: (Builds highway around city.) I wonder if you can make them turn. (Builds highway curving around one corner.) Yeah, okay.

8. H: You remember, you want the highway to be . . . faster than just getting on regular streets. So maybe you should have it go through some parts.

9. J: (Dismisses budget pop-up window. Points to screen.) That's cool! (Inaudible.) I can make it above?

10. H: Above some places, I think. I don't know if they'd let you, maybe not.

11. J: (Moves cursor over large skyscraper.) That's so cool!

12. H: Is that a high rise?

13. J: Yeah. I love them.

14. H: Is it constantly changing, the city? Is it like . . .

15. J: (Builds complicated highway intersection. Looks at H.)

16. H: (Laughs.)

17. J: So cool! (Builds more highway grids in area, creating a complex overlap of four intersections.)

18. H: My gosh, you're going to have those poor drivers going around in circles.

19. J: I'm going to erase that all. I don't like that, OK. (Bulldozes highway system and blows up a building in process.) Ohhh . . .

20. H: Did you just blow up something else?

21. J: Yeah. (Laughs.)

22. H: (Laughs.)

23. J: I'm going to start a new city. I don't understand this one. I'm going to start with highways. (Quits without saving city.)

One sequence during a child's (Jimmy) play with an undergraduate (Holly) is punctuated by moments of engagement with the interface as visual special effect. At a certain point in the game, as his city grows, Jimmy attempts to build highways. "I want to do a highway," he declares, selecting the highway tool. "How do I do a highway?" (line 1). Moving his cursor around, he discusses with Holly where he might put the highway, settling on an area near a commercial district (line 3). He bulldozes to make way for the highway and then builds it around one edge of the city, discovering, at a certain point, that he can make it curve around the corner if he clicks on blocks perpendicular to one another (lines 5-7). As he builds his highway in the foreground, he notices that it is elevated above the level of the regular roadways. "That's cool!" he exclaims. "I can make it above?" (line 9). Holly speculates on whether they can build the highway through the city, and then Jimmy points with his cursor to a tall, blue and white skyscraper: "That's so cool!" (lines 10-11). Holly asks, "Is that a high-rise?" (line 12). "Yeah," Jimmy answers. "I love them," he declares emphatically (line 13). Jimmy goes on to continue his highway and then discovers that if he makes overlapping segments, they result in a cloverleaf. He looks over at Holly with delight when this happens, and she laughs. "So cool!" he exclaims, building further overlapping segments that result in a twisted quadruple cloverleaf (lines 15-17). "My gosh," says Holly, "you're going to have those poor drivers going around in circles" (line 18). Jimmy then bulldozes the whole cloverleaf pattern, blowing up a large building in the process, and then declares that he is going to start a new city (line 23). He closes his city without saving it.

While this sequence begins with certain accountabilities to building a transportation system, by the end Jimmy has wasted thousands of dollars on a highway to nowhere, blown up a building, and trashed his city. Holly draws him back into the accountabilities of building a well-functioning city by pointing out that the highway cloverleaf might look cool but is not going to work very well. Her intervention is subtle, but it has the effect of calling him away from spectacular engagement to the more functional accountabilities of the game. Jimmy responds to her suggestion by trying to fix the highway but eventually decides to start over since he has wasted too much money on playing with the highway as special effect. He apparently has few attachments to the city that he has worked on for more than thirty minutes and, in fact, replicates a pattern of building up cities to a point of difficulty and then getting rid of them, not bothering to save or follow up on his work.

Interactional and Auditory Special Effects

Unlike the media such as film and television that were the targets of Debord's (1995) critique of spectacle and passive consumption, interactive media are predicated on the active engagement of the consumer. This interactivity, rather than negating the spectacular qualities of the medium, actually serves to create a new genre of special effect, an experience of being able to control and manipulate the production of the effect. While visual effects and animations are generally predicated on a somewhat distanced position of spectatorship, interactive effects often foreground auditory effects over visual ones. Most games have a soundtrack, which plays repeatedly in the background and is rarely noted by a player, contrasting with sound as a special effect. A sound *effect* is a result of a particular action and, when initiated by the player, is often the occasion for delight and repeated activation.

One example of engagement with an interactive special effect is with an eleven-year-old, Dean, who is building a city with an undergraduate who is an expert at the game. As he is playing with the budget window, he discovers that increasing taxes causes the sim-citizens to boo and lowering them causes them to cheer. He takes some time out from administering the city to play with this auditory effect (lines 1, 5) before he is called back to his sim-mayor subjectivity by the undergraduate (lines 4, 6) (brackets signify overlapping talk).

1. Dean (D): (Starts bumping up the property tax, big grin.)
2. Undergraduate (UG): What are you doing? No, no, no.
3. D: No, I just [want to see . . .]
4. UG: [Now,] now—[listen].
5. D:(Bumps down the property taxes, making the citizens cheer.) [Yeeeee]eaaah. [I just want to make them happy.]
6. UG: [The best way to make money]—You want to increase your population, right? So you lay down the green, right? So if you put all, make all this all green, then, ahh, your popula-

tion will increase and then you could raise taxes and then you could get up to your five thousand mark.
7. D: Ohh OK. (Closes budget window.)

Dean's apparent pleasure in this interaction can be understood as a kind of computer holding power (Turkle 1984) based on the logic of the interactive special effect. It is the combination of direct interactional engagement with the machine and a unique responsiveness that creates a brief but tight interactional coupling between Dean and *SimCity 2000*. This kind of interactional pleasure occurred

---

Television was a turning point in creating a direct marketing channel between cultural producers and children.

---

numerous times during my observations of kids' play but was only initiated by the children who were controlling the mouse. While surface readings of the interface can invite collaborative interpersonal interpretation, as in the sequence with Jimmy and Holly, the interactive special effect is somewhat antisocial, relying on a tight interactional coupling with human and machine, often at the expense of other interlocutors. As in most examples of this sort, the undergraduate calls him back to the more functional and progress-oriented accountabilities of game play. This undergraduate is more heavy handed than the previous example with Holly, insisting that the kid pay attention: "No, no, no . . . now, now, listen. The best way to make money—you want to increase your population, right?"

Another instance of play, with *DinoPark Tycoon*, exhibits similar dynamics of interactional special effects. At the "Dino Diner," the player is able to purchase items from a menu as feed for the park's dinosaurs. One of the features of this screen is that there is a fly that buzzes around the menu, and if it lands on the menu, and a page is turned, the fly is crushed, emitting a squishing sound, and the player, upon flipping back to the page, sees a bloody smudge. In instance after instance of play with *DinoPark Tycoon*, kids play repeatedly with this game feature. In this day of Ian's play, almost every time he visits the Dino Diner, he spends time smashing flies:

1. Ian (I): (Turns a page, and squishing sound results.) Yeah, I just crunched some more. Yeah, look at all them. They're so dead (laughing). This is rad. Oh, come on fly, I want you to come down here. Come down here puppy. Come to papa. Crunch! (Turns page, and laughs.)
2. Adult (A): That's nasty.

3. I: (Turns page.) Crunchie, crunchie, crunchie. (Turns page.) I crunched him! I crunched
    him! (Turns page.) I'm so mean. I want to go check out my dino. (Leaves Dino Diner.)

As with the case with Dean, this interaction is relatively brief and clearly peripheral
to the primary goals of the game, which are to build and administer the virtual theme
park. Ian takes some time out to enjoy the interactional special effect (lines 1-2) but
returns fairly quickly to the task at hand, checking up on his dinosaur (line 3).

One area of *MSBHB*, involving a simple painting program, is particularly notable as an embodiment of the logic of the interactive special effect. Clicking on the
drawing pad of one of the characters calls forth a screen with a canvas and various
tools, shaped like body parts, along the side. After selecting a body part, the player
can squirt, splat, or stamp blobs and shapes onto the canvas, accompanied by gross
bodily noises appropriate to the body part. Often to the dismay of the accompanying undergraduate, kids will spend excruciatingly long minutes repeatedly squirt-
ing juices from the stomach or emitting a cacophony of farting noises from the
tongue tool. One undergraduate notes, after playing with a group of girls, "Each
different shape or design made its own unique sound. I think the kids get a much
better kick out of the sound than anything else. And they would laugh and laugh
when they found the sound they liked best."

In another instance of play with this program, an undergraduate is working with
a boy who systematically and gleefully goes through each tool, repeatedly emitting
gross sounds. The undergraduate participates happily in this, but she eventually
suggests that they return to the main areas of the game. The boy then suggests that
she is discouraging him from playing with gross sounds and decides that he wants
to stop playing rather than return to the more educational sections of the game.
The undergraduate has actually been remarkably patient through an extended
sequence of play with each drawing tool, suggesting on various occasions that he
try one or another tool. Yet the boy insists that he knows why she suggests that he
move on, " 'Cause you didn't like the sounds." In this case, the boy is more active
than the undergraduate in constructing the opposition between the adult stance
and kid stance with respect to the orientation to gross special effects.

Interactional special effects are similar to the manipulations that are possible
with materials such as clay and finger paints but are mediated by a computational
artifact that uniquely amplifies and embellishes the actions of the user. Like the
visual special effects described earlier, these interactional and auditory effects are
not part of a broader game goal structure but are rather engaged in for momentary
and aesthetic pleasure. These are not the dominant modes of engagement in play
with children's software, but they are small, ongoing breaks in the narrative trajectories of multimedia titles. They are also sites of micropolitical resistance to the
progress-oriented goals and adult values that seek to limit violent and grotesque
spectacles in an educational setting like the 5thD.

Mobilizing Fun: The Micropolitics of Pleasure

Engagements with special effects are not merely an atomized process of individual engagement. They are part of the political economy of cool, a central source of cultural capital in kids' peer relations. Spectacle and fun are mobilized as devices to enlist other kids and to demonstrate style and status, as well as a way of demarcating a kid-centered space that is opposed to the progress goals of adults. A search for all instances of the word *fun* in the video transcript record revealed many instances of *funny* but relatively few instances of children describing something as *fun*. More often, it got used in questions by adults querying whether a child was engaged: "Are you having fun?" "Is this a fun game?" Although adults generally used the term to describe moments when kids were actively engaged, kids tended to use the term to refer to activity that was spectacular in nature, rather than educational or functional. In other words, adults (at least in this progressive educational setting) tend to construct play and fun in relation to developmental goals and engagement, whereas kids see it as something keyed to particular visual and entertainment-oriented idioms.

In the 5thD, an orientation to fun is actively encouraged but ultimately in the service of a reformist educational project. Children mobilize fun as a way of indicating authentic engagement, and fun is celebrated in the 5thD to the extent that it happens in the context of a prosocial learning task. Entertainment is clearly not a monolithic category within mass media forms. While some entertainment idioms are legitimized within the 5thD project, action gaming idioms are explicitly excluded as too patently noneducational. Action entertainment idioms are constantly lurking in the ambient culture that kids participate in. These cultural elements are largely excluded from the 5thD through the selection of nonviolent games and persistent adult surveillance, but they are still present. Due to their illegitimate status in the 5thD, they become a resource for subverting dominant (educational) codes in this local context. I close this article with a case of play with *SimCity 2000* that exhibits this complicated relational dynamic between educational and entertainment idioms.

One day of Ian's play with *SimCity 2000*, captured on video, is a rare case in which action entertainment appears as a social resource in the 5thD, and it enables one to see the tensions around this cultural domain as it appears in an informal learning setting of this sort. The scene opens with Ian sitting in front of the computer, interacting with a well-developed city marked by an enormous airport and waterfalls stacked in a pyramid formation. Another boy is sitting next to him, observing his play and making occasional suggestions; and there is an audience of other club participants, including the videotaper, undergraduates, and other kids and adults walking in and out of the scene. He busily makes a railroad system, water pipes, buildings, and a power plant and worries about such things as whether his people are getting enough water or whether power plants need to be replaced.

Soon, the director of the club appears and tries to get Ian to teach others how to play (line 1), but Ian deftly deflects this accountability to the club norm of collaborative learning, with the support of another kid (line 2):

1. Site director (D): Because you're not going to be sitting here all day just doing it by yourself. So other people watch you. It's not fair to other people.
2. Mark, a younger boy (M): No, we, we, we, we're not supposed to be able to play. We're not supposed to play.
3. D: Why aren't you supposed to play?
4. Ian (I): They're not.
5. M: If you're not a Young Wizard's you can't play this.
6. D: But if you're a Young Wizard's Assistant and you're not teaching anybody else the game, then you can't play it either.
7. M: He's teaching me.
8. I: (Unintelligible) said I could.
9. D: OK good, all right, check it out then.
10. I: Anybody ask me any questions.

Ian's tactic is momentarily successful; he passes as a teacher and resumes his game play. After about twenty minutes, however, he is interrupted by the director of the club again and asked to teach a new undergraduate how to play the game. "I'm not kidding either," the director stresses, "her grade depends on what you teach her, so she'd better do a good job, okay?" After a few moments, Mark suggests, "Show her a disaster. Do an airplane crash." Ian responds with enthusiasm, saves his city, and announces, "Ha ha ha disaster time!!"

Edutainment titles, particularly those that make curricular claims, are generally linear and make much of achieving certain levels and scores. By contrast, entertainment software and elements are exploratory, often repetitive, and generally open ended.

In this sequence of activity, Ian finds himself in the center of a series of interventions and a great deal of social attention, positioned as an expert and asked to teach both an undergraduate and a large audience of other kids about the game. The videotaper and the site director have already intervened a number of times to orient him to his community role as game expert and teacher. His companion is the first to suggest doing a disaster, and he takes it up with a characteristic virtuosity and antiauthoritarianism. Disaster time involves an escalating series of special effects in which the city is first invaded by a space alien, then flooded, set on fire, and subjected to an earthquake and plane crashes. The undergraduate remains pleasant and amused. The videotaper, a longtime participant at the club, is the first to intervene, addressing the undergraduate first. "So, have you figured out how to play?" And then she turns to Ian. "Remember Ian, that Anne has to . . . Ian?!" The videotaper and the undergraduate's protests punctuate this instance of play, and though they do not specifically deny the appeal of destruction, they are clearly trying to redirect the activity. They are overpowered as Mark cheers Ian on and they jointly delight in the spectacles of destruction. "Do another airplane crash!" "Destroy it." Another boy joins the spectacle. "Please do a fire engine." "Put more fire. Fire's cool." "Just burn it all. Burn it. Burn it. Just burn it. Burn it. Burn it. You need more fire, more fire." The site director appears again. "Is he teaching you how to be a constructive citizen?" he jokes. "Another five minutes, and then put Anne on and see what she can do." "Do riots," the third boy continues, not responding to the director's comment.

[I]nteractional and auditory effects are not part of a broader game goal structure but are rather engaged in for momentary and aesthetic pleasure.

After the city is in flames, Ian begins to build large buildings within burning areas to induce more and more spectacular explosions. He turns from blowing up the most expensive of the possible buildings to blowing up colleges, fusion plants, gas power plants, and microwave power plants. His final achievement is to blow up a row of fusion plants lined up in domino formation. "Ian, time, put Anne in there," insists the site director at the conclusion of this performance. "He's into mass destruction at the moment," says Anne, worried. The director assures her, "Yeah, but these guys know a lot about the game." Then he turns to Ian. "I don't want to turn the machine off on you. Be nice to Anne and give her a turn." That is enough of a credible threat for Ian to start a new city for Anne. Here I would like to point to the role of action entertainment idioms in enlisting an audience of other boys and the role of computational media in enabling a virtuosity of the spectacular in the hands of a player. The adults at the club are in the difficult position of trying to validate Ian's technical knowledge but not wanting the destructive scenario to continue. Ian is quite aware of the boundaries of participation in the 5thD and plays to his moment in the spotlight until he is on the verge of disciplinary action. Far from being involved in a regressive and antisocial act, Ian is engaging in a process of enlisting a large and engaged audience in a shared spectacle of technical virtuosity. The unique context of the 5thD enables this to play out in a way that is negotiated rather than either univocally repressive or celebratory; Ian retains his status as game expert and teacher while enlisting the agendas and interests of both adults and kids at the site.

Conclusions

If one resists the impulse to call Ian's activity antisocial, then one is beginning to query the social functions of dysfunctional activity and a certain cultural paradox. While competitive achievement that individuates learning and produces class distinction is considered prosocial and developmentally correct, hedonistic play that creates peer solidarity in relation to consumer culture is considered antisocial and regressive, an attention deficit to the progress goals of certain authoritative institutions. Sutton-Smith (1997) described this tension in terms of private and public transcripts of childhood:

> The adult public transcript is to make children progress, the adult private transcript is to deny their sexual and aggressive impulses; the child public transcript is to be successful as family members and school children, and their private transcript is their play life, in which they can express both their hidden identity and their resentment of being a captive population. (p. 123)

The 5thD is a site that self-consciously works to reengineer this cultural logic by accommodating both child and adult agendas and creating opportunities for cross-generational negotiation and shared discourse. When one adds media industries and high technology to the relational mix, the equation becomes more complicated. Far from being an unmediated voice of a natural childhood pleasure principle, phantasmagoria and spectacle are distributed, engineered social productions that unite children and media industries. They are also sites of virtuosity, connoisseurship, and status negotiation among children as well as between children and adults. What constitutes an authoritative institution is a contingent effect of local micropolitics, where pop culture identification confers status in children's status hierarchies and "fun" gets mobilized vis-à-vis adults as an authenticating trope of a "natural" childlike pleasure principle. This is not a simple story of adult repression of authentic childhood impulses but is a distributed social field that produces the opposition between childhood pleasure and adult achievement norms as a contingent cultural effect, subject to local reshapings as in the 5thD.

The spectacular dimensions of new media deserve special mention as unique materializations of kids' popular entertainment. The atomized consciousness of a player engaging with a special effect is a small moment attached to a large sociotechnical apparatus. Whether in movies or computer games, special effects are what drive budgets and bring in large audiences. This is indicative of a particular kind of industry maturation, where a growing consumer base supports larger production budgets but also increases investor risk, driving the push toward sure-hit products, sequels, formulaic content, and guaranteed crowd pleasers. Special effects also weed out independent developers who do not have the budgets to compete in production value. Entertainment industries participate in the production of institutionalized genres that are packaged and stereotyped into certain formulas that kids recognize and identify with as a libratory and authentic kids' culture. In the titles I reviewed, these appeared as gross bodily noises, explosions, hyperbole, and increasingly, established licensed characters. This "junk culture" is a particular vernacular that cross-cuts media and commodity types, making its way into snack foods, television, movies, school supplies, and interactive multimedia. Just as this junk culture is a site of opposition between adults and kids, entertainment elements in children's software become opportunities for kids to resist adult learning goals in the 5thD and elsewhere.

Although the founders of the children's software industry were looking for a radical break from the existing logics of both entertainment and education, when children's software entered the political and economic mainstream, industrials began reproducing familiar vernaculars that played to mainstream retailing. Kids mobilized these new cultural resources in ways that fit their local peer agendas and intergenerational negotiations. Technology is produced through and productive of structured social and cultural contexts, and any accompanying social change needs to take this as a starting point. Multimedia and interactive media are not inherently "fun" or "educational" but take on these characteristics through a highly distributed social, technical, and cultural apparatus. This research was conducted before the spread of broadband Internet, file sharing, online software distribution, and widespread game hacking and remix. As alternative models for software production and distribution take hold, we may find that the Net is trafficking in forms of children's software that may truly redefine some of the cultural logics of contemporary childhood that were established in the television era. Whatever change happens, it will not be an effect of factors inherent in a particular technology but of a whole complex of discursive, social, political, and economic alignments that link sites of production, distribution, marketing, and consumption.

References

Buckingham, David. 2000. *After the death of childhood: Growing up in the age of electronic media*. Cambridge, UK: Polity.

Cole, Michael. 1997. *Cultural psychology: A once and future discipline*. Cambridge, MA: Harvard University Press.

Debord, Guy. 1995. *Society of the spectacle*. Detroit, MI: Black & Red.

Foucault, Michel. 1978. *The history of sexuality: An introduction*. Vol. 1. Trans. R. Hurley. New York: Vintage Books.

Ito, Mizuko. 2003. Engineering play: Children's software and the productions of everyday life. Ph.D. diss., Stanford University.

Kline, Stephen. 1993. *Out of the garden: Toys and children's culture in the age of TV marketing*. New York: Verso.

Seiter, Ellen. 1995. *Sold separately: Parents and children in consumer culture*. New Brunswick, NJ: Rutgers University Press.

Sutton-Smith, Brian. 1997. *The ambiguity of play*. Cambridge, MA: Harvard University Press.

Turkle, Sherry. 1984. *The second self: Computers and the human spirit*. New York: Touchstone.

Vasquez, Olga A., Lucinda Pease-Alvarez, and Sheila M. Shannon. 1994. *Pushing boundaries: Language and culture in a Mexicano community*. Cambridge: Cambridge University Press.

Audience Construction and Culture Production: Marketing Surveillance in the Digital Age

By
JOSEPH TUROW

This study melds "contextualist" and "resource dependence" perspectives from industrial sociology to explore the implications that audience construction by marketing and media firms hold for the core assumptions that are shaping the emerging media system of the twenty-first century. Marketers, media, and the commercial research firms that work with them are constructing contemporary U.S. audiences as frenetic, self-concerned, attention-challenged, and willing to allow advertisers to track them in response to being rewarded or treated as special. This perspective, a response to challenges and opportunities they perceive from new digital interactive technologies, both leads to and provides rationalizations for a surveillance-based customization approach to the production of culture.

Keywords: marketing; advertising; mass media; production of culture; mass communication; Internet; surveillance

The needs of marketers have fundamentally influenced culture production in the United States since the late nineteenth century. Post–Civil War industrial growth ignited rabid competition between consumer brands. Manufacturers' desire to persuade retailers to carry their brands led them to advertise to consumers in large-circulation newspapers and magazines with the aim (often quite explicit) of having them din retailers for the products. Newspaper and magazine publishers, in turn, realized that

Joseph Turow is Robert Lewis Shayon Professor of Communication and Associate Dean of Graduate Studies at the University of Pennylvania's Annenberg School for Communication. Among several other books, he is author of Breaking Up America: Advertisers and the New Media World *(University of Chicago Press, 1997) and (edited with Andrea Kavanaugh)* The Wired Homestead *(MIT Press, 2003). He has written about media and advertising for the popular press, including* American Demographics *magazine and the* Los Angeles Times. *He currently serves on the boards of the* Journal of Broadcasting and Electronic Media, New Media & Society, *and* Consumer WebWatch, *a consumer-alert project of* Consumers Union.

DOI: 10.1177/0002716204270469

they could make most of their profits from advertisers by charging low subscription rates to garner the huge numbers of readers advertisers wanted (see, e.g., Tebbel 1974). It was the beginning of a lesson for Americans that was repeated with most new media technologies throughout the twentieth century: "Content is cheap—often even free—because advertisers support it."

In the early twenty-first century, marketers, media, and the commercial research firms that work with them are constructing contemporary U.S. audiences as frenetic, self-concerned, attention-challenged, and willing to allow advertisers to track them in response to being rewarded or treated as special.

The implications of this century-long lesson for the production of culture are profound. As many critics of media and advertising have pointed out, turning over the support of much of the U.S. media system to advertisers has ensured that media firms fundamentally shape the main streams of entertainment and news into environments that harmonize with sponsors' desire to sell their products. Critical analysts also recognize that the commodification of audiences is a central feature of media-advertiser relations. Taking cues from advertisers in symbiotic relationships often fraught with tensions, media firms position themselves to attract certain kinds of people in ways that the advertisers consider better or helpfully different from the media firms' competitors. As part of standing out in this competition, media practitioners typically exhort their readers, listeners, or viewers to think of themselves primarily as leisure-oriented consumers of media content and sponsored products. Commercial imperatives rarely encourage media firms to urge their audiences to be engaged producers of a civil society or to expect news and entertainment to contribute toward that goal.

A stream of writings suggests that ongoing relationships between media and marketing firms lead them to define audiences in certain ways. (For an overview, see Whitney and Ettema 1994.) The writings further suggest that the audience definitions lead to the creation of certain kinds of media materials—the production of certain kinds of culture—and not others. A number of studies explore the extent to which and the way in which changing advertiser-media relationships result in changing definitions of audience that, in turn, affect the structure for producing messages directed to those audiences (see Turow 1979; Cross 2000; and Gamson 1997). The studies reinforce the proposition that deliberations by advertisers and media firms about the audience are crucial to the dynamics of mass media culture.

This study takes research on audience construction into the prospective, policy realm. It melds "contextualist" and "resource dependence" perspectives from industrial sociology to explore the implications that audience construction by marketing and media firms hold for the core assumptions that are shaping the emerging media system of the twenty-first century. More than previous studies, it argues that audience constructions by marketing and media firms derive not primarily from "objective" observations of the social world. Rather, the audience categories upon which they focus and the attributes that those choose to highlight relate directly to industrial needs and provide justification for industrial activities.

In the early twenty-first century, marketers, media, and the commercial research firms that work with them are constructing contemporary U.S. audiences as frenetic, self-concerned, attention-challenged, and willing to allow advertisers to track them in response to being rewarded or treated as special. This perspective, a response to challenges and opportunities they perceive from new digital interactive technologies, both leads to and provides rationalizations for a surveillance-based customization approach to the production of culture. An emerging strategic logic encourages media firms and advertisers to cultivate consumers' trust so that their audiences will not object when the companies want to track their activities. The goal of tracking is to store huge amounts of linked personal and lifestyle information in databases with the goal of more efficient "relationship"-oriented marketing that rewards "best customers" with discounts and even story lines designed for them.

The article suggests that the core assumptions of a surveillance-marketing media culture imply the promotion of new forms of consumer anxiety under the rubric of customer satisfaction. There is resistance: concerns about how and why people are watched—and, by implication, about the construction of audiences—are leading advocacy groups to decry it and encourage alternatives. Marketers and media firms, however, have the upper hand in framing the situation for consumers and policy makers. It seems clear that important aspects of media culture produced in early-twenty-first century media will result from the strategies being laid out now under the rubric of giving the (industrially constructed) audience what it wants.

The Industrial Construction of Audiences

A good deal of literature about people who attend to messages emphasizes that their interpretations vary depending upon a wide variety of factors, such as their personalities, family backgrounds, social relationships, context of viewing, and class positions (see, for example, Klapper 1960; Morley 1980; Liebes and Katz 1990). A less trodden, though growing, area of research takes a different tack on the notion of audience. It focuses not on the specific individuals who share programs, articles, or ads but on the ways that the people who create those materials think of those people (Whitney and Ettema 1994).

Writers in this area do not dispute the importance of knowing that the people who receive the messages may differ from one another in their interpretations of the texts. The writers show, however, that the ways media organizations search for and describe their audiences have important implications for the texts that viewers and readers receive in the first place (see Turow 1997, 1-17). The underlying point is that understanding how media organizations think about their audiences—and why in certain ways and not others—is crucial for understanding why particular agendas of news, entertainment, information, education, and advertising and not others are cast up for public consideration.

At the base of this perspective is the notion that audiences are necessarily constructions, whether they are "students" in a classroom, "concertgoers" in a large amphitheater, or "viewers" of a major television network. Typically, these conceptions reflect the reward system under which those addressing the audience work. In school, a teacher is salaried to think of the individuals in her or his class as students who will learn certain subjects from her or him. The jobs of network television officials rise and fall on their abilities to deliver the right numbers and types of people who view TV to sponsors.

Mass media activities are different from other forms of audience construction in the scale of the activities. Mass communication involves the industrialized production, distribution, and exhibition of messages through technological devices. Audience targeting and construction are key parts of the activity, which often involves advertising. Advertising involves the creation of messages to explicitly draw favorable attention to a person, product, or service. Advertising is not the only way that marketers use media to reach people. Another traditional route is public relations, which involves calling favorable attention to the product or service by becoming part of a news story. Yet historically, advertising has been critical to the survival of many U.S. media. In 2002, the one hundred leading companies in U.S. advertising spent an estimated $83 billion (*Advertising Age* 2003). Most of that cash was used to purchase time or space among attractive nonadvertising material on broadcast television, on cable TV, on radio, in magazines, and in newspapers.

An ad-sponsored universe has profound implications for the production of entertainment, news, and information. Creators at all levels realize that the material must be successful in attracting audiences that advertisers want and putting the audience in a mood that makes them maximally persuadable to the sales pitches. Marketing executives continually engage in discussions with their ad agency counterparts about who their consumers are, how to best reach them, and with what messages. Conferences and the trade press are filled with articles discussing trends among American consumers and opining about what types of Americans are most attractive and why. Discussions about the nature of men, women, gays, lesbians, Hispanics, African Americans, teens, and children represent only the tip of an iceberg of constructions that continually take place between advertisers, their agencies, and media firms.

The specifics of these constructions get negotiated through struggles by stakeholders in the process. That is where the resource dependence perspective's focus on interorganizational struggles for power is useful. According to the resource dependence perspective, major goals of organizational leaders are avoiding dependence on other organizations and making others dependent on them (see Aldrich 1979). The general picture is of decision makers attempting to manage their environments as well as their organizations. Power, in this view, is equivalent to the possession of resources. Emerson (1962, 32) added that "influence [perhaps a better word is leverage] is the use of resources in attempts to gain compliance of others." It is through this struggle over resources on several organizational and interorganizational levels that industry strategies toward environmental forces such as audiences develop.

Andrew Pettigrew (1985) provided a helpful way to think about changes in these strategies over time. Pettigrew emphasized the importance of multiple dimensions of context—organizational, social, economic, and political—on organizational activities. Especially important is his suggestion that prominent strategies to face complex new environmental challenges often evolve from organizational activities that have not seemed at all central. A corollary to this idea is the possibility that seemingly unrelated responses to environmental challenges by different organizations might actually share a strategic logic—that is, assumptions by their creators about the best ways to move forward. If leaders across the industry begin to recognize these commonalities, and if technologies allow the interpenetration of the activities, the level of change within the industry may well be profound. So might be the social implications of that change.

Melding resource dependency with contextualism provides a useful lens for examining the way evolving marketer-media relationships are affecting the construction of audiences and, by extension, media content. Resource dependence points to the importance of tracking the ongoing struggles for control over legitimate ways to think about and reach audiences today, struggles that include reciprocal attempts to cultivate dependencies. Contextualism points to the importance of examining organizational, social, economic, and political factors that affect the evolving industrial constructions of audiences and their relations to media culture.

Turn-of-the-century dilemmas

The approach is particularly relevant to understanding how changes roiling through media and marketer organizations at the turn of the twenty-first century are interactively affecting constructions of audience and media culture. Marketers worry that the contemporary hyperfragmentation of media channels—hundreds of cable channels, millions of Web sites—is making it difficult to reach potential customers efficiently with traditional advertising. Even more problematic to marketers is that U.S. consumers seem to be using digital technologies to escape advertisements in ad-supported media. Industry observers fear that pop-up ad killers, spam filters, and ad-skipping buttons in personal video recorders are merely the leading edge of digital technologies that allow audiences to keep the content and zap the commercials without even looking at them.

The possibility that advertising in commercial media may be losing its ability to serve advertisers' interests has created consternation among marketing and media firms. Ranging across many of these difficulties, James Stengel, Proctor and Gamble's Global Marketing Officer, told the 2004 American Association of Advertising Agencies Media Conference that "today's marketing world is broken. . . . We are still too dependent on marketing tactics that are not in touch with today's consumer" (quoted in Neff and Sanders 2004, 1). He made the point quite aptly in his keynote speech. Appearing via video, his remarks were interrupted three times by a TiVo personal video recorder (PVR) screen allowing the viewer to skip ahead—and presumably past any sales pitches.

Commenting about PVRs at a different conference, the chairman of Turner Broadcasting issued similarly dire warnings. He asserted that PVRs were destructive to the TV industry because they contributed to lower ratings, lower ad revenue, and fewer quality programs for TV distributors. "What drives our business," noted Kellner, "is people selling bulbs and vacuum cleaners in Salt Lake City. If you take even a small percentage away, you are going to push this business under profitability" (quoted in Friedman 2003, 13).

The concerns have led to intense discussions within the marketing and media establishments about how to cultivate customers via media in coming decades. Explicitly and implicitly, the discussions link the introduction of new media approaches with changes in the nature of American consumers, either as a guide to certain actions, a justification for them, or both. Guided by contextualism and the resource dependence perspective—and based primarily on interviews with key industry personnel, the systematic reading of trade magazines, and attendance of several marketing-and-media trade conferences—the following pages explore the various forces that are shaping evolving constructions of audience. They also explore ways that these constructions relate to the development of a shared strategic logic among marketing and media personnel that is pushing the production of media culture toward being intimately involved in audience surveillance.

Changing Audience Constructions

To understand the trajectory of contemporary audience construction, it is useful to see how it connects with and diverges from the "audience targeting" approach that media and marketing firms have used for a few decades. Audience targeting by U.S. media dates back to the 1920s and even earlier, but it really took on steam beginning in the 1960s and 1970s. Before those decades, the most common approach to U.S. media audiences emphasized sheer size. The reasons were fundamentally rooted in the nature of manufacturing. Factory activity of the day was based on conveyer systems, rollers, and gravity slides that sent materials through the production process in a continuous stream. The process turned out huge inventories of the exact same goods. It seemed logical to manufacturers to use media vehicles to mass-produce customers in the same way that the factories mass-produced the merchandise (see Pope 1983; Strasser 1995).

The desire to sell to people by "tonnage" (as ad people sometimes describe it) meant that "men," "women," and "children" was about as detailed as most advertisers got in customizing their appeals. Daniel Pope (1983, 139) has written that in the first quarter of the twentieth century, few advertisers "were prepared to recognize and fewer to accept the nation's heterogeneity." Radio, then television, companies became the quintessential crowd catchers. As late as the early 1980s, the Nielsen rating service reported that the three major television networks together reached more than 90 percent of all households viewing television. It pleased marketers as well as the networks that, according to Nielsen, the 90 percent represented more than 50 percent of all homes in the country (see Turow 1997, 26).

By the mid-1980s, ad executives, the marketing trade press, and conference themes had congealed a picture of Americans as much more suspicious, self-indulgent, less unified socially, and leading lives that were much more frenetic than in past decades.

Despite this emphasis on tonnage, some advertisers did aim at smaller slices of the population—for example, immigrant groups and wealthy individuals—quite early in the century. By the 1920s, moreover, new manufacturing initiatives were creating the basis for an approach to marketing that would reward media that targeted segments of the population rather than "everybody." The basic change at work was product differentiation. Economies of scale were now allowing manufacturers to create slightly different versions of the same products to aim at different parts of the marketplace.

Especially after World War II, this sort of logic led manufacturers increasingly to support magazines and radio stations that reached consumer segments that they coveted at the same time that they used television to reach "everyone." Advertisers and their agencies began to support research that allowed them to learn about the buying and leisure habits of listeners to particular radio stations and subscribers to particular periodicals. The work had important implications for the future of marketing. It began to create a model for audience segmentation in other media.

By the late 1970s, many signals indicated that it was television's turn to be trans-formed by market segmentation (Turow 1997, 32-34). In manufacturing, increased competition was pushing product differentiation along so that smaller and smaller numbers of a product could be marketed profitably to certain seg-ments of society. In market research, competition among consumer-analysis firms was leading to findings that differentiated groups in new, unusual, and profitable ways. The manufacturing and market analysis developments meant that advertis-ers increasingly agreed to support the multiplication of broadcast (mostly UHF) and cable television outlets during the 1980s if they reached the kinds of specific audiences the advertisers needed.

The explicit move by mainstream marketing and media firms to consumer tar-geting was accompanied by a shift in their construction of the U.S. population. The view of a segmented society that replaced it was a better fit with the new market-specialization interests of advertisers and the media that wanted to serve them. It also tied in with writings by a small set of social observers in the 1970s and 1980s—especially Daniel Yankelovich, John Naisbitt, Alvin Toffler, and Peter Drucker—who popularized the idea that a profound change in the fabric of U.S. society was taking place (see Turow 1997, 39-43).

At conferences and in trade magazines, ad people explained the change—and justified their increased targeting—in historical terms. They claimed that from the 1940s to the late 1960s, the nation had been united in purpose. The trauma of World War II had created a public that, to quote one ad executive, was "mentally wedded to mutual cooperation and togetherness brought on by [the] conflict" (Maneloveg 1980, 56). About twenty years later, though, pressures such as the civil rights movement and the Vietnam War led the nation to become "less homoge-neous, more splintered." America seemed "split asunder innumerable special interests . . . all more aware of their claims on society." (Maneloveg 1980, 56). In addition, the success of the economic systems of the 1950s and 1960s freed people to experiment with a variety of lifestyles. They privileged the search for their own identities and new types of communities such as the "hippies" that were self-indul-gent and typically not concerned with the larger world. The ideological Right also played its part in unleashing the forces of social division, according to this tale. Ronald Reagan's election to the presidency in 1980 led marketers to conclude that Americans had reinforced their belief in self-reliant attention to market forces along with less confidence in government regulation to solve problems (Crain 1984, 30).

By the mid-1980s, ad executives, the marketing trade press, and conference themes had congealed a picture of Americans as much more suspicious, self-indul-gent, less unified socially, and leading lives that were much more frenetic than in past decades. Research firms convinced marketers that learning as much as possi-ble about the social and social-psychological attributes that drive consumer activi-ties would allow for placing them into audience groupings made of people with similar buying interests and abilities as well as media habits. Cable and magazine executives, desperate to grab ad money from the major networks, asserted that as U.S. society became more divided, it needed more outlets to reflect those divisions—outlets of the sort that cable and magazines were now offering. The target-oriented media firms based their invitation to marketers on two claims. The claim of efficient separation was the media firm's assertion that it could deliver a desired group to advertisers without making them pay for audiences they did not want. The claim of special relationship argued that the target audience felt such an extraordinary tie to the media firm's outlet—the magazine, cable network, newspaper, Web site—that it paid attention to everything about the outlet, including the ads.

Marketers increasingly agreed with these goals in the 1980s and paid research firms to test them. Competition among research firms to refine audience targets for marketers led to an "arms race" that pushed new methods aimed to explore in detail the activities and interests—the lifestyles—that could be associated with people exhibiting certain demographics. In turn, cable, magazine, and other ad vehicles tried to prove that they could target these attractive groups.

By the 1990s, the tide was shifting from general interest to targeted media even in the television realm. The major players remained a few companies. A flurry of corporate combinations created behemoths that controlled major segments of media, including broadcast and cable television. Their response to the fragmentation of channels was to regain control by cornering as many slices of the targeted audiences as possible. Changes regarding CBS provide an example. The percentage of the prime-time audience reached by the CBS television network in 2002 was typically one-third of what it was in 1972. But whereas in 1972 CBS was a company that owned only one TV network, in 2002 CBS TV was one of several video networks owned by Viacom. Viacom therefore sold valuable slices of prime-time viewers to advertisers through MTV, Nickelodeon, Comedy Central, Spike, and UPN as well as CBS. It was a collection of channels that allowed Viacom to move toward controlling the share of viewers CBS reached in the early 1970s, but separated to meet the needs of the new media world.

There was great value in selling the right kinds of audience slices. It was a common industry observation that Disney's ESPN cable networks, aimed at different types of male sports enthusiasts, were far more valuable than its venerable ABC network, with a much larger though broader audience. The new construction of Americans had legitimated the new one hundred channel cable universe to marketers and encouraged media firms to tilt their formats toward the new format to cater to specific interests that attract advertisers. Target marketing and the associated construction of U.S. consumers as segmented and frenetic encouraged a media system increasingly to separate populations from one another particular along demographic, lifestyle, and even psychographic categories rather than "everyone."

Ad skipping and the reconstruction of audiences

In that context of growing abilities of media and marketers to target specific groups through research-guided formats, the realization by mainstream marketing and media practitioners that their future audiences would routinely be able to use technology to eliminate ads aimed at them was disconcerting. Certainly, both groups had known for decades that newspapers and magazines could not guarantee that their readers would actually look at, let alone read, every print ad when they turned the pages. Similarly, advertisers understood that radio and television stations and networks had no way to force people to stay in their seats when the commercials came on. Advertising agencies, in fact, saw getting people's attention through compelling ads as one of their primary challenges.

But marketers, their media planners, and traditional media executives saw spam filters, pop-up filters, new antiad laws for cell phones, and ad-skipping buttons in personal video recorders as collectively representing a fundamentally different challenge to marketers' ability to place commercial messages in front of even the most targeted populations. They ascribed the dangers not just to the ease of erasure or increased channel choice but to a changed nature of large segments of the audience. As early as 1989, executives argued that ad skipping was due to "the limited attention spans and itchy remote control trigger fingers" of the first TV generation grown to adulthood (Benson 1988, S4).

By the turn of the twenty-first century, executives were lamenting that increasing proportions of the public cared nothing about what they insisted was a decades-long contract with media firms that promised attention to ads in return for free or discounted media material. Moreover, they noted that the individuals who were developing technologies to get rid of ads were part of that itchy public and had no vested interests in maintaining the ad-supported world. Agreeing with the CEO of Turner Broadcasting about the dangers of TiVo to the contemporary advertiser-media relationship, a Hollywood talent agent urged marketers to understand that they could no longer present ads through home-based electronic media in traditional ways. "The genie is out of the bottle," he asserted (Friedman 2003, 13).

Clearly, traditional commercial forms in conventional media still represent by far the most prevalent approaches in the first decade of the twenty-first century. Nevertheless, marketers in the early twenty-first century believe firmly that the genie is out of the bottle. They insist that the difficulties of targeting in a hypersegmented media world combined with new digital technologies that allow for the elimination of commercials mean they must be prepared to use new ways to ensure that consumers attend to their electronic solicitations. Increasingly, they are turning to alternatives to standard advertising as instruments to force consumer attention.

As these separate sets of activities develop, they are coming together in a new industry strategy for reaching the public that holds important implications for information privacy and ad-induced anxieties. The model they are developing melds a nontraditional area of advertising—direct marketing—with a selling approach—customer relationship management (CRM)—that has gained much attention in marketing outside the media during the 1990s (see, e.g., Pepper and Rogers 1993). Media and marketing practitioners justify the blending of these unrelated forms in the digital interactive media environment by pointing to what they say is a critical realization about the U.S. media audience that they had no reason to notice in the past. American consumers, they say, are willing to allow advertisers and media firms to collect data about them and track their activities in return for relatively small but useful benefits that make their frenetic, attention-challenged, self-centered lives easier—discounts, entries to media channels, or similar special attention. Converging media and marketing activities based on this proposition are leading to an emerging set of strategic logics in favor of an emerging culture-production system in which surveillance marketing is deeply embedded.

The Rise of Surveillance-Driven Culture Production

A major reason CRM attracts marketers is that it focuses on the quantifiable value of known individuals. CRM is rooted in two insights that are based on the writings of nineteenth-century economist Vilfredo Pareto. One is that a small number of contemporary customers contribute to most of the profits. The second is that it is almost always much more expensive to gain new customers than it is to hold on to current ones. These notions lead to a corollary: "Focus 80% of your efforts on the 20% of customers who provide 80% of your profit" (Cram 2001, 20).

The key to believing it was worth the effort lay in recognizing a repeat customer's lifetime worth. The utility was clearly evident to airlines, whose frequent flyer programs were emblematic of the new approach. Similarly, upscale store and hotel chains saw the utility of keeping updates about their customers and contacting them on regular bases. As the 1990s progressed, manufacturers of inexpensive "package goods"—diapers, cereals, soups, inexpensive cosmetics, over-the-counter pharmaceuticals—also moved toward tracking and wooing individuals one on one. The basic assumption of their activities is, as one *Direct* magazine writer (Levey 2003, 5) put it, "that companies must discriminate among customers."

The process relies on the capabilities of contemporary databases and interactivity. Bloomingdales department store, for example, uses a CRM system to feed data about the store's fifteen thousand "most valuable" patrons straight to the call center or the sales floor. The system provides monthly transaction records on customers in a consolidated marketing database that includes their transactions and promotion history as well as some basic household information. Live links, which go directly to point-of-sale terminals, allow associates to provide access to individual customer photos, with the ability to custom-build merchandise suggestions. Aggregate spending information in each customer's file allows the salesperson to offer customized services. Tailored messages can also be sent by the system to the salesperson as well as to the customer. According to *Direct* magazine (Levey 2004, 1), "When the store hosts one of its 'Girls' Night Out' specials, a sales rep can be alerted that a given customer is particularly desired at the event, and can be fed information about it. That information is printed on the customer's receipt, too."

Marketers' developing desire and ability to discriminate among individual customers based on their contributions to the bottom line has become a badge of honor, a mark of moving with cutting-edge potential of the digital age. When it comes to using media to do that, a clear road map does not exist. Companies are well aware that with the exception of certain personal health information, certain types of personal financial information held by certain types of firms, and personally identifiable information from children younger than thirteen years, marketers have virtually free rein to use individuals' data in the United States for business purposes without their consent. The rise of public outcries over privacy, however, has led many marketers to make at least a nod of getting people's permission for using their information.

A well-known exponent of this point of view, Alan Westin, uses his Privacy and American Business research consultancy to promulgate the idea that most Americans will give it up for a perceived benefit. Westin (2003, 445-46) noted his survey research finding that 58 percent of Americans are "privacy pragmatists" when it comes to information. When asked, he says they "examined the benefits to them or society of the data collection or use, wanted to know the privacy risks and how organizations proposed to control those, and then decided whether to trust the organization or seek legal oversight."

The idea that consumers would make a cost-benefit calculation in giving up useful information about themselves fits the needs of advertisers and media perfectly. Using CRM as a paradigm, advertisers are experimenting with activities that aim to insert themselves unfiltered into their desired customers' domestic lives in ways that encourage surveillance and tailored relationships. Converging on a variety of seemingly unrelated activities, marketers and media practitioners are adapting a business that has historically been looked down upon in traditional media—direct marketing—and reconfigure it to fit the new information-oriented CRM model. The resulting labels that emerge—customized media, walled gardens, and interactive television—are increasingly central to marketers' discussions of the evolving ad world. Though still in their infancy, they represent the strategic future to marketers and are already changing the structure of media culture.

From direct marketing to customized media

For decades direct marketing had a reputation as the less classy, too-obvious part of advertising. A common example of direct marketing was an ad in a magazine that encouraged a reader to write for a free catalog. Another was a set of coupons mailed to the home. In both cases, sales could be tracked by the company giving the discounts. As late as the mid-1970s, though, the elite of the ad world looked down on "direct" work. They associated it with the selling of shoddy or quirky mail-order products—breast enlargers and Ginsu knives—by preying bluntly on the audience's anxieties about being left out socially and desire to be exclusive.

Despite these marked philosophical differences, by 1982 fifteen of the top twenty advertising agencies had bought or started a direct-marketing capability (*Advertising Age* 1983). It was primarily their clients' growing interest in computer-guided targeting of niche markets that brought them to look at direct practitioners with grudging respect. Large direct-marketing firms had been keeping lists of people on computers since the 1960s. Beginning in the late 1970s, their new techniques for dividing and tracking consumers according to an enormous number of demographic, psychographic, and geographic categories led target-minded executives to look at the business anew. At the same time, developments such as the

800 number (for quick responses to TV and catalog offers), ink-jet printing techniques (that allowed mailers to personalize messages to individuals), and the personal computer (which allowed easy data storage and access of sales results) generated a conviction among direct-marketing practitioners that the advertising world was moving their way.

A Dun and Bradstreet executive (in Pagnetti 1983) saw the changes as paralleling the multiplication of U.S. media channels and the distribution of audiences across more outlets than ever. The traditional hallmarks of direct marketing—precise audience identification, individualized media communication, and speedy full-satisfaction order fulfillment—meshed constructively, he said, with the new technologies. Futurist John Naisbitt (in Pagnetti 1983) was even more blunt. "Direct marketers are at the forefront of where everybody is going to be," he predicted in 1983. "We can all learn from them."

The idea that consumers would make a cost-benefit calculation in giving up useful information about themselves fits the needs of advertisers and media perfectly.

As CRM became popular in the off-media world, direct-marketing practitioners began to argue that digital, interactive versions of their craft would allow their clients to reach the customers who count with messages tailored specifically to them. The practice, they knew, implicitly added a crucial assumption about U.S. consumers that went beyond the accepted notion that they are highly differentiated, frenetic, suspicious, self-indulgent, and impatient with any idea that commercials must be part of the media deal. Critical to direct marketing's success in the interactive digital environment is the notion of a new implicit contract between marketers and media firms, on one side, and consumers, on the other: consumers will agree to give up important demographic, psychographic, and lifestyle information about themselves when marketers and media reward them or treat them as special through material that appears tailored for them.

Customized media are those that apply the concepts of one-to-one marketing to help themselves and their advertisers gain the fidelity of desirable audience members. Such media vehicles are still quite expensive using traditional media. Using magazines owned by Time, Inc., for example, it is quite possible to specify that ads should go to certain individual subscribers and not to others, depending on the advertiser's needs and the information about the readers in a *Time* magazine database. Moreover, using ink-jet printing technology, the advertiser can alter on-page copy to reflect the information in the database. The operative phrase, though, is "at a premium price." Even by 2003, producing truly separate versions for different audience segments, let alone individuals, increased costs dramatically. The return-on-investment typically makes the activity unrealistic.

Nevertheless, both print and electronic media firms are increasingly looking for ways to implement customization. Increasingly, they are turning to the Web for customizing relationships with those individuals and those individuals' relationships with advertisers. CNN.com (2004), for example, exhorts users to "personalize your CNN.com page experience today and receive breaking news in your e-mail inbox and on your cell phone, get your hometown weather on the home page and set your news edition to your world region." Such customization allows the site to cultivate a relationship with its audience and to develop data about audience members' interests and movements that it can use for targeting ads.

Using a somewhat different approach toward the same ends, *The New York Times* tries to cultivate loyalty by encouraging users to sign up for a "news tracker" service, which sends them e-mail when articles are published on particular topics. Armed with registration, user-interest data, and information about readers that the *Times* purchases from database firms, the company touts technologies to force ads in front of desired consumers through the ability of "surround sessions": the ability to "own a consumer visit to nytimes.com" by having targeted visitors receive ads almost exclusively from one advertiser during individual sessions on the site (Taylor 2003).

From customized media to walled gardens

The monetary advantage of the personalization approaches used by nytimes.com and CNN.com is that it relies on the user's expressed interest and the depth of content rather than tailored content on the site to generate user interest. That gets around the expenses that it costs to create specifically tailored content. It is an open question, however, whether the costs of even that level of en masse customization can be met by advertising alone. To generate another revenue stream to cover such activities, many online practitioners have begun to engage in a "walled garden" approach to the digital world. A walled garden is an online environment where consumers go for information, communications, and commerce services and that discourages them from leaving for the larger digital world.

The concept initially referred in the late 1990s to a safe place for children on the Web; parents would set their computers so that the kids could visit only those areas. Quickly, however, the concept morphed to mean an area where content providers could induce targeted consumers to enter—sometimes even have them pay for entry—and then track their activities while surrounding them with ads appropriate to their demographic characteristics and actions.

The utility of a walled garden is that the firm running it can charge for it in addition to making money by using information about members to lure advertisers. The marketing trade press has often predicted that this activity would be rejected by consumers because of its association with limited access. In 2003, though, cable systems, phone companies, and America Online began to reframe the concept of walled gardens. In the words of one analyst (Vittore 2003, 9), instead of restricting users from viewing content outside the confines of specific—or preferred—content providers, the new edition of walled gardens "gives users incentives to stay, such as faster access to high-end applications and premium content that others outside the wall can't see."

As a result, cable system owners, major phone companies, Time Warner's AOL, and independents such as Yahoo and Google are rushing into this domain. These players are trying to shape a digital world where walled garden services work faster and better for people than the larger Internet. Moreover, the firms are trying to lure people by proclaiming that these special places protect subscribers and their families from such nuisances as spam, viruses, and pop-up ads more effectively and safely than elsewhere. "The mass market likes a safe, comfortable, supported environment," added a Replay-TV executive (in Moch 2000, 1). "They don't really want the choice and control. They want to be taken care of." An Alcatel phone company executive (in Vittore 2003, 9) agreed. Going online, he said, is "kind of like going to a flea market. There's some good stuff laying on the table, but it's generally not a good shopping experience. We think this is a better way to organize the marketplace and monetize the network."

This transformation of the Internet into a privatized and monetized custom domain is beginning to take place. For example, in 2003 BellSouth started offering a $4.95 per month add-on package of content from ABC for its FastAccess DSL subscribers. Among the choices were 700-kilobit encoded videos of movie trailers, extreme sports, game trailers, music videos, celebrity interviews, short films, and fashion videos. Also, during the Iraq War the company provided a satellite feed from ABC Live. Only the sites that were party to revenue deals with BellSouth could be reached at these speeds. The purpose of these attractive spaces was to bring elite customers to an area where BellSouth could present both general advertisements and customized appeals to them.

From walled gardens to interactive television

The logic of walled gardens has also carried over to discussions of the least advanced area of electronic media: interactive television. In industry discussions, the term is quite elastic, ranging from already available PVR and video-on-demand devices such as TiVo to over-the-horizon technologies that encourage even more radical changes in the way people use TV. When it comes to the latter, advertiser and media executives have expressed consensus about the direction of major changes, if not the time it will take to see them implemented. They are pretty well unanimous that the future of television in the twenty-first century lies in presenting viewers with menus of programs that they can watch at times of their choosing— often for a small fee. Not only will the twentieth-century notion of linear network programming be challenged, but viewers will be guided into their own program choices and flows by "intelligent navigators" that learn what they like and search for programs that fit those characteristics. Moreover, say the futurists, viewers who would like to interact with programs could do that, to change the plot, perhaps, or to find out about—and even purchase—the clothes or objects that the characters use on the programs.

Some of these capabilities are already here. Wink is a firm with a device that allows viewers to interact with, and order from, programming (Elkin 2003, 6). Another firm is involved in differentially placing commercials into New York City cable homes based on collected information about the households (Friedman 2001, S2). Still another firm has mastered the capability of digitally placing brands into programs themselves (Mandese 2004). Doing that in real time based upon individual or household lifestyle or demographic information is technically possible but is still expensive and unlikely because so few households subscribe to digital TV. The basic infrastructure for garnering the required information for this sort of data-driven product placement is developing rapidly, however. TiVo already minutely tracks and categorizes the viewing habits of its users as part of its service contract. The company sells the data in aggregate to potential advertisers. For its own purposes, it analyzes the habits of individual subscribing households. It then recommends, and even records, programs for the households based on preferences inferred from the computer data as well as deals with advertisers who want TiVo viewers to watch those shows and commercials.

Discourse about interactive television's future suggests a movement from tracking and customizing for the household to doing that for the individual. In these discussions, the language used to picture future TV merges with the language of walled gardens, customized media, and loyalty programs. "Television in the interactive world is going to have a world of walled gardens," noted one marketing executive (in Moch 2000, 1). He argued that multiple cable systems operators and satellite providers will be able to create the high-quality, complete media environments. "They'll give [consumers] so much information in this walled garden that [they] don't desire to leave."

Getting them to not want to leave will be particularly useful to media and marketers when the viewers provide enormous amounts of data about what they do in the electronic environment, when, and where. Here is where the strategic logic of CRM loyalty programs kicks in. The goal of media firms in this interactive environment will be not only to instill loyalty to their own brands; it will be to cultivate relationships with their advertisers who will, despite the subscription nature of walled gardens, pay a substantial part of the programming freight. Product placement through sponsorship and embedding will be one step in the process. Another step, already being tried by content sites such as Salon.com on the Web, is to give desirable viewers discounts to content if they view commercials. Still another is to simply give them advertiser-sponsored discounts to premium content so as to emphasize goodwill and encourage the transfer of consumer data.

Concluding Remarks

It is in this convergence of strategic logic that some may feel the social rub lies regarding this approach to the production of culture. The combined language of direct marketing and CRM suffuses discussions of trusted media, walled gardens, and interactive television. The digital world marketers and media firms are building consequently has as its core in the belief that success will come from seducing customers to release their personal data in the interest of rewarding relationships with media and marketers. Marketers will claim to reward consumers' distinctiveness. Purposefully and not, they may well also encourage feelings of anxiousness and anger.

The circumstances are not hard to imagine. They are, in fact, common topics in consultancy reports, trade articles, and conference discussions. Using detailed audience surveillance, digital marketers would like to be able to track the media activities of their target audience in quite a lot of detail. To ensure that customers they value view targeted, perhaps even customized, commercials on the Web or on TV, marketers may offer those audience members discounts to programming, even "sponsor" certain media materials, or even embed certain products and characters into programs they view. Such seemingly benign relationships can quickly lead to feelings of discrimination, anger, and suspicion if viewers believe that they are not getting the discounts, or the opportunities to attend to material, that others receive.

CRM specialists, however, have learned how to manage such anger. One way is to make the customer see tension-inducing rules as almost an interpersonal issue between company and customer. "Failure" to get benefits or offers within the scheme would then be a private issue resulting from the rules of collaboration rather than one needing public remedy. In the best of cases, customers try to show by their purchases that they deserve to be treated at a higher level of service. Some customers exit the "relationship," which because of low volume may suit the company fine. The approach could still blow up into public trouble, as when Victoria's Secret was accused of charging more in its West Coast than East Coast catalogs. Still, loyalty programmers believe that properly configured programs based on one-to-one interactions can keep legal discrimination in the interest of marketing a private matter. Moreover, they believe that inducing anxiety that causes unwanted customers to feel they do not belong to a consumption group is good business. Efficient marketing increasingly means "managing" the customer roster—"rewarding some, getting rid of others, improving the value of each of them (Peppers and Rogers 1993)."

There are those who do not believe that this approach to audiences should be the basis for the production of culture in U.S. society's mainstream media. At this point, however, media advocacy groups are opposing contemporary developments in new media around issues of privacy invasion and hypercommercialization (Turow forthcoming). As this article has shown, however, the emerging strategic logic of mainstream marketing and media organizations is to present their activities not as privacy invasion but as two-way customer relationships, not as commercial intrusion but as pinpoint selling help for frenetic consumers in a troubling world. Clearly, as developments progress, the contours of the emerging media environment will change. It seems clear, however, that much mainstream production of culture will have audience surveillance intimately woven into it.

References

Advertising Age. 1982. *Direct marketing. July 19*.
————. 2003. National advertisers report. June 24.
Aldrich, H. 1979. *Organizations and environments*. Englewood Cliffs, NJ: Prentice Hall.
Benson, J. 1988. Trouble corralling the grazers. *Advertising Age*, November 28.
CNN.com. 2004. CNN.com preferences. http://www.cnn.com/services/preferences/.
Crain, R. 1984. Reagan to keep ship on the same course. *Advertising Age*, November 15, p. 30.
Cram, T. 2001. Marketing society—How to care for customers who count the most. *Marketing*, July 12.
Cross, G. 2000. *An all-consuming society*. New York: Columbia University Press.
Elkin, T. 2003. New technology: Mediaedge "living room" simulates consumer experience for clients. *Advertising Age*, June 16.
Emerson, R. 1962. Power-dependent relations. *American Sociological Review* 27:31-40.
Friedman, W. 2001. Eagle-eye marketers find right spot, right time; product placements increase as part of syndication deals. *Advertising Age*, June 22.
————. 2003. Panel discussions: Marketing in a TiVo world. *Advertising Age*, February 10.
Gamson, J. 1997. *Freaks talk back*. Chicago: University of Chicago Press.
Klapper, J. 1960. *The effects of mass communication*. Glencoe, IL: Free Press.
Levey, R. 2003. The trouble with points programs. *Direct*, April 1.
————. 2004. Bloomingdale's goes for the best. *Direct*, January 1.
Liebes, T., and E. Katz. 1990. *The export of meaning: Cross-cultural readings of Dallas*. New York: Oxford University Press.
Mandese, J. 2004. VOD feature promises to make ad-skipping DOA. *MediaPost's MediDaily News*, March 30. http://www.mediapost.com/.
Maneloveg, H. 1980. Marketing—and all society—affected by media changes. *Advertising Age*, November 13.
Moch, C. 2000. Great wall of content: Controlled climates may be creeping into interactive TV. *Telephony*, May 29.
Morley, D. 1980. *The nationwide audience: Structure and decoding*. London: British Film Institute.
Neff, J., and Lisa Sanders. 2004 It's broken; P&G's Stengel takes industry to task for clinging to outdated media model, *Advertising Age*, February 16.
Pagnetti, A.1983. Sales sprout from the seeds of segmentation. *Advertising Age*, January 17.
Peppers, D., and Martha Rogers. 1993. *The one to one future*. New York: Doubleday.
Pettigrew, A., 1984. Examining change in the long-term context of culture and politics. In *Organizational strategy and change*, ed. J. M. Pennings. San Francisco: Jossey Bass.
Pope, D. 1983. *Making of modern advertising*. New York: Basic Books.
Strasser, Susan. 1995. *Satisfaction guaranteed*. Washington, DC: Smithsonian Institution Press.
Taylor, C. 2003. Interactive quarterly: Independent agency; Avenue A; Proving that expertise pays, this media agency; retained clients and increased revenues. *AdWeek*, February 3, via Nexis.
Tebbel, John. 1974. *The media in America*. New York: Crowell.
Turow, J. 1979. *Getting books to children: An exploration of publisher-market relations*. Chicago: American Library Association.
————. 1997. *Breaking up America: Advertisers and the new media world*. Chicago: University of Chicago Press.

———. Forthcoming. Cracking the consumer code. In *The new politics of surveillance and visibility*, ed. K. Haggerty and R. Ericson. Toronto, Canada: University of Toronto Press.

Vittore, V. 2003. A broadband hierarchy of content kings. *Telephony*, May 12.

Westin, A. 2003. Social and political dimensions of privacy. *Journal of Social Issues* 59 (2): 431-53.

Whitney, D. C., and J. Ettema. 1994. *Audiencemaking*. Thousand Oaks, CA: Sage.

Remote Control: The Rise of Electronic Cultural Policy

By
SIVA VAIDHYANATHAN

Since the early 1990s, the United States has been formulating, executing, and imposing a form of "electronic cultural policy." This phrase means two things: a state-generated set of policies to encourage or mandate design standards for electronic devices and dictate a particular set of cultural choices; and the cultural choices themselves, which have been embedded in the design and software of electronic goods. The goal of electronic cultural policy has been to encourage and enable "remote control," shifting decisions over the use of content from the user to the vendor. The intended macro effects of such micro policies are antidemocratic. Their potential has created the possibility of a whole new set of forms of cultural domination by a handful of powerful global institutions. Yet so far, the actual consequences of these policies have been different from those intended, igniting activism and disobedience on a global scale.

Keywords: copyright; encryption; trade; cultural imperialism

The relationship between digital technology and creative imagination is becoming more complex and less predictable every day. While once it seemed obvious and easy to declare the rise of a "network society" in which individuals would realign themselves, empower themselves, and undermine traditional methods of social and cultural control, it seems clear that networked digital communication need not serve such liberating ends (Castells 2000). In fact, the struggles between extreme forces—information anarchy and information oligarchy—have rendered any simple formulation of the new creative age almost immediately archaic (Vaidhyanathan 2004).

Siva Vaidhyanathan is an assistant professor of culture and communication at New York University. He is the author of Copyrights and Copywrongs: The Rise of Intellectual Property and How It Threatens Creativity *(New York University Press, 2001) and* The Anarchist in the Library *(Basic Books, 2004). He received a Ph.D. in American studies from the University of Texas at Austin and has taught at Wesleyan University, the University of Wisconsin–Madison, and New York University.*

DOI: 10.1177/0002716204270663

A fierce global battle is raging over the terms of access, use, reuse, combination, recombination, execution, and distribution of cultural materials. It is not necessarily aligned along a North-South axis; it is more often a struggle between individuals and communities that are reaching out and puncturing the fragile, permeable membranes of state-set cultural limits. At stake is Antonio Gramsci's notion that "all men are intellectuals" in that they may work to "sustain a conception of the world or modify it; that is, to bring into being new modes of thought" (Gramsci and Forgacs 2000). While inexpensive digital technology has exponentially expanded the power of individuals to master their own media spaces and manipulate texts and images in ways that seem to signal an age of "semiotic democracy" (Coombe 1992), powerful forces have acted to reengineer—one might say "reimagineer"— from above these otherwise liberating and empowering systems.

The nexus of such reimagineering is electronic cultural policy. It is a particular flavor of cultural policy that guides the architecture of interfaces, networks, standards, protocols, and formats that house and deliver cultural products. Cultural policy is itself an understudied factor in global cultural change (and stasis). Only recently have scholars such as Toby Miller, George Yúdice, Stanley Katz, Gigi Bradford, and Lawrence Rothfield taken seriously the systematic interactions between states and cultural practices, between the bureaucratic and the creative. Although it is common in the United States to assume that culture is in general subject to minimal state influence (with the obvious counterexamples of lightly funded yet oddly controversial national endowments), much of the mechanics and economics of culture are subject to heavy levels of governance from the state. Trade policies, defense policies, and educational policies all have cultural elements to them and depend on complementary cultural policies to generate consensuses and mobilize support. As Toby Miller and George Yúdice (2002) wrote, "National cultural policies are, then, a privileged terrain of hegemony."

The Goblin Edit

Increasingly, digital creators are puncturing this hegemony. They are employing tools that allow them to evade some of the most powerful instruments of cultural policy. They are undermining many of the explicit goals of nationalism and capitalism. And they have tripped political alarms in ways that make powerful interests demand more expansive means of enforcement. One example of such practice is the work of the Goblin.

The Goblin is the pseudonym of an amateur Russian digital video editor named Dmitri Puchkov. Not satisfied with merely watching illegal copies of Hollywood films, he has differentiated some products within the rather crowded Russian video market. The Goblin redubs non-Russian films into colloquial Russian, trumping the rather unsatisfying subtitle translations available on the market (Walsh 2003). The Goblin's greatest hits are redubs of the first two of the *Lord of the Rings* trilogy. By rewriting the script and recording the soundtrack, he turned Frodo Baggins into Frodo Sumkin and the rest of the "good" characters into caricatures of incompetent Russian officials. The evil Orcs became Russian gangsters. Gandalf the Wizard constantly quotes Karl Marx. The Goblin is doing what Gramsci celebrated. He is "bringing into being new modes of thought." He is remastering the cultural signs that are given him and refashioning them to fit his daily concerns and specific political environment.

By any reasonable measure, recent changes that expanded the powers and lengthened the terms of copyrights in the United States have been complete failures.

Puchkov originally made these new versions for his friends, but they made copies and spread them widely. Pirate video merchants all over Russia are distributing Goblin edits, which are in high demand, for about $10. By throwing out the old soundtrack and revising the characters completely, the Goblin has produced a new work, one that does not directly compete with the original in the marketplace. No one who wants to watch the original "good" Frodo Baggins would want the Goblin version in its stead. But the real value of the Goblin edit is that it uses a familiar English text and Hollywood production (and New Zealand settings) to comment on Russian politics and society. This is multilayered cultural criticism and revision that cleverly surpasses the influence of the original in its relevance to current events. It should make some feel queasy and others giggle. It should make everyone pause and think. It makes Hollywood nervous and angry (Vaidhyanathan 2004).

What are the implications to the cultural, political, and economic status of Hollywood if all films are to be considered permanent "works in progress"? Should creativity be reserved for professionals and experts? Or will teenagers in their basements and libraries be able to soup up or strip down the signs, symbols, and texts that make up such an important part of their lives? Should the major companies in the global motion picture industry, bolstered by the political power of the United States government, be able to dictate the form and format of distribution around the globe? What are the implications for local cultural forms if powerful media companies use law and technology to ossify their advantages? In lawsuits, congressional hearings, and international negotiations, Hollywood studios claim they need maximum and near-permanent control over their products to justify the massive investments they make in production, marketing, and distribution. The commercial film industry and the governments that do its bidding are willing to go to extreme measures to preserve their global cultural and commercial standing. What does a consideration of practices such as the Goblin Edit and the predictable policy backlash from Hollywood reveal about the notion of "cultural imperialism"?

Not Exactly "Cultural Imperialism"

"Cultural imperialism" has become a cliché. The academic "cultural imperialism thesis" is in severe need of revision. Once dominant among leftist critics in the 1970s and 1980s (Schiller 1976), it has been supplanted and modified by the rise of cultural studies (Tomlinson 1991). Yet it still resonates in North-South public discourse and some anxious corners of academia (Feld 2001). While those who complain about cultural imperialism cite the ubiquity of KFC in Cairo and the McDonalds in Manila, anxious cultural protectionists in the United States quiver at the sound of Spanish spoken in public or mosques opening in Ohio. Some American nationalists argue that cultural imperialism would be good for the world, as we Americans have so much figured out (Rothkopf 1997). Others dodge its complications by celebrating "Creolization" at all costs, while ignoring real and serious imbalances in the political economy of culture (Cowen 2002). While the evidence for cultural imperialism is only powerful when selectively examined, the evidence for infrastructural imperialism is much stronger. There are imbalances of power in global flows of culture, but they are not what traditional cultural imperialism theorists claim.

Instead, it seems that if there is a dominant form of cultural imperialism, it concerns the pipelines, not the products—the formats of distribution and the terms of access and use. It is not exactly "content neutral," but it is less necessarily "content specific" than cultural imperialism theorists assume. The texts, signs, and messages that flow through global communications networks do not carry a clear and unambiguous celebrations of ideas and ideologies we might lazily label "Western"—consumerism, individualism, and secularism. These commercial pipelines may carry texts that overtly hope to threaten the tenets of global capitalism, like albums by the leftist rock band Rage against the Machine, films by Michael Moore, or books by Naomi Klein. Time Warner does not care if the data inscribed on the compact discs it sells simulate the voice of Madonna or Ali Farka Toure. What flows from North to South does not matter as much as how it flows, how much revenue the flows generate, and who may reuse the elements of such flows.

Domestic Electronic Cultural Policy

The battle over formats and terms of delivery and distribution date back to the struggles to regulate early radio in the United States. From the beginning of "mass" electronic media in the United States, it became clear that major industry players were wise to capture regulatory initiatives to limit competition. By moving technical standards into the realm of licensing, fewer voices could influence public deliberation and distract consumers from the loudest calls for their attention (McChesney 1993).

This model of industry-state synergy extended through the twentieth century to broadcast television, cable television, and telecommunication. In stark contrast, the Internet developed as a content-delivery network with minimal state oversight and no dominant firms dictating standards or restricting entry into the content markets. (Microsoft's late, triumphant entry into the browser market and Google.com's dominance of the search engine are the major exceptions to the early hypercompetitive nature of the Internet, yet neither achieved dominance with the aid of the state; Lessig 1999.)

As the Goblin has demonstrated, the combination of a relatively open, relatively inexpensive medium such as a global, expanding, packet-switching digital network and powerful, adaptable, customizable, portable personal computers has generated some remarkable opportunities for democratic creativity. Panic over such radical democracy has also pushed established content producers to try to rein in the democratic nature of both the personal computer and the Internet (McChesney 1993; Vaidhyanathan 2004).

In one sense, such widespread democratic cultural production (peer-to-peer production, one might say) seems less than revolutionary. It merely echoes how cultural texts have flowed through and been revised by discursive communities everywhere for centuries. Texts often undergo a process similar to a game of "telephone," through which a text is substantially—sometimes almost unintentionally—distorted through many small revisions. In some cases like the Goblin Edit, however, something more is going on. This is an example of a direct ideological challenge to an oppressive and corrupt political system. A disempowered member of that system is using democratizing technology (digital editing software, a personal computer, an optical storage drive, the Internet, etc.) to revise a dominant, global, and powerful commercial product for local needs. This is occurring within a context of increased partnership and cooperation between the Russian and American governments in matters of cultural and technological policy (i.e., global intellectual property treaties and the instruments designed to enforce them). Such radical textual revisions have occurred in other contexts and have helped build political critiques, if not movements. For instance, historian Lawrence Levine (1988) has documented how working-class players and audiences in nineteenth-century America adapted and revised the works of William Shakespeare to their local contexts, concerns, and ideologies. And historian Eric Lott (1993) has shown how *Uncle Tom's Cabin* was reworked by working-class white communities to aid the cause of racial dominance instead of the Christian liberationist message the book was intended to serve. Whether serving progressive ends or regressive, racist ones, cultural democracy (and thus the technologies on which it depends for revision and distribution) can have profound political effects in the real world. Elements and themes from such recaptured and reworked texts may serve as raw material in the development of ideologies or agendas. And they may stir hearts and minds toward actions.

Sites of Electronic Cultural Policy

By the end of the twentieth century, major cultural industries in the United States decided that copyright was obsolete and insufficient to protect their interests and expand their markets. Copyright, as it had emerged in much of the world, granted strong public interest safeguards such as "fair use" or "fair dealing," nonprotection of facts and ideas, and eventual expiration and entry into the public domain (Vaidhyanathan 2001). Frustrated with the longevity and strength of these democratic safeguards, the leaders of copyright-producing industries started a steady movement to shift the site of regulation from civil courts to machines themselves. Understanding that multilateral policy-making bodies had the power to impose policies on sovereign states without deliberation or compromise within them, industry leaders and representatives from the U.S. Patent and Trademark Office and Department of Commerce employed forums like the World Intellectual Property Organization (WIPO) and the World Trade Organization (WTO) and regional organs such as the European Union (EU) and the Free Trade Area of the Americas (FTAA) to gain leverage and avoid public interest nongovernmental organizations (Sell 2003). They sought to standardize intellectual property across the globe as more nations joined the ranks of the industrialized and consumptive. American and European companies seeking new markets did not want to see their products copied in countries with weak or no intellectual property protections. So the developed world pushed for the establishment of WIPO and the Trade Related Aspects of Intellectual Property Rights (TRIPS) accord. WIPO members generate treaties and agreements about global intellectual property standards. Signatories of the TRIPS accord may, through the WTO enforcement mechanisms, seek retribution for a violation of intellectual property standards or enforcement by another.

In the 1980s, the United States tried to use WIPO, under the auspices of the United Nations, to negotiate the first round of global electronic cultural policy treaties. After encountering resistance, and realizing that such a forum allows developing nations the ability to form blocs and act in concert to protect their interests, the United States moved its intellectual property efforts into the mainstream trade negotiations through the General Agreement on Tariffs and Trade (GATT). As GATT morphed into a permanent resolution body, the WTO, in the 1990s, the United States used it to force nations that sought favorable trade in other areas to sign the Agreement on Trade Related Aspects of Intellectual Property (TRIPs), a set of global minimal standards for copyright, patent, trade secret, trademark, semiconductor, and geographic marker regulations (Sell 2003).

But by 2001, the United States found that its leverage at the WTO was weakening, most significantly because of failures to standardize intellectual property regimes. In this case, however, it was the patent system instead of the copyright system that stifled the global reach of American policy. Many developing nations—some overwhelmed by the spread of HIV and AIDS—stood their ground on measures to allow production of generic versions of expensive HIV-retarding drugs.

The Doha Round of the WTO negotiations made it clear that the United States and Western Europe could not globally dictate the terms of intellectual property. The efforts of these developing nations were bolstered by a large, vocal, and growing human rights campaign that focused on how the U.S. patent system rendered essential drugs unaffordable to millions of needy people throughout the world (Mayne 2002).

What are the implications to the cultural, political, and economic status of Hollywood if all films are to be considered permanent "works in progress"? Should creativity be reserved for professionals and experts?

Such globalization and standardization efforts have generated much consternation among developing nations. But most of the opposition has laid within areas of regulation that have much clearer life-or-death ramifications, such as agriculture, pharmaceuticals, and the exploitation of natural resources and rare biological material. Farmers do not always appreciate being told they must respect limits on the use and replantation of patented seeds and plants, and gestational publishing and media companies must play by rules written by their more powerful and established global competitors. Yet Northern concerns that developing nations serve as havens for software and video pirates (and huge potential markets for cultural goods and pharmaceuticals) has kept the pressure on their governments to adopt and enforce laws that resemble those of the United States and Western Europe.

As a result of the 1997 WIPO Treaty, many countries, including the United States, have passed laws forbidding the distribution of any technologies—even simple mathematical algorithms—that might evade or crack access or copy-control mechanisms that surround digital materials. Such digital rights management technologies protect not only copyrighted material but also material that is already in the public domain and facts and data that are not covered by copyright law. Digital "lockdown" grants far greater control over works than traditional copyright law ever did. Through such laws as the U.S. Digital Millennium Copyright Act (DMCA), information regulation is leaving the realm of human judgment and entering a technocratic regime instead.

By any reasonable measure, recent changes that expanded the powers and lengthened the terms of copyrights in the United States have been complete failures. The changes have done nothing to stem real piracy and nothing to prevent widespread file sharing. Yet they have burdened scientists, librarians, scholars, students, and engineers. They have chilled some political speech, art, and Web linking. These radical changes have been hard on the legitimate users of copyrighted materials and irrelevant for those who flaunt laws and technological controls. Librarians worry while pirates flourish. Where once users could assume wide latitude in their private, noncommercial uses, now a layer of code stands in the way of access to the work itself, preventing a variety of harmless uses. Because access controls allow content providers to regulate use, they can set all the terms of use. The de facto duration of protection under legally protected technological restrictions is infinite. While U.S. copyright law in 2001 protects any work created today for life of the author plus seventy years, ninety-five years in the case of corporate "works for hire," electronic gates do not expire. This allows producers to "recapture" works in the public domain. This also violates the constitutional mandate that Congress pass copyright laws that protect "for limited times." The DMCA and other such global legal regimes work over and above real copyright law (Lessig 2004).

Most dangerously, the DMCA ensures that producers may exercise editorial control over the uses of their materials. They can extract contractual promises that the use will not parody or criticize the work in exchange for access—many Web sites already do this. Just as dangerously, the DMCA could enable producers to contractually and electronically bind users from reusing facts or ideas contained in the work. Despite the ineffectiveness and counterproductivity of the law and the technology it supports, the copyright industries insist on defending the DMCA as if their futures depend on it. Despite its failures to protect music and video, some have found a use for the DMCA. It is more important than ever in garages, offices, and living rooms as a method to restrict competition. Increasingly, hardware industries (industries outside what are generally considered "software" or copyright industries like film, music, text, and computer code) are using the DMCA to lock in monopoly control over secondary goods. These are goods that have nothing to do with copyright, nothing to do with creativity, knowledge, or art. Because it is possible to put a computer chip into almost anything, companies do. If a company puts software on a chip that sits on a removable part of a machine, and puts some other software on a complementary chip in the larger device, the DMCA prevents another company from developing a replacement for that part (Vaidhyanathan 2004).

Regulating Global Broadcasting

The most ambitious attempt at imposing electronic cultural policy on the rest of the world involves a draft treaty considered through 2003 and 2004 by WIPO. It is officially called the Consolidated Text for a Treaty on the Protection of Broadcasting Organizations and colloquially the Global Broadcast flag provisions. This draft treaty would bind all its signatory states to create a sui generis property right over broadcasted video content. Broadcasters (not copyright holders) would control the distribution rights to the material. Consumers would have no established rights to copy for home use, later viewing, or adaptation and alteration to cope with sensory disabilities. Even the broadcasting of public domain works would "recapture" them so that the broadcasters would have control not unlike maximum copyright protection. As with the DMCA, anyone who circumvents copy control or distribution control technologies would face severe penalties. Such provisions, if globally adopted, could shut down independent video-recording firms like TiVo and ReplayTV and replace them with recorders owned by, controlled by, and monitored by broadcasters such as News Corporation (WIPO 2004).

[The Global Broadcast flag] provisions, if globally adopted, could shut down independent video-recording firms like TiVo and ReplayTV and replace them with recorders owned by, controlled by, and monitored by broadcasters such as News Corporation.

The American broadcast flag story is less alarming (if only because consumer advocates and the electronic industry tempered it) but just as important. The big movie studios, through their lobbying organization the Motion Picture Association of America (MPAA), claim they need to rein in the rampant sharing of digital files over peer-to-peer networks, even though such sharing will continue as long as there are hackable DVDs on the market. To gain a remarkable amount of control over personal mediascapes, the major studios and broadcast networks have come up with proposed technological standards that would guide the use of the digital signals in broadcast television. These FCC-mandated standards would require electronics manufacturers to build into their televisions devices that would regulate the access to and copying of encrypted material. They would determine which devices could and could not play material that contains a small bit of code called a "broadcast flag." The presence of the flag would tell a digital device (computer, home digital recorder, television, etc.) whether the content is authorized to be played. One may still record *The Sopranos* for later home viewing using an old analog machine such as a VHS recorder. But VHS is a dying medium. Electronics stores are considering dropping VHS players from shelves in favor of digital video recorders like TiVo and nonrecording devices like DVD players. Video stores are expanding their DVD offerings and shrinking VHS space. So as they break, VHS machines will find their way to landfills and museums. And with them, substantial consumer autonomy will go as well. The U.S. broadcast flag has two major problems. The first has to do with consumer rights. The second—and perhaps the more important issue in the long run—concerns creativity and innovation. One of the basic tenets of U.S. media law in the past two decades has been that users have a certain amount of autonomy to make choices about how, when, and in what form they will use lawfully acquired content within their homes. Private, noncommercial, noneducational uses are generally considered noninfringing. Among users, the concept of fair use has grown into a penumbra of rights that copyright users confidently enjoy without fear of being sued. Either the law does not explicitly forbid such uses (such as making mixed tapes or CDs), or it explicitly allows them (such as time-shifting television programs) (Vaidhyanathan 2001).

U.S. leaders are considering even more extreme electronic cultural policy measures. One bill introduced to Congress in 2003 would allow copyright holders to hack in and disrupt a computer's ability to communicate with others if they suspected it might be distributing their material—all without due process. Another bill would require all machines that work with digital code—from microwaves to MP3 players to mechanical pets—to include copy-control technology that would restrict their customizability. As each effort to install new controls into digital infrastructure fails, industry leaders clamor for more intrusive and restrictive measures. Each of these proposals pushes the global information ecosystem toward a condition of disequilibrium, igniting unpredictability where all yearn for stability and proprietary restrictions where many yearn for openness. Understandably, there is a creative and political backlash.

Cultural Anti-Imperialism

In early 2004, word quickly spread among Internet-connected music fans that a mysterious producer known only as DJ Danger Mouse had, in a flash of recombinant brilliance (or Creole creativity) mixed the lyrical tracks from Jay-Z's recent *Black Album* with the harmonic bed of the Beatles's 1968 album, *The Beatles*, known widely as the "White Album." Danger Mouse, whose real name is Brian Burton, made a particularly bold and witty move by blending two entire albums, making them talk to each other and discover their common rhythmic core. While bold, "The Grey Album," as Danger Mouse called it, was only the most recent and most high-profile example of the phenomenon of "mash-ups" or "mashes." For more than five years, amateur producers have been using inexpensive mixing software such as ProTools to create stunning and surprising mixes of temporally disparate music. One noteworthy example combines the guitar riffs from Nirvana's 1991 hit "Smells Like Teen Spirit" with Destiny's Child's 2001 hit "Bootylicious." Another features the hook from the Clash's 1983 song "Rock the Casbah" with Pink's "Get the Party Started." Mashes have attracted the attention of lawyers representing major music publishers and record labels. Danger Mouse agreed to cease distributing copies of "The Grey Album" after lawyers from the Beatles's label, EMI Music, demanded he do so or face civil penalties. Despite Danger Mouse's willingness to conform to legal demands, his work continues to move through Internet music communities. In fact, in February 2004, dozens of Web sites flaunted EMI's authority and made statements about the cultural value of digital remixing and sampling by openly posting the songs from "The Grey Album." Their coordinated protest was known as "Grey Tuesday" (Walker 2004).

This phenomenon seems fresh and almost revolutionary when examined exclusively through the medium of the Internet and its effects on the major commercial music industry (Walker 2004). But it is merely the latest incarnation of a widely shared, deeply embedded cultural habit of cultural recombination across time and space. This habit has found voice in works as canonical as Mark Twain's *Adventures of Huckleberry Finn* (1884) and *A Connecticut Yankee in King Arthur's Court* (1891) and as disposable as David Shire's "Night on Disco Mountain" from the soundtrack of *Saturday Night Fever* (1977). It was central to the development of hip-hop culture in the 1970s, when DJs challenged themselves to surprise and tickle audiences with odd and unexpected live mixes of beats lifted from Kraftwerk, the Beatles, or Led Zeppelin with elements of rhythm and blues hits or funny sounds captured from television. But now such recombinant "creative destruction" is harder and more expensive than ever. The only room for it is underground or through anonymous channels of distribution like peer-to-peer file sharing networks or global piracy trade routes (Vaidhyanathan 2001).

A Global Free Culture Movement?

Because of recklessly designed multilateral policy initiatives, global information regulatory systems are absurd. Participating in a pirate economy is easier than ever. Participating in a legitimate, competitive economy is easier than ever. Participating in a legitimate information or cultural economy is harder and more expensive than ever. Such absurdity stems from a widespread anxiety that digitization and networking would wreak havoc on cultural industries. To some extent they have. To an equally important extent, they have locked winners into place and chilled legitimate free markets of technology and creativity while granting prominence to illicit and subversive creativity and distribution. The spread of such top-down global electronic cultural policy has the potential to chill both technological and cultural experimentation.

References

Castells, M. 2000. *The rise of the network society.* Oxford, UK: Blackwell.

Coombe, R. J. 1992. Author/izing celebrity: Publicity rights, postmodern politics, and unauthorized genders. *Cardozo Arts and Entertainment Law Journal* 10.

Cowen, T. 2002. *Creative destruction: How globalization is changing the world's cultures.* Princeton, NJ: Princeton University Press.

Feld, S. 2001. A sweet lullaby for world music. In *Globalization*, ed. A. Appadurai, 344. Durham, NC: Duke University Press.

Gramsci, A., and D. Forgacs. 2000. *The Gramsci reader: Selected writings, 1916-1935*. New York: New York University Press.

Lessig, L. 1999. *Code and other laws of cyberspace*. New York: Basic Books.

———. 2004. *Free Culture: How big media uses technology and the law to lock down culture and control creativity*. New York: Penguin.

Levine, Lawrence. 1988. *Highbrow/lowbrow: The emergence of cultural hierarchy in America*. Cambridge, MA: Harvard University Press.

Lott, Eric. 1993. *Love and theft: Blackface minstrelsy and the American working class*. New York: Oxford University Press.

Mayne, R. 2002. The global campaign on patents and access to medicines: An Oxfam perspective. In *Global intellectual property rights: Knowledge, access, and development*, ed. R. Mayne. New York: Palgrave.

McChesney, R. W. 1993. *Telecommunications, mass media, and democracy: The battle for the control of U.S. broadcasting, 1928-1935*. New York: Oxford University Press.

Miller, T., and G. Yúdice. 2002. *Cultural policy*. Thousand Oaks, CA: Sage.

Rothkopf, D. 1997. In praise of cultural imperialism? *Foreign Policy* 107 (Summer): 38-53.

Schiller, H. I. 1976. *Communication and cultural domination*. White Plains, NY: International Arts and Sciences Press.

Sell, S. K. 2003. *Private power, public law: The globalization of intellectual property rights*. Cambridge: Cambridge University Press.

Tomlinson, J. 1991. *Cultural imperialism: A critical introduction*. Baltimore: Johns Hopkins University Press.

Vaidhyanathan, S. 2001. *Copyrights and copywrongs: The rise of intellectual property and how it threatens creativity*. New York: New York University Press.

———. 2004. *The anarchist in the library: How the clash between freedom and control is hacking the real world and crashing the system*. New York: Basic Books.

Walker, R. 2004. Consumed: The Grey Album. *The New York Times Magazine*, p. 32.

Walsh, N. P. 2003. Russia's cult video pirate rescripts Lord of the Rings as gangster film. *The Observer*, June 22. http://observer.guardian.co.uk/international/story/0,6903,982487,00.html/.

World Intellectual Property Organization (WIPO). 2004. Consolidated text for a treaty on the protection of broadcasting organizations. Standing Committee of Copyright and Related Rights, Geneva, Switzerland.

The Changing Place of Cultural Production: The Location of Social Networks in a Digital Media Industry

By
GINA NEFF

This article examines the role of place and placemaking within cultural industries in the digital era. The data for this article are drawn from a data set of attendance at more than nine hundred social networking events over a six-year period in New York City's Internet, or "new media," industry. These data confirm that place became more, not less, important to cultural production over this period. Networking, or the processes of the formation of social network ties, is concentrated in activities within narrow geographic clusters. This study suggests that the networking events within the industry—cocktail parties, seminars, ceremonies, and the like—mediate access to crucial resources within the industry.

Keywords: Internet industry; social network analysis; creative industries; high-technology districts; industrial districts; work and occupations; network formation

If you keep schmoozing something will surely come out of it: maybe a job, an investor, a new customer, love, inspiration or a brilliant new hire who will save your dot-com.
—"Bernardo's List" e-mail, March 7, 2001

Digital media and information technologies have enabled work and organization to occur at a distance. There is, however, a paradox in the changing place of production. As distance work becomes technically easier, employees remain bound to place through their social networks, or the set of people and organizations linked by social relationships (Castilla et al. 2000), which

Gina Neff is an assistant professor of communication at the University of California, San Diego. Her research focuses on work in creative industries and the changing role of information technologies in social organization.

NOTE: I wish to acknowledge the University of California's Institute for Labor and Employment for a postdoctoral fellowship that supported the writing of this article. Valuable comments and suggestions from Philip Howard, David Kirsch, and Jennifer Lena greatly improved this article. This study would not have been possible without the help of Courtney Pulitzer, who generously made available her personal archives.

DOI: 10.1177/0002716204270505

mediate entrée into organizations and industries. Even within the industries that create the technologies for distance work, the core business activities often cluster in relatively small geographic areas. Technology has not rendered work and organization "spaceless"; nor have we seen the "death of distance" (Cairncross 1997) as earlier critics predicted. However, technology has changed the place of production. In the case of New York's Internet industry—or "Silicon Alley," as it was commonly called—the designers and front-office employees clustered around a very narrow swath of Manhattan. Firms were tightly colocated, and as I argue below, this allowed productive activity to occur outside the boundary of individual firms and outside office walls.

Geographic boundaries legitimated membership within the industrial community of Silicon Alley. For example, employees reported difficulty moving between New York and other centers of Internet production (such as San Francisco and Austin), even though the portability of their in-demand skills suggested otherwise. One programmer who moved from San Francisco to New York discussed the importance of having the "right" address for establishing that he was serious about landing a job within Silicon Alley:

> I had a phone number. I had an address. I was living on Long Island, but I had the West 25th Street address which was great.... [It] established that I had my own office ... in the right district [the Flatiron District]. I was going out. I was meeting people. I was interviewing in various places.[1]

The "right district" in New York's Internet industry was near the Flatiron building at 23rd Street and Broadway in Manhattan, and this particular respondent saw location as a marker of his seriousness and legitimacy as much as his experience and contacts garnered from years of employment in San Francisco.

What forces shape the formation of regional clusters within creative industries? Scholars have pointed to the social ties that link companies together across a geographic region as the foundation of innovative, creative, and emergent industries and social networking as the process in which these creative milieus form (Florida 2002; Kadushin 1974; Piore and Sable 1984; Saxenian 1994; Storper 1997; Uzzi 1996). An industry's cocktail parties, seminars, and informal gatherings form its social backbone and are especially important to innovative industries that rely on the rapid dissemination of information. Few scholars, however, have studied in any depth the *formation* of social ties within these sorts of industries. This article does this through an examination of what could be called the microprocesses of locational logic: a pattern of individual-level occurrences function to structure industrial location. The spatial processes of the Internet industry owe much to the practice of "networking," as business-oriented meetings outside of work are commonly called, and networking shapes the location decisions of industry actors. That is, being in the so-called right district means being where the action is. Within Silicon Alley, that action was located in after-hours networking events.

Few studies exist that actually use a source of data on the practice of creating an industry's informal social network. Although scholars have long recognized the importance of social tie formation in informal, off-hours settings, they have tended to ignore studying the actual practice tie creation. Given that scholars credit informal social ties as (1) linking organizations across firm boundaries, (2) being "new forms of labor market intermediation" (Benner 2002), and (3) establishing positive economic externalities of regional production, this analysis of tie formation is sorely needed. As I argue below, social ties are *constitutive* of productive milieus within cultural industries, and the work central to maintaining these social ties happens outside of the formal boundaries of organizations and inside industrial social settings. Unfortunately, events, the critical unit of analysis for understanding this process, lack academic attention.

In Silicon Alley, the absence of other organizational and industrial supports meant one's social network became the main resource for maintaining employability.

This article uses a novel type of network data—reporting on social events—to analyze the informal organization of New York's Internet industry from 2000 to 2002. Social events reporting is a relatively underused form of social network data that avoids many of the methodological concerns of network specification: it does not rely on participant recall, is collected contemporaneously, and can capture the best and widest net over a rapidly changing field of actors. Social reporting, society columns, and the like are not commonly associated with scholarship on industrial organization. However, there is both precedent for studying social structure using social reporting or "society pages" (Brieger 1974; Davis, Gardner, and Gardner 1941) and widespread reporting of this sort in trade publications covering other industries.

In the next section, I outline theories of informal social ties within regional industrial districts. Then I describe some of the particularities of the Internet industry in New York and the data and methods used in this article. Next, I analyze the ways in which networking events geographically circumscribed Silicon Alley. These findings suggest that even within a digital media industry that relies on the technologies that enable distance work, social networks can lead to tight geographic clustering. The data below show a tight localization of a particular strata of people within New York's Internet industry, even though they are more likely than the average worker with the technologies of distance work.

Informal Ties within Silicon Alley

Theories of regional growth have focused on how social networks encourage economic growth (Florida 2002; Saxenian 1994). "Regional systems of creativity and innovation" emerge from the "dense localized production complexes that function as the essential economic backbone of thriving cities and regions" (Scott 2000, 35, 16). Comparatively, regions that develop these rich social networks within local industrial systems are better able to adapt to changing markets and technologies than other regions (Heydebrand 1999; Powell et al. 2002; Saxenian 1994).

While *regions* have been the focus of much of this scholarly attention, how networks form among individuals within regions (on which economic growth ostensibly relies) is less well understood, even as employees, companies, and scholars alike recognize the value of such networks. Much of the research to date has focused on how organizations are cosituated to share resources across firm boundaries. The geographic proximity of firms within neighborhoods, districts, and cities can foster a "recurrent collaboration and mutual interdependence of money and ideas," especially in innovative and high-technology industries (Powell et al. 2002, 303). The strongest innovation effects of colocation, however, may actually be from individual actors linking *across* organizational boundaries. This kind of "networked individualism" (Wellman 2001, 238) fosters a community approach to production, links firms to one another through the social ties of their respective employees, and draws upon the social practices associated with artists, "neobohemians" (Lloyd 2002), and the "creative class" (Florida 2002) to bring innovation inside the firm.

Social networking is certainly not unique to the Internet industry. Other industries—and media industries in particular—also rely heavily on the networks of those working within the industry. Professional and middle-class workers readily report increased pressures to "network," or make potential business contacts through social engagements (Neff 2004; Smith 2001). Nor are the structures that emerge from social networking new—certainly the "old boy's club" metaphor and the image of the three-martini lunch predate post-Fordist changes in employment structure that encourage workers' reliance on network resources in the face of shrinking organizational supports. Kadushin (1974), for example, identified "lunch distance" as a force that concentrated the American intelligentsia in a radius around midtown Manhattan from which a writer could reasonably travel for a lunch date with his or her editor. There is also a body of research on the relational ties among entrepreneurial companies and the legal and financial services companies that support them (Castila et al. 2000; Powell et al. 2002, Patton and Kenney 2003). Less is written, however, about the kind of project-based and temporary organization among creative workers and firms that Grabher (2002a, 208) has called a "pool of resources" that "'gels' into latent networks."

Several scholars have suggested that networks increase workers' mobility within industries that rely on network forms of organization, and regional networks may substitute for types of workforce support that used to be found within organizations, such as internal labor markets, job training, and job security. How workers fare within regional networks is still unclear. Scholars of technology industries have noted that regional networks provide many resources for workers as well as for organizations but may also prevent workers' mobility across regions. Silicon Alley workers, for example, were more dependent on local market information and connections than were other types of project-based media workers for information about work and continued employability (Christopherson 2002, 2012). Social networks serve as a new form of labor market mediation for workers (Benner 2002) and provide workers with a type of job security in which personal connections serve as conduits for information about new jobs and new technologies (Batt et al. 2001). These connections however, may increase the experience of labor market inequality, as workers unable to access or maintain these networks may be at a disadvantage (Batt et al. 2001; Neff 2004). In Silicon Alley, the absence of other organizational and industrial supports meant one's social network became the main resource for maintaining employability.

Regionally based networks encourage collaborative practices across and within organizations, help diffuse continually changing technical information, and build environments of innovation that provide positive economic externalities for firms and workers. From New York's Silicon Alley to San Francisco's "Multimedia Gulch," producers of Internet-related goods and services formed clusters in regionally based local economies that adopted brands linking them to specific geographic regions.[2] The next section examines the link between locations, neighborhoods, and identities.

Neighborhood, "Noise," and Identity

The shift to postindustrial production has resulted in the reinvestment of urban space with "symbolic" capital (Zukin 1995), creating "new geographies of centrality in which cities are the key articulators" (Sassen 2002, 2). The technology industry in the late 1990s proved an interesting hybrid of two processes that shape cities. On one hand, global capitalism exacerbates the need for technology industries to move some production activities to lower-wage areas and in the developing world (Castells 2001; O Riain 2000). On the other hand, there is an incredible investment into the association of certain types of creative and high-technology production with particular cities and districts. The spatial effects of technological change create at once "enormous geographic dispersal and mobility" and "pronounced territorial concentrations of resources" to manage that mobility (Sassen 2002, 2). These same forces reshaping urban spaces gave rise to an Internet industry balanced between intensified forces of concentration and dispersion.

Given this balance, how did local production markets and fluency in local knowledge come to predominate the industrial organization of the Internet industry? What were the pressures that led to intensified concentration within specific industrial districts in a digital era? Industrial districts are not new, of course—even within the boundaries of what is now considered the center of Silicon Alley, one could find the remains of previous urban manufacturing districts. Social connectivity, though, may be amplified in the digital era (Sassen 2002, 21), making the effects of neighborhoods even stronger for the development of urban zones of industrial production. Within highly technically linked industries, cities "are effectively nourished by strong electronic links to a wider world, but simultaneously prize their differences from other places, their local institutions and hangouts, and their unique ambiences and customs" (Mitchell 1995, 170). Rather than being a zero-sum trade-off, technological links and social links may complement one another, especially in cultural industries that "rely on the spatial logic of territorially concentrated milieux of innovation, with a multiplicity of interactions, and face-to-face exchanges at the core of the innovation process" (Castells 2001, 228). Advances in telecommunications technologies may actually increase the demand for ongoing, face-to-face meetings (Thrift 1996a), which occur in a "re-embedded set of meeting places" within cities that support the "discourse networks" critical to the functioning of contemporary global capitalism (Thrift 1996b, 231, 249).

The parties and nightlife of Silicon Alley helped to constitute the production of the industry, not the other way around.

Symbolic capital can also be invested into economic activities through association with particular locations. The association of warehouse space with artists' living lofts (Zukin 1982) meant that office spaces within formerly industrial neighborhoods could be invested with an image of creativity and innovation, helping to establish what Kotkin and DeVol (2001, 30) termed "knowledge-value neighborhoods." Local governments and business leaders reinvested cities and districts with symbolic capital through "branding campaigns devised by place marketers" emphasizing "the promise of a reborn city that had left behind a polluted and blue-collar past for a future in which it was vibrant, stylish, confident, cosmopolitan, and innovative" (Hannigan 2003, 354). In the postindustrial economy, the growth of creative industries both depends upon this process of placemaking and magnifies it.

The buzz or noise available inside of tightly located innovative industries also drives colocation within creative milieux. (Grabher 2002b, 254). While sharing information is important, the social practices around precognitive information or "noise"—"rumors, impressions, recommendations, trade folklore, strategic misinformation"—may tie the workforce of creative industries together through a process of negotiating meaning and of sensemaking (Grabher 2002b, 254). Although they were writing of the proximity of workers within a firm, Girard and Stark's (2002, 1947) observation that the noise generated in innovative work heightens tolerance for heterogeneous ideas and practices and creates a forced intimacy seems aptly applied to Silicon Alley as a whole. Noise socializes and enculturates workers, transmitting the norms, practices, and stories of the community (Grabher 2002a, 208-9). Telecommunication advances that increase information may make the instinctual interpretation of noise even more important, heightening "the salience of proximity" for interpretive advantage (Beunza and Stark 2003, 155). The move toward electronic trading on Wall Street, for instance, meant that trading rooms became less dependent on their physical proximity to a centralized stock exchange but, rather, became "a web of trading rooms in which each node is anchored to the area by its proximity to others" (Beunza and Stark 2003, 158). Colocation persists, in part, because of the interpretive advantages of noise.

Neighborhoods play a significant role in this process. In particular, neighborhoods with the reputation for fostering artistic production provide individual cultural producers with "both material and symbolic resources that facilitate creative activity, particularly in the early stages of a cultural producer's career" (Lloyd forthcoming). Far from being "the other of productive practice," consumption within these industrial structures forms the basis of creative production (Lloyd 2002). The art galleries, bars, restaurants, and other nightlife venues represent new intersections of consumption and production in urban space that "potentially operate as key features in a new regime of capital accumulation" (Lloyd 2002, 518-19). These venues give spatiality to what Brown and Duguid (1991) have termed "occupational communities of practice" and have precedent in other industries and eras: neighborhood bars catering to a clientele of newspapermen, cops, or dock workers have functional similarities to the sleek lounges that attract fashion models or coffee shops that host screenwriters.

Venues such as these make it easier for cultural producers to recognize and establish contact with one another, while simultaneously establishing the spatial markers for creative industries. Creative neighborhoods with "funky" nightlife form the core of a "cultural industrial complex" that lures creative people to certain places (Kotkin 2002, 130). Silicon Alley in particular benefited from a kind of "industrialization of bohemia" in which "pace and rhythms of industry [were] reprogrammed to accommodate an artist's work mentality that once flourished in defiance of industrial routine" (Ross 2003, 124). Silicon Alley, I argue, became a thriving cultural space and incorporated the creative values of its workforce into industry practice through the nightlife events that occurred with dizzying frequency within the industry.

Silicon Alley: The Geography of an Industry's Nightlife

The parties and nightlife of Silicon Alley helped to constitute the production of the industry, not the other way around. The purported decadence of dot-com

FIGURE 1
STYLIZED MAP OF SILICON ALLEY

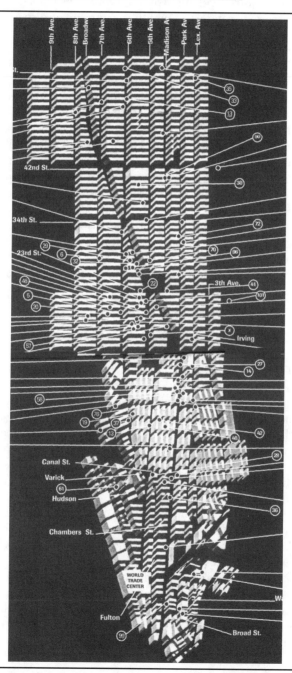

SOURCE: *Silicon Alley Reporter*, no. 8, October 1997. Used with permission.

nightlife with its requisite launch parties, evenings spent with coworkers at the bar, and the flurry of industry-wide networking events was not simply a result of the youthfulness of a creative industry. Nightlife events linked disparate producers in a rapidly changing industry together into a community of practice that disseminated information, generated "noise," and channeled artistic lifestyles and practices into a commodifiable form palatable to demands of venture capitalists and Wall Street. The intensified social networking that occurred within the industry suggests that social network events themselves have become an important place of production within creative industries.

Initially, Silicon Alley was defined as being the collection of technology companies clustered in and around Manhattan's Flatiron District. The *Silicon Alley Reporter* regularly published a map in its early issues that served as both a business directory and a boundary marker for a growing industry. The map showed the lack of conceptual clarity about what the Internet industry was—it listed of many different kinds of business ventures such as Internet cafes, wired nightclubs, Internet service providers, advertising firms that specialized in the production of World Wide Web pages for corporate clients, educational facilities, public relations firms, magazines, and so on.[3] The map from the October 1997 issue listed 137 Silicon Alley companies and their locations (see Figure 1). As an indication of the rapid growth in Silicon Alley, the number of companies listed on the map had doubled in five months.

On this map, each dot indicates a particular building hosting one or more Internet-related companies, thus indicating how firms clustered in the neighborhood around 23rd Street and Broadway. The *Silicon Alley Reporter* included the following note with an earlier map: "FYI: Silicon Alley is loosely defined as the area from 28th Street to Spring Street along Broadway, and three blocks East and West of Broadway along that stretch. Silicon Alley is ever expanding so in this issue we have redesigned the map to include the uptown and downtown contingent."[4] As can be seen, the largest concentration of Internet companies was clustered around 23rd Street and Broadway. In the Flatiron District, Doubleclick posted a billboard advertisement at the intersection of Broadway and 22nd Street, across the street from the Flatiron Building, that read, "Doubleclick welcomes you to Silicon Alley." That billboard came down in March 2002.[5]

Regardless of its center, the concentration of the production of Internet content in New York reflected "a remarkable degree of clustering despite its much ballyhooed spacelessness" (Zook 2000, 418). The New York metropolitan region had one of the country's highest concentrations of registered commercial Internet domains, and within the region the highest concentration of commercial Internet domains were clustered in Manhattan around the Flatiron District, along with smaller centers of production in the Financial District and Midtown East (Zook 2000). As I will show below, this concentration is reflected in the clustering of nightlife venues of industry events.

Data and Method

Social events reporting, or the gossip column, is an underused corpus of social network data with precedent in social network theory (see Brieger 1974; and Davis, Gardner, and Gardner 1941). For this article, I analyze the location of industry events using more than three years of reporting in a weekly online Silicon Alley trade newsletter.

"The Cyber Scene" began as a biweekly column in *AtNewYork*, a weekly e-mail newsletter about New York's nascent Internet industry. The newsletter, along with its competitor, *Silicon Alley Reporter*, circumscribed the field of Silicon Alley through a process of including (and excluding) within its coverage ideas, technologies, companies, and personalities. These early trade publications included reporting on the myriad of industry-related networking events, and *AtNewYork* began coverage of Silicon Alley events in September 1996. By April 1997, the weekly column was written by Courtney Pulitzer,[6] who continued covering events for *AtNewYork* and later for her own newsletter through 2002. These weekly columns covered approximately one-tenth of the events held each week,[7] and coverage extended to the most important industry gatherings, such as meetings of the New York New Media Association (NYNMA) and the World Wide Web Artists Consortium, as well as smaller public and private gatherings. Events included conferences, panels, seminars, and workshops; private social events such as going-away dinners and birthday and engagement parties; and perhaps most important, public social events such as award ceremonies, company launch parties, parties celebrating new offices, and even "closing" parties to mark company failures. For simplicity's sake, all these types of events are referred to in this article as "social events," and after-hours events held in restaurants, bars, and nightclubs are referred to specifically as "nightlife events."

There was a continuity in Pulitzer's coverage of events over the six-year period that was surprising given the turmoil in the industry. For example, in one of the first columns, the launch party for Total NY was covered; less than a year and a half later, its "closing" party was also featured. Birthday parties, anniversary parties, going away parties—in the early years of coverage, Silicon Alley, at least through the eyes of its social reporters, was a community that celebrated rituals together. Even otherwise staid business public relations functions or informal panels became opportunities for a bit of frolicking, and frivolity found its way into Pulitzer's reporting. Dancing, drinking, and flirting were as much of a part of these columns as were companies' business models. In the excerpt below, Pulitzer captured a bit of the "rowdy" behavior that occasionally occurred:

"Where are the cheese sticks! We want more cheese sticks!" You'd think this sort of a chant would come from the football-watching crowd in a sports bar (no offense!) but instead it came from selected attendees at the Art Director's Club roundtable "Revenge of the Nerds: Chic Geeks in New Media" on Tuesday, February 2nd. Anthony Vagnoni of *Adver-*

tising Age kept the rowdy panelists in tow. . . . John Carlin of Funny Garbage, Rich Lefurgy of the IAB, Kyle Shannon of Agency.com, and Howard Fishman of Real Media were among the panelists. . . . Meanwhile, I overheard a very artistic-looking gentleman tell Jaime Levy of Electronic Hollywood that "I love computers" and "I also like chat rooms." Alayna Tagariello of Peppercom mingled about, and bubbly journalist Pamela Parker and adorable Kit Cody, executive producer of Concrete Media, were perched at the door as the event was ending and small sanctions were deciding to head off to one of a handful hip, underground bars. ("The Cyber Scene," *AtNewYork*, February 5, 1999)

Pulitzer's column attempted to inscribe the diversity of businesses within Silicon Alley and functioned to legitimate business models and businesses through reports:

> I met Catherine Winchester, CEO of Soliloquy, Inc., whom I'd heard about before, but never met. She explained the nature of her company to me. It's an interesting company in that the name indicates speaking alone and the product is about conversing with a computer. Standing by Oven Digital's display table, I saw Michael Hughes of Oracle, who sent me a most interesting link the other day about Oracle and its new $100 million venture fund to foster companies that leverage its Oracle Internet computing platform. ("The Cyber Scene," *AtNewYork*, January 29, 1999)

Event reporting formed a contemporaneous who's who of Silicon Alley in which new businesses were introduced, personalities were created, and associations among business models were made. In the process, individuals marked themselves as "regulars on the scene" in Pulitzer's description and established their own legitimacy within Silicon Alley. Events also provided Silicon Alley organizations access to potential employees and clients, as well as access to people working in other industries, such as arts and media (which were predominant in the early years of Silicon Alley), and later business and finance. Through the regularity of the column, the issues, companies, people, and events important to Silicon Alley were documented as they changed over time. The reporting of who hosted and attended Silicon Alley events helped to circumscribe what companies considered themselves a part of the "community" and, in turn, the industry. Comparing the more social Silicon Alley to the older networks around Silicon Valley, Pulitzer commented that social events in New York "propel the scene forward and give it validity" ("The Cyber Scene," *AtNewYork*, November 14, 1997). Other industry participants also equated the parties of Silicon Alley with membership in the industry. As one respondent told me, "We're not a Silicon Alley company—I mean, we're not a dot-com, those parties, that life, that's not us. We're just computer geeks."

Social networking was an industry, literally, in Silicon Alley. Weekly e-mail lists emerged with the sole purpose of telling people about the Silicon Alley events of the week, and at least one of these lists survived the dot-com crash. Event planners and "event management firms" were hired to handle the details of company parties, from the invitations to the venue to the guest list to the gift bag.[8] A hierarchy of events emerged later in Silicon Alley's history, with smaller, more exclusive events replicating the early "insider-y" feel of "old" Silicon Alley.[9] The number of these events meant that the time required to stay "connected" within the field was enormous, and many workers felt they needed to attend events to maintain their employability within the field (Neff 2004).

Method of analysis

For the analysis of participation in Silicon Alley events, I compiled a dataset of all "The Cyber Scene" social columns from September 1996 through 2002 when the column ended.[10] The resulting database contained more than 9,000 participants at 941 New York City area events over the six-year period. For this article, I am using only data from 2000 through 2002, which represents the period of the industry's maturation and its struggle to recover after the 2000 crash in technology stock prices.

Over this period, Pulitzer reported on 456 events with 4,430 participants at 280 unique venues.[11] On average, the columns in this period reported on the attendance of 9 people per event and roughly 4 events covered per week.

Information about event venues was also collected and coded by type, including offices, bars, nightclubs, restaurants, private homes, hotels, museums, and educational facilities. Of the participants included in this analysis, approximately 85 percent, or 3,783, attended an event at an identifiable venue. The addresses of these venues were collected using nightlife directories, telephone and Web directories, business event planning guides, and New York City real estate databases.

Once the address and zip code of a venue were determined, the venue was coded by neighborhood using the definitions of New York City neighborhoods as defined by the New York City Department of City Planning. Zip codes for venues were used to create geographical information system maps locating nightlife and office venues for Silicon Alley events.

Locating Silicon Alley

The sheer number of all Silicon Alley social events—not to mention the industry of planners for them and the multiple outlets for reporting upon them—points to the central role that social events played in linking Silicon Alley companies and workers. Roughly 70 percent of the events reported were parties, receptions, dinners, and the like, with conferences, panels, and seminars making up 27 percent of the reported events. As such, the bulk of Silicon Alley social events were held in bars, nightclubs, restaurants, or private events spaces such as lofts and other facilities for hire. These nightlife activities (as opposed to, say, office parties or seminars) were concentrated around the Flatiron District. The parties and nightlife were not restricted to those working in start-up companies: Wall Street investment banks (JP Morgan, Salomon Smith Barney, UBS), venture capitalists, corporate law firms (Brobeck and Thelen, Reid), top-ranked business schools (Wharton and MIT), industry associations (NYNMA and the New York Software Industry Association), large technology companies (Oracle and IBM), advertising and entertainment firms (MTV, TBWA\Chiat\Day, Sony, AOL/Time Warner), and foreign consulates

TABLE 1

LOCATION OF SILICON ALLEY VENUES BY ZIP CODE

		All Venues		Nightlife Venues		Office Venues	
Zip Code	Neighborhood	n	% Total	n	% Total	n	% Total
Flatiron and adjacent areas							
10003	East Village; Gramercy	23	8.2	17	12.1	3	5.9
10011	Greenwich Village; Chelsea	22	7.9	16	11.3	3	5.9
10001	Chelsea; Flatiron	21	7.5	9	6.4	6	11.8
10010	Flatiron; Madison Square; Gramercy	19	6.8	13	9.2	3	5.9
Total	Flatiron and surrounding area	85	31.8	55	38.7	15	29.4
Rest of Manhattan							
10022	Midtown East; Madison Avenue	28	10.0	8	5.7	9	17.6
10019	Midtown West; Columbus Circle	20	7.1	5	3.5	2	3.9
10036	Midtown West; Times Square	19	6.8	9	6.4	6	11.8
10013	SoHo/Tribeca	19	6.8	10	7.1	3	5.9
10017	Midtown East	13	4.6	5	3.5	2	3.9
10012	Greenwich Village	10	3.6	8	5.7	1	2.0
10002	Lower East Side	10	3.6	10	7.1	0	0
Total	Outside of the Flatiron and surrounding areas	182	68.2	87	59.1	36	70.6

TABLE 2

NUMBER OF PARTICIPANTS IN FLATIRON AREA EVENTS

Zip Code	Neighborhood	Participants Reported
10003	East Village; Gramercy	448
10011	Greenwich Village; Chelsea	353
10010	Chelsea; Flatiron	327
10001	Flatiron; Madison Square; Gramercy	209
	Total	1,337
	Percentage of all participants	35.4

(the Swedish and Canadian consulates in particular) all played host to Silicon Alley nightlife events over this period. To the extent that being close to this evening action was important for positioning a company within Silicon Alley, the location of these events shows the microprocesses of agglomeration. Parties built industrial networks.

TABLE 3
ORGANIZATIONS HOSTING MIDTOWN OFFICE EVENTS

Industry	Company
Advertising	TBWA\Chiat\Day, agency7
Entertainment	AOL/Time Warner, MTV, Sony
Finance	JP MorganChase, Morgan Stanley, UBS
Law	Brobeck, Phleger & Harrison; Dorsey & Whitney; Thelen, Reid, & Priest; Schulte Roth & Zabel
Public relations	Cone Communications offices
Venture capital	VantagePoint
Internet and technology	
Advertising & PR	SiegelGale; e-Media
Broadband	Excite @Home
Technology	IBM, Oracle
Industry association	NYNMA
Start-up	Kizna.com & InfiniteFace.com

Bars, restaurants, nightclubs, and events spaces compose the category of "night-life venues" in this analysis. As shown in Table 1, almost 39 percent of nightlife events were held in the Flatiron District. By contrast, only 29 percent of the events in offices were held in the Flatiron District. Table 2 shows that more than 35 percent of the participants were at events located in the four zip codes that compose and are adjacent to the Flatiron District. Working with neighborhood codes, the concentration of nightlife events in the small Flatiron District is even more noticeable. Twenty-five percent of all the events held in bars were within a five-block radius of the Flatiron Building.

Office venues for events, surprisingly, were not in the concentrated in the open-space lofts of start-up companies in the Flatiron District and neighboring Chelsea. Instead, the largest number of office-based events was in Midtown. More than a third, 37 percent, of the office venues were located north of 42nd Street and south of 59th Street. Table 3 shows the hosting organizations for these events. Notice that most of the midtown office events are sponsored not by Internet start-ups but rather by corporate finance, law, adverting, and entertainment firms—established business more likely to have offices with conference and catering facilities.[12]

Figures 2 and 3 show, respectively, the location for Silicon Alley social events that were held in nightlife venues and in office venues. While the Flatiron District and its environs clearly has the highest concentration of nightlife events, there are other clusters of social activity to notice, namely, around the Midtown East section where corporate headquarters in advertising and other fields are located, as well as in the Financial District. The clustering of events around these districts shows how organizations from other industries attempted to affiliate with Silicon Alley's start-up companies through hosting events for their clients and potential clients.

FIGURE 2
LOCATION OF NIGHTLIFE VENUES FOR
SILICON ALLEY EVENTS, 2000-2002

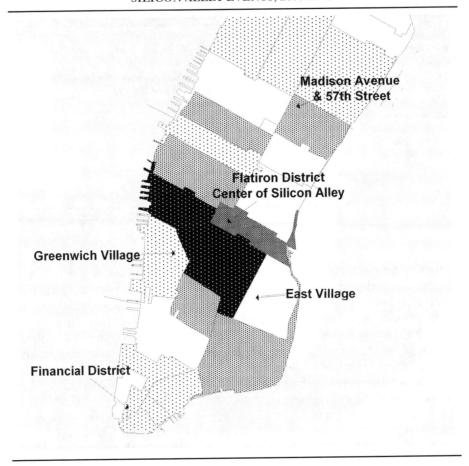

Where Production Occurs

Andrew Ross (2003, 89) wrote of the parties that Razorfish, a Silicon Alley design firm, threw: "The hedonism of company culture was carefully crafted; it could be as articulate in expressing a company's profile and aspirations as the corporate portfolio." The effort, resources, and time that went into creating a "cyber scene," as Pulitzer aptly termed it, reflect this attention to crafting corporate images through social events. These dot-com social events, at times seemingly extravagant, constituted the industrial organization of Silicon Alley by creating the spatial environment for building social ties.

If the place of cultural production could be said to have shifted during the digital era, it was from the confines of offices to the bars and nightclubs of after-work

FIGURE 3
LOCATION OF OFFICE VENUES FOR
SILICON ALLEY EVENTS, 2000-2002

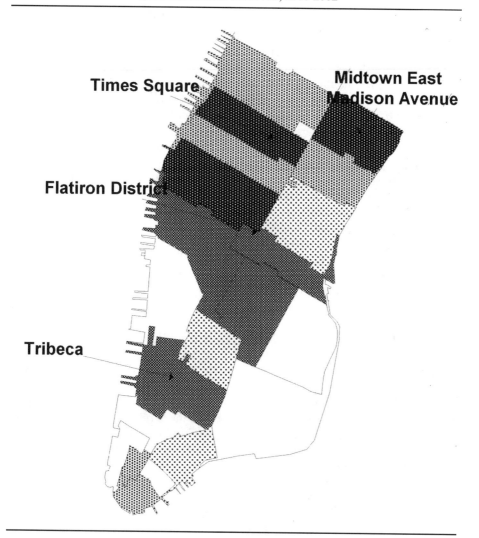

socializing, at least in terms of the network economy of Silicon Alley. The maps of
Silicon Alley events show how social networks clustered within particular neighborhoods in Manhattan. The patterning of these venues points to a new location for
industrial districts—a location that is not so much in geographic space as in the cul-
tural-social space of the after-hours events that play a crucial role in linking
together creative producers. The persistence of these colocation forces under the
pressures of geographic dispersion suggest that social networks dynamically shape

the contours of regional economies, especially with regards to the professional employees of innovative industries. Parties can make industries from otherwise disparate actors.

Industry actors heard the "noise" of the industry at these events. Outside the firm, in the tightly interlinked social settings, the network economies of production that fuel creative industries emerged. Parties were not play: they offered the chance to establish ties, gather information, and become a part of an occupational community of practice that spanned Silicon Alley. Indeed, employees considered after-hours events a part of their working life. The productive practices of social events point to a changing place of production, from within organizational boundaries to the industrial settings that foster the emergence of geographically based social networks. These networks were bound to place to such an extent that mobility for employees between cities was difficult.

City and business leaders looking to foster creative industries should consider how to encourage the formation of ties across organizations as a way to harness innovation. At the same time, the microprocesses of the location of creative industries could exacerbate inequalities in geographic development—that is, some spaces, even *within* cities, will continue to be more important, more central to the process of social networking, than other spaces. Employees within the creative industries that rely on the productive work of social events could also face severe disadvantages if they are unable to participate in the frenzy of nightlife activity.

Studies of social networks have been criticized for missing out on the richness of the content of social ties—that is, while the *existence* of links among industrial actors have been the object of analysis, less scholarly attention has been paid to the ways in which these ties represent the relations that build markets, much less to the process of building those relations. If we are to fully understand markets and economic processes as "tangible social constructions" (White 2002, 9), then the relational richness of social ties must be studied simultaneously with the structures that organize industries. This article shows that much more research needs to be done on the social events that link the personal networks of individuals to the structures that shape their industries, and studying the emergence of informal organization across industry actors is one mechanism for doing so.

Notes

1. For more interview data with Silicon Alley workers and for the research methodology for the qualitative data discussed here, see Neff (2004).

2. "Siliconias," or names for regional technology districts evocative of Silicon Valley, erupted with the rise of the Internet industry. See Brad Wieners, "Silicon Envy," *Wired*, 6.09, September 1998.

3. Tellingly, the map excluded the New York headquarters of established technology companies such as IBM and Sony.

4. Anon., "The Map," *Silicon Alley Reporter*, no. 4, May 1997.

5. Denny Lee, "A Once-Evocative Name Falls Victim to the Bursting of the High-Tech Bubble," *The New York Times*, March 24, 2002, 14:4. It is interesting to note that Lee's article was written as part of the weekly "Neighborhood Report" section of the Sunday *New York Times*. The neighborhood heading for the

article was "Silicon Alley," not the Flatiron District or Chelsea, the more general and more widely accepted names for the neighborhood.

6. Among her qualifications for the job as a social columnist, Pulitzer had been a party organizer for one of the industry associations.

7. Bernardo Joselevich's weekly e-mail featured more than fifty Internet industry events in New York City per week in March 2001, a full year after the beginning of the dot-com crash. "The Cyber Scene" reported on an average of 4.6 events per week that month.

8. While corporate event planning predates the Internet industry, several of the events hosted by Internet companies were covered in the trade newsletters for event planners. See the coverage in *BizBash* of *The Industry Standard*'s June 21, 2000, rooftop party at http://www.bizbash.com/content/editorial/e222.asp (accessed February 18, 2004).

9. See Tom Watson, "What the Industry Needs: Real Representation from NYNMA," *AtNewYork*, no. 3.16, December 19, 1997; and Amy Harmon, "Trying to Put a Little Soul Back into Silicon Alley," *The New York Times*, October 19, 1997, 14:4.

10. Data about digital phenomena are especially ephemeral and at danger of being lost to researchers. The current lack of availability of Pulitzer's column online is emblematic of this problem.

11. In this article, *participant* refers to a person at an event, not a unique person. The average is less than 1.5 events per person for the entire 1996 to 2002 data set.

12. For example, Pulitzer described a dinner hosted by Swiss investment bank UBS as a "four-course extravaganza complete with a ceremonial dance between each course," cooked by the bank's private chef. The founder of GetAbstract.com and the CEO of LivePerson were on the exclusive guest list ("The Cyber Scene," *AtNewYork*, April 28, 2000).

References

Batt, Rosemary, Susan Christopherson, Ned Rightor, and Danielle Van Jaarsveld. 2001. *Net-working, work patterns and workforce policies for the new media industry.* Washington, DC: Economic Policy Institute.

Benner, Chris. 2002. *Work in the new economy: Flexible labor markets in Silicon Valley.* Malden, MA: Blackwell.

Beunza, Daniel, and David Stark. 2003. The organization of responsiveness: Innovation and recovery in the trading rooms of lower Manhattan. *Socio-Economic Review* 1:135-64.

Brieger, Ronald L. 1974. The duality of persons and groups. *Social Forces* 53:181-90.

Brown, John S., and Paul Duguid. 1991. Organizational learning and communities of practice: Toward a unified view of working, learning, and innovation. *Organization Science* 2:40-57.

Cairncross, Frances. 1997. *The death of distance: How the communications revolution will change our lives.* Cambridge, MA: Harvard Business School Press.

Castells, Manuel. 2001. *The Internet galaxy: Reflections on the Internet, business and society.* New York: Oxford University Press.

Castilla, Emilio J., Hokyu Hwang, Ellen Granovetter, and Mark Granovetter. 2000. Social networks in Silicon Valley. In *The Silicon Valley edge: A habitat for innovation and entrepreneurship*, ed. Chong-Moon Lee, William F. Miller, Marguerite Gong Hancock, and Henry S. Rowen. Palo Alto, CA: Stanford University Press.

Christopherson, Susan. 2002. Project work in context: Regulatory change and the new geography of media. *Environment and Planning A* 34:2003-15.

Davis, A., B. Gardner, and M. R. Gardner. 1941. *Deep South.* Chicago: University of Chicago Press.

Florida, Richard. 2002. *The creative class.* New York: Basic.

Girard, Monique, and David Stark. 2002. Distributing intelligence and organizing diversity in new media projects. *Environment and Planning A* 34:1927-49.

Grabher, Gernot. 2002a. Cool projects, boring institutions: Temporary collaboration in social context. *Regional Studies* 36:205-14.

———. 2002b. The project ecology of advertising: Tasks, talents and teams. *Regional Studies* 36:245-62.

Hannigan, John. 2003. Symposium on branding, the entertainment economy and urban place building: Introduction. *International Journal of Urban and Regional Research* 27:352-60.

Heydebrand, Wolf. 1999. Multimedia networks, globalization and strategies of innovation: The case of Silicon Alley. In *Multimedia and regional economic restructuring*, ed. Hans-Joachim Braczyk, Gerhard Fuchs, and Hans-Georg Wolf. London: Routledge.

Kadushin, Charles. 1974. *The American intellectual elite*. Boston: Little, Brown.

Kotkin, Joel. 2002. *The new geography: How the digital revolution is reshaping the American landscape*. New York: Random House.

Kotkin, Joel, and Ross C. DeVol. 2001. Knowledge-value cities in the digital age. February 13. The Milken Institute. http://www.milkeninstitute.org/pdf/kvdc.pdf (accessed September 30, 2003).

Lloyd, Richard. 2002. Neo-bohemia: Art and neighborhood redevelopment in Chicago. *Journal of Urban Affairs* 24:517-32.

———. Forthcoming. Living like an artist. *City and Community*.

Mitchell, William J. 1995. *City of bits: Space, place and the Infobahn*. Cambridge, MA: MIT Press.

Neff, Gina 2004. Organizing uncertainty: Individual, organizational and institutional risk in New York's Internet industry, 1995-2003. Unpublished Ph.D. diss., Columbia University, New York.

O Riain, Sean. 2000. The flexible developmental state: Globalization, information technology, and the "Celtic tiger." *Politics & Society* 28:157-93.

Patton, Donald, and Martin Kenney. 2003. The spatial distribution of entrepreneurial support networks: Evidence from semiconductor initial public offerings from 1996 through 2000. Berkeley, CA: Berkeley Roundtable on the International Economy, BRIEWP153, March 1. http://repositories.cdlib.org/brie/BRIEWP153 (accessed March 1, 2004).

Piore, M. J., and C. F. Sabel. 1984. *The second industrial divide*, New York: Basic Books.

Powell, Walter W., Kenneth W. Koput, James I. Bowie, and Laurel Smith-Doerr. 2002. The spatial clustering of science and capital: Accounting for biotech firm-venture capital relationships. *Regional Studies* 36:291-305.

Ross, Andrew. 2003. *White collar: The human workplace and its hidden costs*. New York: Basic Books.

Sassen, Saskia. 2002. Locating cities on global circuits. In *Global network, linked cities*, ed. Saskia Sassen. New York: Routledge.

Saxenian, AnnaLee. 1994. *Regional advantage: Culture and competition in Silicon Valley and Route 128*. Cambridge, MA: Harvard University Press.

Scott, Allen J. 2000. *The cultural economy of cities*. London: Sage.

Smith, Vicki. 2001. *Crossing the great divide*. Ithaca, NY: Cornell University Press.

Storper, Michael. 1997. *The regional world: Territorial development in a global economy*. New York: Guilford.

Thrift, Nigel. 1996a. New urban eras and old technological fears: Reconfiguring the goodwill of electronic things. *Urban Studies* 33:1463-93.

———. 1996b. *Spatial formations*. London: Sage.

Uzzi, Brian. 1996. The sources and consequences of embeddedness for the economic performance of organizations: The network effect. *American Sociological Review* 61:674-98.

Wellman, Barry. 2001. Physical place and cyberplace: The rise of personalized networking. *International Journal of Urban and Regional Research* 25:227-52.

White, Harrison C. 2002. *Markets from networks*. Princeton, NJ: Princeton University Press.

Zook, Matthew A. 2000. The web of production: The economic geography of commercial Internet content production in the United States. *Environment and Planning A* 32:411-26.

Zukin, Sharon. 1995. *The cultures of cities*. Cambridge, MA: Blackwell.

Zukin, Sharon. 1982. *Loft living: Culture and capital in urban change*. Baltimore: Johns Hopkins University Press.

Deep Democracy, Thin Citizenship: The Impact of Digital Media in Political Campaign Strategy

Digital media strategies are a crucial component of contemporary political campaigns. Established political elites use database and Internet technologies to raise money, organize volunteers, gather intelligence on voters, and do opposition research. However, they use data-mining techniques that outrage privacy advocates and surreptitious technologies that few Internet users understand. Grassroots political actors and average voters build their own digital campaigns, researching public policy options, candidate histories, lobbyist maneuvering, and the finances of big campaigns. I examine the role of digital technologies in the production of contemporary political culture with ethnographic and survey evidence from four election seasons between 1996 and 2002. Democracy is deeper in terms of the diffusion of rich data about political actors, policy options, and the diversity of actors and opinion in the public sphere. Citizenship is thinner in terms of the ease in which people can become politically expressive without being substantively engaged.

Keywords: political communication; information technology; campaign strategy; Internet; data mining

By
PHILIP N. HOWARD

When one considers the role of digital technologies in contemporary political life, it is easy to be caught up in the rhetoric about the potential of technology for keeping the public sphere healthy. What makes a healthy public sphere, and, rhetoric aside, how has the public sphere fared in the first decade of the digital age? Theorists such as Gabriel Tarde, Jurgen

Philip N. Howard is an assistant professor in the Department of Communication at the University of Washington in Seattle. His research focuses on the role of new media in political communication and the application of new media technologies in addressing social inequalities in the developing world.

NOTE: I am grateful for fellowship support from the Pew Internet and American Life Project and its director, Lee Rainie. For research assistance, I wish to thank Diane Beall, Maria Garrido, and Angie Vu. For their helpful comments, I wish to thank Lance Bennett, Robert Entman, Eric Klinenberg, Gina Neff, and Michael Schudson.

DOI: 10.1177/0002716204270139

Habermas, and Benedict Anderson have enunciated useful ways of assessing the health of the public sphere. Perhaps the best way to assess the health of the public sphere in the digital age is through analysis of how political campaigns go about producing political content and how citizens in turn consume this content.

The public sphere is a space where people exchange ideas and challenge one another's opinions. First, it requires shared text, regularly published and generally accessible. Obviously, "text" in this sense does not refer simply to the printed word but includes the multiple forms of content we now consume—offline and online— that contain information about political campaigns and public policy options. Citizens must be confident that everyone has access to the same quality of information. Second, it requires the act of conversation, through which we constitute the public sphere when we discuss the affairs of state and share the floor without discrimination. For practical reasons, we agree to mediators such as pollsters and newspaper editors, who assist the act of conversation by distilling opinion and presenting distinct, coherent policy options. Third, it requires a place for action: legislatures, courts, voting booths, and places of administration where decisions are made and enacted (Tarde 1898; Anderson 1991; Habermas 1991; Katz 1992). The more of these spheres the better, says Calhoun (1998), so that different people can communicate their needs to one another.

Increasingly, digital technologies are used to organize political information in the public sphere, and unlike those used in traditional media, these interactive tools allow for both the production and consumption of political content. The way digital technologies are used for decades to come will be patterned by today's design choices, and understanding the normative structures and assumptions of the architects of political information systems will help us develop some theories about what democracy and citizenship mean today.

To understand the implications of digital technologies such as the Web sites, listservs, and electronic polls for the health of the public sphere, it is important to study both the production and consumption of political culture. To help understand how political culture is produced by contemporary campaign managers, I analyze data from ethnographic observations of political consultants specializing in new media campaign strategies and a social network analysis of how this professional network developed between 1995 and 2004. To help understand how contemporary citizens consume political culture, I compare data from a series of nationally representative election surveys conducted during four campaign seasons: 1996, 1998, 2000, and 2002.

Information Technology inside the Campaigns

The process of producing political culture has changed significantly over the past decade. Political victories have often been won or lost by the quality and quantity of information that campaigns have access to—polling information about constituents, details about political competitors generated by opposition research, and status reports from different parts of campaign organization. Until recently, only larger, well-financed, national campaigns could afford the computing infrastructure and consulting services to make relational databases work toward political ends. Today, both campaigns and citizens can buy relational databases online, databases that match voters' names and addresses with voter registration records, credit card purchases, and more.

The campaign consultant's instinct is to fully manage the interaction between a candidate and a constituent, sheltering the candidate from tough questions, prompting and coaching as possible, and ending the interaction as soon as the candidate drifts off message or falters (Stromer-Galley 2000). As Larry Purpuro, the Republican National Committee (RNC) deputy chief of staff and webmaster in the 2000 campaign, explained, "Anybody involved in a campaign, regardless of their ideology, is always concerned about control. Chat is difficult to control" (quoted in Jagoda 2000, 48). Thus, while one may imagine scenarios in which digital technologies may help meet deliberative goals, campaign managers have very specific uses and gratifications for the online tools they build. One of the managers at a conservative political action committee (PAC) reveals that he has the same goals as well-known groups like MoveOn.org and MeetUp.com. "I have the same goal as the activists," he says. "I'd like to get a million people. I want the Speaker of the House to be able to send an e-mail to a million people about how the latest tax package benefits them. I want to be able to circumvent Peter Jennings." He is particularly angry about how the liberal media spins his campaigns, though he does not think of himself as a kind of information gatekeeper. "Constituents always complain about feeling disconnected from Congress because the media doesn't transmit a GOP politician's message clearly." In a sense, he is a classic republican, expressing dismay at the idea that digital technologies can be used to invigorate the public sphere by reducing the transaction costs of participating in public life:

> These people are assuming that the obstacle to participation is the labor; I think the obstacle is personal interest. Why is it better to have more people participating if their level of interest is so low that they can't even get off their butts to get a stamp and write Washington? Are their opinions really valuable if they can't afford 33 cents for that opinion? If they will blubber in front of the local TV cameras but not be bothered to actually vote? Or worse, like in Florida, they try to vote but don't take care to learn how the ballot works?

Even though he expresses cynicism at the idea that digital technologies can or should be used to engage the public, he and his colleagues working on campaigns that are more liberal increasingly integrate the technologies into campaign strategies.

Campaign consultants have developed a number of models for predicting political outcomes, and the new digital technologies help improve the accuracy of these models. Whether activating citizens or channeling the rancor at policy makers, they make increasingly reliable calculations about public elections or legislative votes on issues important to their campaigns. A high-profile consultant with Democratic Party causes joked, "We do grasstops, not grassroots," when he described his new campaigning science:

We've organized 60,000 telegrams in the last three months through our Web site. But that's because I know if I pay Western Union to deliver the telegrams, and if I buy this many banner ads with this kind of message, I can take this many impressions and convert them into this many telegrams, from these specific states, districts, or zip codes. Say we have four senators who are inclined to vote our way but not willing to commit just yet. We dig up the data on the zip codes in their districts. It should cost me $350,000 to buy 3,000,000 banner ads a month in those districts. On average, 1 percent of viewers click through a banner ad to learn more about the campaign, and on average 9 percent of those buy a message and get outraged enough to write a telegram. That gives me 270 telegrams from angry constituents to deluge four key congressional offices in the week before my vote. That's usually enough to tip a leaner [senator]. We know how much it costs to recruit an activist.

Figure 1 summarizes the political principles behind this consultant's political strategic calculations. Digital technologies make possible a very refined science of campaigning, a science that permits ever more predictable electoral or legislative outcomes. Of course, the specific ratios between campaign funding, advertising reach, and response rates vary by issue area. For example, even though about one in ten people who view a solicitation to join a campaign will join the campaign (regardless of the issue area), and one in ten of those members will be passionate enough to write letters on behalf of the campaign, these response rates are slightly higher for issues that appeal to retired adults. What makes this modeling possible is a relatively new informational product: digital political information. Political campaigns have always invested in good data, but data records of surprising detail can be quickly collected and distributed over digital technologies, and these data have become the means of creating and sorting political messages.

Digitized political information as a product. For the most part, political consultants with expertise in digital information either work for clients who want to survey the public about commercial products and services, target the public with political messages, or approach the public through particular political campaigns. They usually offer three kinds of services to their clients.

When lobby groups form, political consultants with expertise in digital technology build legitimacy for the cause by identifying members unaware of the need for representation. For example, a lobby group will often claim to represent both the firms in an industry and the consumers of that industry's goods. Increasingly, they make these claims sound legitimate by presenting data about the importance of their industry to the economy or consumers. Second, these firms do *direct-inference* public policy polling for clients. In other words, they run survey instruments that field clear questions about political topics. For example, a direct-inference question might ask, "Do you support the president?" or "Should the government offer universal health care?" and pollsters can use basic demographic features to explain variation in responses. Third, these firms increasingly do *indirect-inference* public policy polling. In other words, they collect data from survey questions, demographic data, credit card purchases, Internet activity, or voter registration files and make inferences about opinion. They might infer, without actually fielding survey questions, that a woman who is older than fifty-five, living in New

FIGURE 1
CALCULATING A POLITICAL CAMPAIGN

$350k buys 3 million online ads	4 districts for 1 week
1% click-through rate for online ads	30,000 people learn of campaign
9% accepts message and joins campaign	2,700 people join campaign
10% passionate enough to write letters	270 telegrams to Congress

4 Congressional votes moved

York, registered as a Democrat, and spending a significant amount of her income on pharmaceuticals is very likely to think the government should offer universal health care. Moreover, purchases of guns, birth control, or other consumer goods can help researchers make indirect inference about a consumer's political attitudes.

With new media tools, political campaigns can amass data from so many sources that complex relational databases can be used to extrapolate political information without ever directly contacting a respondent. In important ways, the data is "cleaner" than that taken from traditional survey methods because the contact, cooperation, and completion rates are higher. Depending on how campaigns use new media for research, they are more likely to contact exactly the people they want to sample, more of these contacts are likely to participate, and more of the survey is likely to be completed by respondents. The raw data may be cheaply purchased by anyone through the Web sites that consultants maintain, though more advanced analysis and premium data are available at greater costs. In sum, today's commercially available political information is multisourced; nuanced; and scaled from named individuals and households to residential blocks, zip codes, and electoral districts.

Digitized political information in the marketplace. The contemporary market for political information now includes a diverse population of actors, including advertising and public relations agencies, media and entertainment companies, university research institutes, pollsters, nonprofits and private foundations, political parties, Internet service providers, and PACs. Most of these organizations make deliberate efforts to associate with academic research institutions to appear more legitimate. They cohost conferences, work with academic data sets, and use university names liberally throughout their business plans and corporate identity literature.

They buy, sell, and trade political information, which in its raw form can be sold cheaply to any citizen with Internet access. In other forms, aggregated and relational political information is more expensive and priced at a point that only the more high-end lobby groups can afford. The cost of polling has dropped substantially, such that political information is not just available to presidents and political parties; it is now available to anybody who can afford it. Thus, competition between organizations in this market has driven down the price of political information, made the product more widely distributed, and made the range of products more diverse. The market for political information is more open—in a sense, democratized—than ever before, in that more people buy and sell political information. Elite political lobbyists, grassroots movements, established political parties, and "after-work" activists have access to the same informational market. Most campaigns, however, use informational products to meet one particular goal: rather than broadcasting their political messages, they seek to *narrowcast* their political message. Narrowcasting is the practice of sending particular political messages to particular people and ensuring that supporters or constituents receive the campaign messages. Has the new depth and breadth of digital information had an impact on our political sophistication? How is the public responding to the changing opportunity costs of citizenship in a digital democracy?

Consuming Political Information Online

One of the critiques of digital politics has been that citizens would choose to view political content they already know and not expose themselves to challenging ideas (Sunstein 2001). But has the consumption of political news changed this way since digital technologies became a part of our media system? It turns out this is a difficult question to answer because few sources of nationally representative data are comparable over time. Data from the Pew Center for People and the Press and the Pew Internet and American Life Project help reveal the role of digital technologies in the consumption of political culture.

Part of the analytical challenge of studying digital communication technologies in the political sphere is that these technologies are not simply a means of mass communication, easily comparable with television, radio, newspapers, or other ways of delivering news content. By definition, these technologies are interactive, allowing us to both produce and consume political content and engage with the public sphere in a way not possible with broadcast technologies. Supporters of McCain, Bradley, Dean, and other challenger candidates have effectively used tools like the Internet to organize, volunteer, and donate money. As former Governor of Minnesota Jesse Ventura's campaign manager famously quipped, "Ventura didn't win because of the Internet, but he would not have won without it." Beyond the success stories of particular online campaigns, how widely do citizens use tools like the Internet for political communication?

Between 1996 and 2002, the proportion of the adult American population who reported that the Internet was "very important" to helping them decide how to vote increased from about 14 to 20 percent (Howard 2005). A small but growing group reported that something they learned online made them decide to vote for or against a particular candidate, and in 2002, almost a quarter of the population reported having visited a Web site to research specific public policy issues. The number of people who visit Web sites that share their point of view is smaller (8 percent) than the number of people who visit Web sites that have different views (13 percent). In other words, more people report visiting Web sites that challenge their opinion than report visiting Web sites with perspectives they share. About a quarter of the adult population goes to Web sites on specific issues that interest them. Sixteen percent of the population has participated in political culture by engaging with political Web sites through several kinds of interaction, such as joining campaigns, volunteering time, donating money, or participating in polls. Similarly interesting, 16 percent of the population has reported "learning something new" from the political Web sites they visit (Howard 2005).

[Political consultant firms] collect data from survey questions, demographic data, credit card purchases, Internet activity, or voter registration files and make inferences about opinion.

More people online, doing more political activities. Table 1 reveals patterns in the rise of the Internet as a communication tool over the past four election cycles. Until recently, it made sense to present such data as percentages of the subsample of Internet users alone. Currently, however, the Internet is an integral part of campaign communications, and a significant proportion of the population uses it to learn about politics. Since the Internet is increasingly embedded in the daily lives of many U.S. citizens, it makes sense to review these data as percentages of a total sample.

In 1996, the Internet was a new political communication tool, but by 2002, two-thirds of the adult population had access to the Internet. Over this time, a growing portion of the population has chosen to learn about and contribute to political life through digital technologies.

Since 1996, the portion of the public reporting to have read a daily newspaper dropped from 50 percent to 39 percent. The proportion of people listening to news radio and watching the news or a news program on television also declined. Between 2000 and 2002, the proportion of people going online on a daily basis increased from 30 to 35 percent. This question was not asked in prior surveys, but in each of the four survey periods, the interviewers inquired if respondents had "ever" gone online, and this proportion rose from 23 percent in 1996 to 61 percent in 2002.

TABLE 1

CONSUMING POLITICAL CULTURE IN THE DIGITAL AGE—MEDIA USE
DURING FOUR ELECTIONS, 1996-2002 (IN PERCENTAGES)

	Election Year			
Media Use	1996	1998	2000	2002
Comparative media use				
Newspaper—read a daily newspaper yesterday	50[a]	47[a]	40	39
Radio news—news about election campaigns mostly provided by radio[b]	44	41	17	13
Television news—watched a news program on television yesterday	59[a]	65	64	61
Internet use, ever—ever been online to access the Internet or World Wide Web or to send and receive e-mail	23[c]	41	54	61
Internet use, yesterday—went online to access the Internet or World Wide Web or to send and receive e-mail yesterday	—	—	30	35
Online news, ever—ever been online to get news	—	—	12	41
Online news, yesterday—went online to get news yesterday	—	—	12	17
Active political research online, ever—ever been online for news or information about politics or the campaign	4	6	16	24
Active political research online, yesterday—went online for news or information about politics or the campaign yesterday	7	9	9	8
Combined media use				
Number of different sources of political content used on a daily basis[d]				
No media	—	17	14	11
One medium	—	33	29	27
Two media	—	35	36	36
Three media	—	15	20	24
Four media	—	0	1	2
Total	—	100	100	100
Voting-age population who voted[e]	49	36	51	40
Total weighted *N*	4,360	3,184	13,343	2,745

SOURCE: The author's calculations with data from the Pew Center for the People and the Press and the Pew Internet and American Life Project.

a. This question was fielded in April of that year.

b. For 1996 and 1998, radio use is based on the number of people who reported listening to news on the radio in the previous day. For 2000 and 2002, this was extracted from a multiple response question, "How did you get most of your news about the election campaigns in your state and district? From television, from newspapers, from radio or from magazines or from the Internet?"

TABLE 1 (continued)

Two responses were solicited, and a "radio" variable was created if either response was for radio. A very small fraction of respondents chose "magazine," so this category is not used in this analysis.

c. This question was fielded in July 1996.

d. Of the people who go online to access the Internet or World Wide Web or to send and receive e-mail, the number of who have the following specific media for political news: they watched the news or a news program on the previous day; they read a newspaper on the previous day; they identified radio as one of the two most important sources for information and news about the election campaigns in their state and district or reported listening to the news on the radio the previous day; they researched news online, whether a general news topic, a political news topic, or news specific to a political campaign.

e. Source: http://www.fec.gov/elections.html.

Currently, about one-third of the adult population reports having gone online sometime the previous day. Specifically, in comparison to other news media, about 41 percent of the population reports having consumed news online, and 17 percent of the population reports getting news sometime the previous day. The proportion of people who deliberately go online for political or campaign news during elections grew from 4 percent in the 1996 elections to 24 percent in the 2002 elections. The portion of adults who look for news or information about politics on a *daily* basis during campaign periods seems to be consistently less than 10 percent of the total adult population, though the proportion doing so on a weekly basis has increased modestly over the past four elections. These questions were fielded when candidate and issue campaigns would have been prominent in the news, between October and December during election years. In each survey period, however, respondents were asked if they had ever gone online to look for news or information about a specific election period, and the population who responded positively to this query doubled from 6 percent in 1996 to 13 percent in 2002.

According to the survey data, the four most commonly used media for information about politics are television news and news programs, radio, newspapers, and the Internet. Increasingly, these media reference each other, and many publish political news and campaign information in multiple formats. Still, they are for the most part distinct technologies used for consuming political culture. The Internet, additionally, allows users to help produce political culture through blogs, personal campaign sites, and other forms of content creation. Over the past four election cycles, almost two-thirds of the adult population in the United States had some online experience with political news, information, or other content.

Over this period, several interesting changes in the way we produce and consume political news took place. First, the proportion of people who never look for political information has diminished. Second, a sizable proportion of the population consistently consults at least two media types for political news. Third, the proportion of people who consult three or four other kinds of media for political news

TABLE 2

THE PUBLIC SPHERE IN THE DIGITAL AGE: MORE TEXT, SHARED LESS
(IN PERCENTAGES)

| | Election Year | | | | |
Type of Political Web Sites Visited	1996	1998	2000	2002	Change
Local political Web sites—devoted to news or information about local community	34	31	24	7	−27
Political office Web sites—leaders holding political office, such as House of Representatives, the Senate, or the White House Web sites	35	15	10	—[a]	−25
Nonpartisan Web Sites—such as those run by groups with no declared political affiliation, for example, the League of Women Voters	46	43	32	24	−22
Political candidate Web sites—set up by a candidate for political office or on behalf of a candidate for office	21	11	17	5	−16
Partisan Web sites—such as those run by the national political parties, for example, the Democrats or Republicans	24	11	18	22	−2
Issue-specific Web sites— providing information about specific issues or policies of interest, such as the environment, gun control, abortion, or health care reform	42	49	—[b]	65	+23
U.S. adults online who visited at least three of above types	31	21	16	14	−16
U.S. adults online weighted *N*	993	3,465	11,824	2,783	

SOURCE: The author's calculations with data from the Pew Center for the People and the Press and the Pew Internet and American Life Project.
a. In 2002, no question about office-holding politicians was fielded.
b. In 2000, a different phrasing was used: respondents were asked if they visited "Special Interest or Issue Specific Web Sites," and 11 percent responded yes. The phrasing, "special interest," probably discouraged responses, while providing examples such as "environment" and "health care reform" prompted responses in other years, so the number for this year is not comparable and not reported in this table.

has increased steadily, from 15 percent in 1998 to 21 percent in 2000 to 26 percent in 2002. The two clear implications from Table 1 are that the size of the group that never searched for political news decreased while the size of the group that liked consulting multiple media for news increased.

Table 2 reveals much about what kind of political content is being viewed online. Outside of news providers, six types of Web sites provide content about politics and public policy options: special interest groups, political office holders, candidates for office, partisan groups, nonpartisan groups, and community activist groups.

Figure 1 and Table 1 reveal that overall, the number of people using digital tools for political ends is increasing. Table 2 suggests, however, that the range of political actors in the public sphere whom we turn to for political information is changing. Over time, the proportion of people who visit the Web sites of elected leaders, political candidates, political parties, nonpartisan groups, and local community groups has declined significantly. Over this time, the Web sites of special interest groups have captured most of the attention of citizens looking for political content. In the 2002 campaign season, fully 65 percent of the public had turned to special interest groups to research politics and policy, while parties, leaders, candidates, and nonpartisan groups were consulted less frequently. In 1996, just less than a third of Internet users visiting political Web sites actually visited at least three different types of political Web sites. More recently, the proportion doing this has been halved.

Even though television is still the single most dominant medium for election news, those who have used the Internet for political information report different kinds of reasons for preferring it as a medium. They find the information more convenient, feel that other media do not provide enough news, get information not available elsewhere, and find that online news sources reflect their personal interests. They augment their understanding of current events, research records of political candidates, or deepen their understanding of particular issues by visiting the Web sites of national and local news organizations; commercial online services; and government, candidate, or issue-oriented Web sites. Users must invest in computers and an Internet connection, but the transaction costs of doing political research are significantly less in the digital age.

Deep Democracy, Thin Citizenship, and Social Control

One of the ironies of the digital age is that even though media sources seem to be consolidating, their success depends on their ability to deliver customized content to differentiated, issue-specific social groups. A few of these social groups are sophisticated and self-defining—social control is exercised by political campaigns that use information technologies to parse the public sphere into issue-specific constituencies as needed.

When social scientists began to treat mass media structures and content seriously, they exposed a range of social functions behind large technical systems for collecting and distributing text in the public sphere. For example, Lazarsfeld and Merton (1948) described several sources of bias and problematic outcomes, arguing that the social function of mass media was status conferral, the enforcement of social norms, and the narcotizing dysfunction. Digital communication technologies, however, are fundamentally different from mass media structures. Whereas mass media systems for broadcasting content had distinct roles for the elite producers of content and the mass consumers of content, digital communication technologies are networked, and digital media systems for narrowcasting content blur the distinction between producers and consumers of content. Despite the difference between mass and networked media systems, some scholars expected that the Internet would become a mass communication technology as more people used it. Such "massifycation" would not be a quality of the technology but of the cultural content available online. The digital age, however, does not appear to be marked by mass communication technologies in form or mass culture in content. Thus, it may surprise some observers that the proportion of people producing and consuming political content online has increased, not decreased, with the diffusion of digital technologies. Others will be surprised that the number of people who visit political Web sites for which they already feel an affinity is smaller than the number of people who visit Web sites with content that challenges their convictions. The public sphere actors we seem to turn to most appear to be specialized and issue specific.

The new market for digital political information. Most of the scholarship assessing the political role of new media has concentrated on individual users as solitary voters who collect and evaluate political information or who decide that collecting and evaluating political information is a low priority (Howard and Milstein 2003). The common analytical frame for this work situates these users within an abstract public sphere. In contrast, one of the most important roles for new media in politics has been in opening up *the market for political information*. Political information often includes details about personal identity and opinion that allow researchers to make relational and explanatory inferences. This information about individuals is collected from a variety of sources, including credit card purchases, Internet activities, and academic surveys. It is used to infer, for example, political preferences based on gender, race, or consumer activity.

Several companies now amass and market detailed profiles of citizens using traditional survey and data-mining methods, but both have also developed powerful new media tools to complement traditional methods. Their spider programs crawl through the Web, automatically collecting Web site content, such as personal contact information or an organization's press releases. They often deploy unsolicited e-mails to gather or spread information for commercial or political marketing campaigns.

Spyware, a kind of software that is covertly installed on users' computers during Internet use, reports a user's Web activities back to the sponsoring organization. Spyware can be covertly installed on a user's computer, but even if it is consensually installed, the user rarely understands how the software works and often forgets that it is recording activities. Many companies have developed variations of these tools, but political consultants now apply them to gathering information about political preferences. Consultants combine the latest statistical methods with Web-based sampling techniques to generate reliable information about how political characters and policy options play in the public sphere.

Whereas traditional survey methods took several weeks to generate results, Web-based surveys collected more nuanced polling data in less time (Witte and Howard 2002). Most digital campaigns claim to only share aggregated, not personally identifiable, information with other campaigns, but a surprising amount of data leaks as political consultants take their talents—and data—from campaign to campaign. In the 2000 campaign season, several politicians simply altered their Web sites' privacy policies when campaign managers realized that they had collected politically and commercially valuable data from their supporters.

But these consultants have a problematic role in this new marketplace for political information: they mislead people into surrendering personal information by promising participants that expressing an opinion to business leaders and politicians will greatly influence corporations and government, guiding the ways products and services are developed. Digital campaigns commonly tell prospective participants they will be joining a revolution in research that will irrevocably alter approaches to the collection and application of information and that participation is part of a citizen's duty to help good governance. After several months, many panelists forget that spyware is installed on their machines.

Political data-mining companies take advantage of legal protections for their product. An example of a move in this direction can be found in the dozens of words that pollsters, political consultants, and political data miners have already trademarked, including *belief, communication, connectedness, deliberative, empathy, fairness, inclusiveness,* and *learner.* Thus, digital campaigns take advantage of the rhetoric about new media technologies to excite citizens into sharing data. Moreover, it conflates the incentive to participate as a consumer with the incentive to participate as a citizen. Finally, the political information that used to circulate in the public sphere now circulates in a marketplace where it is priced, trademarked, and sold.

The vast majority of U.S. legislators, presidential candidates, and both Democratic and Republican parties (at both the state and national level) have used political data-mining firms to modernize their campaigns. Lobbyists also combine databases and software to target potential constituents and supporters; generate campaign awareness; solicit contributions through the Internet, telephone, mail, and door-to-door efforts; and improve press relations and public relations. They use databases and software to reach audiences based on demographic, geographic, or political criteria. Digital campaigns also accept, process, authenticate, analyze, and disclose contributions received through the Internet.

Many political databases came from companies that provided free e-mail service and required subscribers to fill out questionnaires. Initial questionnaires collect the demographics of database members, such as age, gender, income, expected major purchases, hobbies, interests, family size, and education. This information is supplemented using spyware to track database members' patterns of computer use. The largest political databases, in fact, now include the information of more than 150 million registered voters in the United States, as culled from state and local boards of elections, departments of motor vehicles, municipal licensing agencies, and social science survey data. Relational databases commonly include dates of birth, dates of voter or motor vehicle registration, residential addresses, family details, political jurisdictions, and party affiliations. Through digital technologies, data some of us consider private information—from e-mail addresses and telephone numbers to credit card purchases, political preferences, and income status—have been added to these databases. Moreover, specialist lobby organizations buy, sell, and trade data regularly, and several political consulting houses have detailed, expanding information on more than three-quarters of the American voting public, as well as on hundreds of thousands of unregistered voters.

The vast majority of U.S. legislators, presidential candidates, and both Democratic and Republican parties (at both the state and national level) have used political data-mining firms to modernize their campaigns.

Most of these firms have compiled their digital resources without the explicit or informed consent of the people in the databases, and even though some of the data is from public records, a significant amount of it is *not*. In other words, most of the data is not being used in ways that we would imagine serve a public interest. On the contrary, combining various sources of information paints a highly detailed picture of our private interests.

The combined relational databases are used to serve the private interests of political candidates or lobbyist campaigns—to uniquely customize messages to manipulate certain responses from particular individuals in the database. Even if some citizens initially gave consent for the use of their political information, most would not have consented to its continuous aggregation and applications in unexpected ways. Both political organizations and commercial industry are able to drive traffic to their Web sites by directing customized banner and e-mail advertisements via the political, demographic, and commercial characteristic profiles of members of the database. In addition, partner or affinity campaigns share data on prospective sympathizers, members of the public, or elected officials.

Voter registration records are governed by complex regulations. More than twenty-five states, including California, prohibit the commercial use of voter registration records. Yet campaigns run by PACs are registered as nonprofit charities and are exempt from many of these restrictions. This allows for the distribution of political information through Web sites that deliver raw data processed as mailing labels, telephone sheets, walk lists, polling samples, or any files suitable for import into many current software programs.

In the digital age, political information has become a highly marketable, easily collected, quickly distributed, cultural product. That this political information is bought and sold is not new. However, the quality of the product and the structure of the market evolved significantly once political campaigns started using new media technologies to collect and distribute information.

Direct democracy through the market? The market for political information has grown significantly and now includes a more diverse group of actors buying and selling a wider and deeper range of informational politics. While I have been speaking in the abstract about consumers, citizens, and users, it is important to note that they are real people. All too often, literature that searches for the positive, negative, or neutral political implications of new media tools also speaks of abstracted, isolated technology users, missing interesting changes in the qualities of political information and the structure of the market in political information.

While political lobbyists have profiled the majority of readers of this article, four of every ten readers are profiled in exhaustive detail in terms of identity and political opinion. These detailed profiles are used to draw direct and indirect inferences in the commercial and political sphere. Political actors then use this information to design the messages we receive. In the end, this means a growing amount of the political and consumer content we see has been tailor-made for us alone and that others are getting messages uniquely tailored for them.

Smaller data-mining firms and consulting houses have also begun to collaborate internationally, starting in the United Kingdom, Canada, and Australia, seeing a potential opportunity for using international databases to implement U.S.-style political campaigns in established and emerging democracies. Thus, the details of the identities and opinions of citizens of other countries are also being gathered and traded to create a global market for political information.

Such detailed knowledge about individuals is used to exercise panoptical and discursive power (Foucault 1977, 1999; Poster 1990, 1995), but political information is also a key component of the long-observed surveillance duty of governance (Giddens 1987; Webster 1995; Scott 1998). Contemporary political theorists may agree that the state is defined as a social organization with legitimate control of both the machinery of violence and the machinery of surveillance, but I find that, increasingly, other entities have purview over political information. The raw political data are available to both powerful lobbyists and individual citizens, so even though some organizations have more resources to bear on analyzing political data, individuals can increasingly use the same data to observe organizational behavior in the political context.

With new media, both political and commercial organizations conduct surveillance of citizen opinion on public policy questions. Even though individuals' identities and opinions are bought and sold in the open electronic marketplace, the technologies that allow indirect inference about opinions make it less necessary for political organizations to attend to freely voiced views. Customizing political and commercial messages is an old marketing trick, but the degree of tailoring possible with new media is so much more powerful that political information today is a significantly different product.

Customizing political messages to the degree possible with new media reduces the quality and quantity of shared text in the public sphere, restricting our future supplies of political information based on assumptions about the opinions and identities of our past. Increasingly, an important part of our political participation occurs somewhat beyond our control, co-opted into a highly privatized and often covert sphere, one that trades, channels, and filters our political information, thus denying a forum for its direct, free, and deliberate exchange.

Even if some citizens initially gave consent for the use of their political information, most would not have consented to its continuous aggregation and applications in unexpected ways.

Where is the shared text? The competition between political campaigns is one of the central acts of democratic discourse. This competition results, however, in smaller pieces of text being shared by smaller and smaller groups of people. Experienced Internet users, for instance, self-segment by programming their news services to provide particular content; nonusers generate other kinds of electronic information that reveals political preferences to tech-savvy lobbyists. The information technologies that are available to the public are those that prevent random encounters with political content. They are designed to entrench a citizen's political norms through software that privileges some content over other content. Some citizens make the original expression of preferences by visiting political Web sites and self-identifying as fiscally conservative, environmentally progressive, or socially liberal, for example. They develop their news accounts with political parties or PACs such as the National Rifle Association, Christian Coalition, or Sierra Club.

The campaign managers of these organizations take great interest in preparing content for their membership by reducing their members' exposure to content from groups with competing political agendas, decreasing the amount of random exposure to content that might provide evidentiary challenges to the group's norms, and editorializing a context to even the most innocuous news events. Internet search engines privilege some content over other content, political webmasters have developed tricks to direct the results of casual searches for politi-cal information, and there are a wide range of hurdles to seeking information from government agencies (Introna and Nissenbum 2000; Hargittai 2003).

If a shared text is important to the public sphere, journalists have a key role in editing content on behalf of the public. Obviously, no text can be universally shared among the citizenry, and practically speaking, media systems distribute political content to most people, most of the time; a degree of randomness ensures that everybody is exposed to some new ideas some of the time. Digital technologies remove the random distribution of content, something that occurs when people casually pick up news stories from the newspapers they read and television they watch. Internet users either choose to consume political content or they do not. Campaigns either choose to produce content for you or they do not. More people are sharing less. Moreover, in the digital age, technologies like the Internet are hav-ing a significant impact on the quality and quantity of shared text in the public sphere. For those who know how to find it, there is more rich detail on public policy options and a range of interesting new tools for expressing and measuring diverse political opinions.

In the abstract, a healthy public sphere needs shared text and acts of conversa-tion. Survey research suggests that Americans increasingly use digital tools to research politics and engage their friends, family, and political leaders in discus-sion. Ethnographic observation suggests, however, that political campaign strate-gies are increasingly geared toward fragmenting the public sphere, either by send-ing particular messages to particular people or by designing tools for citizens to encode their personal interests and sequester their consumption of news. Although the excitement of the digital age was based in technological potential, we can be less confident that everyone in our polity has access to the same quality of regularly published, generally accessible, political information.

References

Anderson, B. 1991. *Imagined communities: Reflections on the origin and spread of nationalism.* London: Verso.

Calhoun, C. 1998. Community without propinquity revisited: Communications technology and the transfor-mation of the urban public sphere. *Sociological Inquiry* 68 (3): 373-97.

Foucault, M. 1977. *Discipline and punish: The birth of the prison.* New York: Pantheon.

———. 1999. Power as knowledge. In *Social theory, the multicultural and classic readings*, ed. C. Lemert, 475-81. Boulder, CO: Westview.

Giddens, A. 1987. *Social theory and modern sociology.* Stanford, CA: Stanford University Press.

Habermas, J. 1991. *The structural transformation of the public sphere.* Cambridge, MA: MIT Press.

Hargittai, E. 2003. Serving citizens' needs: Minimizing online hurdles to accessing government information. *IT & Society* 1 (3): 27-41.

Howard, P. N. 2005. *Politics in code: Franchise and representation in the age of new media.* Cambridge: Cam-bridge University Press.

Howard, P. N., and T. J. Milstein 2003. Spiders, spam, and spyware: New media and the market for political information. In *Internet Studies 1.0*, ed. M. Consalvo. New York: Peter Lang.

Introna, L., and H. Nissenbum. 2000. Shaping the Web: Why the politics of search engines matters. *The Information Society* 16 (3): 1-17.

Jagoda, K. 2000. *E-voter study 2000: Measuring the effectiveness of the Internet in election 2000*. Washington, DC: E-Voter Institute.

Katz, E. 1992. On parenting a paradigm: Gabriel Tarde's agenda for opinion and communication research. *International Journal of Public Opinion Research* 4:80-85.

Lazarsfeld, P. F., and R. K. Merton. 1948. Mass-communication, popular taste, and organized social action. In *The communication of ideas*. ed. L. Bryson, 95-118. New York: Harper & Brothers.

Poster, M. 1990. *The mode of information*. Cambridge, UK: Polity.

———. 1995. *The second media age*. Cambridge, UK: Polity.

Scott, J. C. 1998. *Seeing like a state: How certain schemes to improve the human condition have failed*. New Haven, CT: Yale University Press.

Stromer-Galley, J. 2000. Online interaction and why candidates avoid it. *Journal of Communication* 50 (4): 111-32.

Sunstein, C. R. 2001. *Republic.com*. Princeton, NJ: Princeton University Press.

Tarde, G. 1898. *Opinion and conversation. L'opinion Et La Foule*. Paris: Alcan.

Webster, F. 1995. *Theories of the information society*. London: Routledge.

Witte, J., and P. N. Howard 2002. The future of polling: Relational inference and the development of Internet survey instruments. In *Navigating public opinion: Polls, policy and the future of American democracy*, ed. J. Manza, F. L. Cook, and B. I. Page, 272-89. New York: Oxford University Press.

How do civic associations in Eastern Europe organize themselves online? Based on data collected on 1,585 East European civil society Web sites, the authors identify five emergent genres of organizing technologies: newsletters, interactive platforms, multilingual solicitations, directories, and brochures. These clusters do not correspond to stages of development. Moreover, newer Web sites are more likely to be typical of their genre, suggesting that forms are becoming more distinctive. In contrast to the utopian image of a de-territorialized, participatory global civil society, the authors' examination of the structure of hyperlinks finds that transnational types of Web sites are not inclined to be participatory. Whereas other paradigms focus on inequality of users' online access, the authors probe inequality in the accessibility of Web sites to potential users through search engine technology and show how this varies across different types of civil society Web sites.

Keywords: technology; Internet; civil society; Eastern Europe; participation; Web site analysis

Organizing Technologies: Genre Forms of Online Civic Association in Eastern Europe

By
BALÁZS VEDRES,
LÁSZLÓ BRUSZT,
and
DAVID STARK

After "Internet and Society"

One of the challenges of exploring the coevolution of organizational forms and emergent technologies is to take seriously the expectations triggered by a new technology. Taking them seriously does not mean accepting their sometimes wildly exaggerated claims but, instead, understanding the underlying assumptions about technology and society that give rise to them. The popular as well as the scholarly literature on the Internet and the public sphere is filled with excitement about the transformative potential of new information and interactive

Balázs Vedres is an assistant professor at the Department of Sociology and Social Anthropology, Central European University, and received his graduate training at the Department of Sociology, Columbia University. He is an international fellow of the Santa Fe Institute and a junior fellow of Collegium Budapest. His research interests include economic sociology, economic transformation, social networks, and historical and discourse analy-

NOTE: Research for this article was supported by NSF Grant N 0115378 and by the Open Society Institute Information Program (Budapest).

technologies that, it was believed, would open a new era of an expanded and vibrant global civil society.

The possibility for connectivity was seen as the key element in this transformation. The new technologies would overcome the one-to-many character of the once-dominant mass media in favor of unmediated connections among the new global citizens. They would revive a dormant public sphere by creating new domains for deliberation. Because connectivity was interactive, the virtual public sphere would be a new field that was, above all, participatory. In place of the passive consumers of the mass communication model or of the tired electorate of the old polity, the cybercitizen would be a user as producer, contributing to online debates and interacting directly with others. Connectivity, moreover, would not only reshape the citizen but would also reshape the topography and the geography of the public sphere. Because technology provided the means for anyone with a network connection to link to someone similarly networked anywhere else on the planet, the virtual public sphere would become increasingly de-territorialized. In the e-topic visions, an imaginary premodern polis became fused with the globally interactive technologies of the twenty-first century (for a critical discussion of this literature, see Hand and Sandywell 2002).

Amid this overheated rhetoric, sociologists posed the sobering question, Is connectivity really so ubiquitous? Who has access? How are patterns of usage such as hours online and types of online activity (e-mailing, browsing, shopping, gaming, instant messaging, etc.) stratified? And how do these patterns correlate with other demographic or social class variables such as gender, age, occupation, income, level of education, and so on? The resulting body of work represents an already

sis methods. His recent publications concern the interdependence of strategizing agents and evolving network structures in large-scale social change in the fields of business networks, political discourse, and civil society organizations.

László Bruszt is a professor at the Department of Social and Political Sciences at the European University Institute (Florence). In his earlier research, he has dealt with issues of institutional transformation in the postcommunist countries. His more recent studies focus on the interplay between transnationalization, institutional development, and economic change. He is currently conducting research on the evolution of regional interorganizational networks in Central Europe and the formation of regional developmental regimes. Together with David Stark and Balázs Vedres, he is involved in an ongoing research on the technologies of civil society. His recent publications include "Making Markets and Eastern Enlargement: Diverging Convergence?" in West European Politics *(2002/2) and "Market Making as State Making: Constitutions and Economic Development in Postcommunist Eastern Europe" in* Constitutional Political Economy *(2002/1).*

David Stark is Arthur Lehman Professor of Sociology and International Affairs at Columbia University where he directs the Center on Organizational Innovation (www.coi.columbia.edu/). He is an external faculty member of the Santa Fe Institute. Stark has carried out field research in Hungarian factories before and after 1989, in new media startups in Manhattan before and after the dot-com crash, and in a World Financial Center trading room before and after the attack on September 11, 2001. Supported by grants from the National Science Foundation, he is currently conducting research on the evolution of interorganizational networks in Hungary and on new technologies of deliberation and representation in the rebuilding of Lower Manhattan. Stark's publications and recent working papers are available online at www.sociology.columbia.edu/people/faculty/stark/index.html.

well-developed framework that many refer to as the "Internet and Society" paradigm.[1] Exemplary in its relentless determination to chart the demographics of Web usage has been the research undertaken under the sponsorship of the Pew Project on "Internet and American Life" (see http://www.pewinternet.org/reports.asp), as indicated by this sample of titles in its recent reports:

"Asian-Americans and the Internet: The Young and the Connected"
"Wired Seniors: A Fervent Few, Inspired by Family Ties"
"Hispanics and the Internet"
"African-Americans and the Internet"
"College Students and the Web"

If the Internet enjoys a special distinction, it might be that its end-users are the most systematically studied (both for commercial and scholarly purposes) of any newly introduced technology in history.

The Internet and Society paradigm offers an important corrective to the utopian promises of the early literature on the virtual public sphere. But as the flip side of the utopian framework—both emphasizing connectivity, one pointing to transformative potential, the other pointing to obstacles (whether in access or skills)—the Internet and Society approach fails to challenge widely held assumptions about technology. Our objection, to pose it succinctly, is less with the terms "Internet" or "Society" than with the "and,"[2] signaling that technology is something external to society.[3] As sociologists, we agree that our task is to study the social, but we argue for a sociology in which technology is a constituent part of the social.[4] While we reject the utopian approach that tries to deduce social effects from the properties of technology, we also depart from approaches that focus solely on the effects of the properties of social structure. Instead of trying to understand the structure of civic organization mechanistically from the properties of the new technology, and instead of analyzing the ways social structures might limit these effects, we propose to study combinations of technologies, actors, and types of actions yielding different emerging structures of online civic association.

In this departure, we are strongly influenced by insights from science and technology studies. As Bruno Latour (1991) and Michel Callon (1991) have argued, social network analysis, as practiced by American sociologists, typically focuses only on ties between persons (or anthropomorphized organizations) ignoring the sociotechnical features of organizations as ties among persons and things. Similarly, Hutchins (1995) argued that intelligence is socially distributed—the "social" includes humans and their nonhuman artifacts—as he demonstrated in a painstakingly detailed analysis of how a navy destroyer is navigated into harbor after a power failure. In a pathbreaking study of the relationship between organizational form and technology, Yates (1989) pointed to the importance of such prosaic artifacts as the file folder and the filing cabinet in the emergence of bureaucratic organizations. Eisenstein (1993) demonstrated that the organization of modern science is inseparable from print technology; Orlikowski (2000) criticized the "appropriationist" view that uses are inscribed in technology; and Barley (1986) provided a set of theoretical tools to grasp how technology interacts with organizational structure. As Boczkowski (2004) demonstrated in his study of online newspapers, technologies offer "affordances." Although you cannot do just anything you want with a given technology, a given technology typically "affords" more than one application. The history of technology, and of communication technologies in particular, is replete with examples of how technologies, such as the telephone (Fischer 1992), coevolved with social practices in ways that departed dramatically from the usage originally inscribed by their designers.

The history of technology, and of communication technologies in particular, is replete with examples of how technologies . . . coevolved with social practices in ways that departed dramatically from the usage originally inscribed by their designers.

The postsocialist societies of Eastern Europe provide an extraordinary laboratory for exploring the coevolution of organizational forms and interactive technology: the emergence of voluntary associations in the region coincides with the digital revolution. Prior to 1989, there were almost no nongovernmental organizations (NGOs) in the conventional sense in Eastern Europe, and the Internet was in its infancy. Before 1989, the small number of beleaguered voluntary associations communicated by samizdat. With no access to photocopy machines, they attached special springs to typewriter keys to produce up to seven carbon copies of their documents. In Prague, for example, it was not uncommon for the members of an underground philosophy seminar to circulate texts that were literally in manuscript—some in the handwriting of elementary school children who had painstakingly copied a parent's writings so it could circulate more widely. Today, both NGOs and the Internet are experiencing exponential growth throughout the region. In Hungary, for example, the number of NGOs jumped to about fifteen thousand in the first year after the democratic transition and now stands at more than fifty thousand, while at the same time, by conservative estimates, the number of people online doubles every year, and the number of Web sites doubles every six months (Kuti 2001). In little more than a decade, the technological framework in which voluntary associations are operating has gone from the limitations of a pre-Guttenberg setting to the opportunities of advanced communication technologies.

Our task in this article is to examine civil society Web sites. As our title, "Organizing Technologies," suggests, we study technologies of organizing and, in doing so, study how these technologies are organized. Web site technologies can be deployed by civic associations and social movements for organizing civil society. From the array of available technologies, which are featured on their Web sites? Just as we can think about conventional (offline) organizations as particular bundles of routines, we think here about online organization as particular bundles of features. If technology was determinant, then we would expect to find little systematic variation in that array. But as we shall see, we do find identifiable patterns of variation suggesting that civic associations are organizing technologies in distinctive ways. Restated, we are examining a new field of political representation: with the emergence of NGOs, we find new types of actors making new kinds of representational claims outside of electoral politics within a new representational medium. In asking how organizations re-present themselves online, we are examining the technologies of politics. In charting the characteristic patterns of how particular features are combined, we are examining the organization of technology.

Data

To chart structuration processes in the web of civil society in East Central Europe, we gathered data from 1,586 prominent civil society Web sites across the four countries in the region. Table 1 shows the distribution.

Web site data for each of the four countries were collected between March and June 2002 by native-language speakers whom we trained in the sample selection and coding procedures.[5] We visited each Web site and used a questionnaire to record data on specific features, adopting a procedure that we had refined in a previous pilot project of six hundred Web sites. In that pilot project, we found that many site features involved different ways of organizing relations with other actors: visitors, members, clients and/or potential constituents, actual or potential donors, other organizations, and so on. These features are the elementary forms of online civic organizing. They allow for different forms of activity: from getting in touch with the NGO; to consulting information about its activities, its field of action, or its allies; to more active forms of participation in online and offline actions.[6] Our task is to identify the distinctive patterns in which these relational features are combined.

For each Web site, we recorded the presence or absence of thirteen features, yielding the following variables:

1. Offline reachability: whether a user could find a street address or a phone number of the sponsoring organization listed on the Web site.[7]
2. The Web site includes an e-mail address to reach the organization.
3. The site includes a mission statement.
4. The site includes a feature of downloadable annual reports or accounts of fund-raising.
5. The presence of a distinct news section.
6. The site includes a calendar of events or a list of scheduled meetings.
7. The Web site posts information about conferences.

TABLE 1

THE DISTRIBUTION OF WEB SITES BY COUNTRIES

Country	Number of Web Sites
Czech Republic	484
Hungary	405
Poland	314
Slovakia	383
Total	1,586

8. Whether the site is available to readers in different languages.
9. The site includes a separate page or dedicated section specifically for links to other Web sites.
10. Whether a user/visitor to the Web site can sign up online to join the group or organization or to register online to join listservs or receive e-mailings of various kinds.
11. The potential to participate online through such features as bulletin boards and chat rooms or to post documents directly to the site.
12. An online database of any kind that can be used on the Web site or downloaded from it.
13. The Web site includes an online survey.

Table 2 reports the overall frequencies of the feature variables in our population of prominent civil society Web sites.

Clusters of Civil Society Web Sites

How are these features selected and combined in actual Web sites? The logical permutations of the thirteen variables make it possible that we could find as many different types of Web sites as the total number in our population. That would be a finding of no pattern at all. Another possibility is that a single model or blueprint is encoded in the technology of the Web. The topology of such a field would be smooth and single-peaked. At its apex would be the modal Web sites that conform most fully to that blueprint. Scattered randomly around the center would be those Web sites that have not yet realized the full potential for civil society Web sites, whether because the creators of these Web site have not yet learned how to use the technology efficiently or whether, because of limited time or lack of resources, they have not been able to complete their site construction. In the single-mode model, these Web sites are expected to converge to the blueprint.

To chart the landscape of Web sites, we used cluster analysis. The result of the Ward-clustering (Ward 1963) partitions our cases into five groups, explaining 38 percent of the variance of Web site features. Table 3 presents the five clusters and the percentage of Web sites within each cluster that have a given feature. For each feature, we also present an adjusted residual that indicates whether the given feature is significantly more or less common in the given cluster than in the overall population. An adjusted residual greater than two indicates that Web sites in that

TABLE 2

THE FREQUENCIES OF WEB SITE FEATURE VARIABLES

Variable	Description	Percentage
OFFREACH	Offline reachability (address, phone number indicated)	86.6
EMAIL	E-mail address indicated	85.5
MISSION	Mission statement	63.7
REPORT	Annual report, information about funders	36.5
NEWS	News section	42.2
CALMEET	Calendar of events, information on meetings	41.7
CONF	Information about conferences	16.1
MORELANG	Site fully or partly available in other languages	33.4
LINKPAGE	Separate link-page	31.0
SIGNUP	One can sign up for alerts, newsletter or e-mail lists; or one can register as member, join the organization online	31.5
PARTICIPATE	There is a bulletin board, chat room, or users can post documents on the site by other means	21.1
DATABASE	Online database	15.9
SURVEY	Online survey	5.1

cluster are significantly more likely to have that feature than average. A residual less than minus two indicates that Web sites in the cluster are significantly less likely to have the feature (Agresti 2002).

Each of the clusters represents a distinctive form of online organization. That is, in place of a single model to which all Web sites conform to a greater or lesser degree, we found five relatively coherent models or blueprints. The creators of civil society Web sites are neither rigidly following a single model nor randomly selecting features. They actively shape their Web sites, but they do so along clearly identifiable types or scripts. As we shall see on closer inspection, four of these types have precursors in print genres: newsletters, solicitations, brochures, and directories. A fifth type, the interactive platform, is an emergent online genre. Faced with new technologies, the creators of Web sites turn to already-existing cultural forms as templates for action. Genre structures organization.

Online Genres

1. Newsletters. Making up nearly one-third of the NGO Web sites, this cluster is the most numerous online organizational form. Web sites of this type have a much higher than average probability of including calendars of events or information about meetings. In fact, 90.3 percent of these Web sites do include such a feature, and almost 28 percent of them (higher than any of the other clusters) provide information about conferences. These Web sites are also the most likely to have a "news" feature about the activities of the NGO. Web sites in this cluster function as *online newsletters* of ongoing activities, regularly reporting on activities that have

TABLE 3
GENRE FORMS OF CIVIL SOCIETY WEB SITES

	Clusters of Web Site Features										Total
	1. Newsletter		2. Interactive		3. Solicitation		4. Directory		5. Brochure		
	a	b	a	b	a	b	a	b	a	b	a
CALMEET	90.3	+ +	29.1	- -	36.3		1.1	- -	5.5	- -	41.7
NEWS	62.4	+ +	47.2	+	32.5	-	19.6	- -	23.7	- -	42.2
CONF	29.0	+ +	13.1		21.8	+	0.5	- -	3.8	- -	16.1
PARTICIPATE	16.1	-	61.9	+ +	6.8	- -	2.7	- -	0.7	- -	21.1
SIGNUP	34.6		63.7	+ +	13.7	- -	9.0	- -	13.8	- -	31.5
SURVEY	3.8		12.0	+ +	3.0		2.7		1.7	-	5.1
DATABASE	16.3		21.3	+	17.1		10.6	-	10.7		15.9
MORELANG	27.4	-	29.3		95.3	+ +	24.9	-	4.8	- -	33.4
REPORT	41.7	+	18.7	- -	52.1	+ +	17.5	- -	50.5	+ +	36.5
EMAIL	90.3	+	79.5	-	92.3	+	92.1	+	75.3	- -	85.5
LINKPAGE	31.2		38.4	+	23.1	-	64.0	+ +	6.2	- -	31.0
MISSION	60.2		60.8		74.8	+	38.6		81.1	+ +	63.8
OFFREACH	88.7	-	71.7	- -	96.6	+ +	84.1	- -	95.9	+ +	86.6
Total	100		100		100		100		100		100
n	497		375		234		189		291		1,586
Percentage	31.3		23.6		14.8		11.9		18.4		100

NOTE: a column = percentage of Web sites within the genre form that has the feature indicated. b column = pluses and minuses represent the adjusted standardized residual of the frequency of the given feature. One plus means that the residual is greater than two, two pluses indicate that the residual is greater than four. One minus, accordingly, indicates a residual of at least minus two, while two minuses indicate a residual less than minus four.

178

already taken place and providing information about the possibilities for participation in upcoming offline events. Consistent with this orientation to a user who is an actual or potential member, these Web sites frequently make use of technologies of registration, allowing constituents to join the organization online and sign up to receive more specific information about the activities of the NGO. Significantly less likely to translate their materials into other languages, these Web sites are oriented to domestic users, whom they seek to get involved in their offline activities. Involvement in this case does not, however, extend to online participation, because these Web sites are significantly less likely to include such features. These online newsletters select, among the affordances on the Web, those features that target their members and constituents with information that encourages them to participate in the offline activities of the organization.

2. Interactive platforms. This is the second largest cluster in our population of civil society Web sites with nearly 24 percent of the NGOs grouped in this category. Almost 62 percent of these Web sites include features that allow online participation—by far the highest among our five clusters. The user they are targeting seems to be active and experienced in the online environment: these Web sites are likely to have link-pages for their users and, more significant, they are most likely to allow users to join the organization online or sign up for various kinds of online services (almost two-thirds of their Web sites include such features), to provide online databases, and to use the Web to survey their members or constituents. Consistent with this orientation to individual members, these sites are least likely to provide formal annual reports or information about funders, and they are unlikely to translate their materials into foreign languages. Moreover, consistent with their online orientation, they are least likely to provide information about their offline reachability (more than 25 percent of these Web sites contain neither an offline address nor a phone number). When compared to the average Web site, these sites are significantly less likely to provide an e-mail address, a finding that may seem curious given their otherwise strong online sensibility. But this finding is meaningful in light of the full ensemble of features: perhaps even more important than *reaching the "organization,"* users of these interactive sites might want—and by the ensemble of features presented are most encouraged—to *reach each other.* As the Web sites among our population with the richest opportunities for online conversation with other users, for online participation, for using online databases, and for posting materials online, the format of these Web sites is as a *platform for online interactivity.*

3. Multilingual solicitations. The most distinguishing feature of the Web sites grouped in this cluster (representing about 15 percent of the population) is that nearly all of them (95.3 percent) post their site in more than one language version. Across all clusters in the overall average, only one in three Web sites adopts this feature. In addition to this pronounced multilingual character, Web sites in this cluster are more likely to use the Web to establish their professional standing as the beneficiaries of donors and the (formally accountable) spenders of money. On one hand, they are more likely to have their annual reports and fund-raising information on the Web; on the other, they are less likely to provide an ongoing news feature and to provide for forms of online interactivity. The contrast with the interactive platforms is telling. Solicitation Web sites are three times more likely than the interactive platforms to post reports that establish their legitimacy on a standardized professional basis. Conversely, they are nine times less likely to adopt features that allow for online participation and nearly five times less likely to attempt to attract new members by allowing them to use online forms or join the organization online. Although about 22 percent of these sites post information about conferences, they are far less likely than the more activist newsletters to post calendars or announcements about meetings (36 percent compared to 90 percent). Thus, whereas the Web sites in our first and second clusters appear to be organizing members for online or offline activities, these multilingual solicitations are *oriented to other organizations*, perhaps especially to foreign donors. The organizations creating these Web sites are highly reachable: 97 percent provide an address or a phone number, and 92 percent provide an e-mail address where they can be contacted. But when you reach their Web sites, you are less likely than on the average site to find a link-page feature from which you can reach other (potentially competitor?) organizations.

4. Directories. Among the civil society Web sites in our population, about 12 percent are grouped in our fourth, and smallest, cluster, distinguished by the finding that nearly two-thirds of these Web sites post a link-page. Apart from one other variable, an e-mail contact address, these sites are below average on every other feature (that is, the adjusted residuals are negative). They are significantly less likely to have information about conferences and meetings, provide online databases, and adopt various forms of online registration or participation; and among all the clusters, they are least likely to post mission statements and include features of formal accountability. These Web sites are *virtual directories*. Thus, they differ markedly from the online newsletters: Web sites in this cluster are ninety times less likely to have a calendar of events or information about meetings than the sites of the newsletter cluster. They also differ from the sites of the interactive platform cluster in that they are twenty-three times less likely to use the most interactive features of Web technology: bulletin boards, online chat rooms, and sections for member uploads. Finally, they differ from the multilingual solicitors in that they are much less likely to have an annual report or information on fund-raising on their Web sites. About one-quarter of these Web sites have a version of the Web site in more than one language; one in five has a "news" feature; and one in ten provides an online database. These sites are oriented to a user who is expected to be neither a prospective member nor a prospective donor (at least not of, or to, the hosting NGO itself). When you visit these Web sites, what you are most likely to be able to do is *move on to other Web sites* by means of an organized collection of links. In that respect, these Web sites maintain the avenues of online civil society by creating hyperlinks that keep other Web sites connected and accessible.

5. *Brochures*. About 18 percent of our NGO Web sites are grouped in this last cluster characterized as *digital brochures*. The features of the Web that they are most likely to combine are information on offline reachability, a mission statement, and features of formal accountability. Across all the clusters, these Web sites are least likely to include any of the other available features of Web technology. In comparison to the virtual directories, they are ten times less likely to have link pages. Although they do provide more information about their offline activities than the directories, they are much less eventful when compared to the Web sites of the online newsletters—considerably less likely to have a news feature (24 percent compared to 62 percent) and seventeen times less likely to post information about meetings. When compared to the multilingual solicitations, they make even less use of the interactive affordances of Web technology; but the most salient difference between these two clusters is that whereas 95 percent of the Web sites in the former cluster have multilingual versions, only 5 percent of the sites in the pure brochure cluster offer versions in more than one language. This group of Web sites represents a minimal participation in the web of civil society.

Age of Web Sites and Genre Forms

Consistent with the idea that combinations of technological affordances, actors, and actions yield emerging structures, we interpret the clusters of Web site features that we have found as distinct genre forms for organizing technologies. Technology is enacted, rather than encoded. An alterative explanation is that these typical combinations of features are simply stages of development in building a civil society Web site, whereby actors "appropriate" technology. Thinking of the brochure cluster, for example, one might be tempted to assume that this constellation of Web site features signifies a first phase, a temporary placeholder on the Web until further features can be added. In a similar vein, the participatory cluster of interactive platforms could be thought of as an advanced stage where civil society Web sites arrive once their creators are thoroughly familiarized with the potential of online technologies. Whereas a brochure is a first step in the life course of a civil society Web site, interactive platforms come later as the full realization of the promise of the technology.[8]

To test this stage hypothesis, we collected information about the age of each Web site in our population. A chi-square test finds no difference between Web site clusters in terms of age (chi-square = 1.358, p = .852). Based on this finding (and other related tests with various statistical controls), we can reject the hypothesis that Web site feature clusters are stages in Web site development or progression along the path to realizing the one real civil society Web site. It is more likely that Web site features clusters are indeed emerging genre forms of civil society Web presence.

If clusters do not correspond to stages of development toward a blueprinted ideal civil society Web site, is the web of civil society in Eastern Europe evolving toward or away from the five genre forms we have found? That is, although Web sites are not converging to a single ideal type, do Web sites within a given cluster come to resemble an ideal typical site that represents their cluster? Operationally, are Web sites that were created later more likely to approximate their cluster centroid than Web sites that were designed earlier?

To test this hypothesis, we created a measure of closeness to the genre ideal types using discriminant analysis. If the Web is evolving toward the five genre forms, then we would find a significantly higher discriminant score for the newly designed Web sites than for the older ones. An F-test of this hypothesis finds that the newer Web sites do have a significantly higher discriminant score ($F = 3.765, p = .053$). Newer Web sites more closely approximate their cluster centroid (within cluster ideal type).

Faced with new technologies, the creators of Web sites turn to already-existing cultural forms as templates for action. Genre structures organization.

The finding suggests that genre forms are robust and that they are likely to continue to structure online organization in the near future. A likely explanation of the finding is that the creators of Web sites learn from Web sites they have seen and use them as models. Instead of being instructed simply to "make us a Web site," webmasters, it seems, are being told to "make us *this kind* of Web site." But this indexical ordering does not yield a rigid copying. To be clear, our findings here are not that newer Web sites resemble older Web sites within their genre but that *the newer are more likely to be typical of the genre*. At the outset of the process, differences among Web sites were perhaps slight; but based on these initial differences, forms emerged that are becoming more rather than less distinctive. Genre structures. But it does not do so mechanically. In this case, it is reproduced precisely as new actors make modifications that shape the genre form.

The Field of Online Civic Organization

Having examined how genres structure online organization, we turn now to the structure of the organizational field of civil society Web sites. Figure 1 presents the correspondence analysis of the field as represented in a two-dimensional space.

FIGURE 1

THE SPACE OF GENRE FORMS AND WEB SITE FEATURES

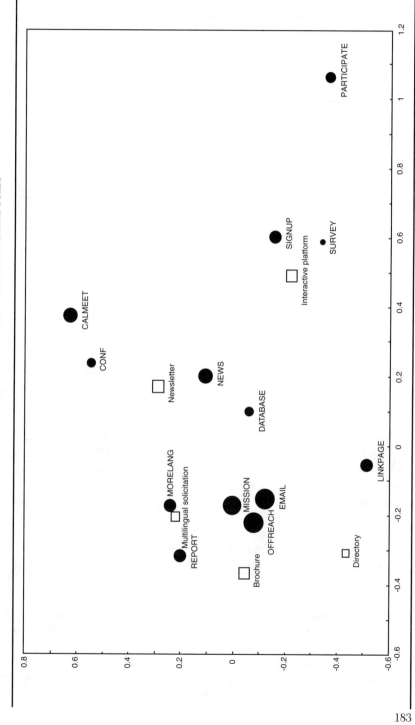

One of the advantages of correspondence analysis is that it allows us to represent the clusters and the features of each Web site in a single space. We can thus represent the distance of the various features from each other (understood as the probability of their co-occurrence on the sites) as well as represent the relationship between the clusters as given by their relative proximity/distance from the various features.

Whereas the Internet and Society paradigm focused on inequality of users' access to various aspects of the Web, we now add the problem of inequality in the accessibility of Web sites to potential users.

As a model, Figure 1 is a simplified representation of the original data. The adequacy of the two-dimensional space is measured by the proportion of variance the two dimensions represent of the original variance in the distribution of features across genre forms. In this case, the proportion of variance explained is 59.6 percent, indicating that this two-dimensional model is a good fit to the original data.[9] On our two-dimensional figure, we indicate the overall frequency of each feature by the size (area) of its circular marker, and the number of Web sites that have been grouped in a given cluster is represented by the area of the respective squares.

We interpret structure in this field as follows: The horizontal axis is organized (reading left to right) as information versus participation. The vertical axis is organized (reading top to bottom) as offline activity versus online activity. Thus, to the right side of the origin, we find Web sites that are oriented to members. Web sites in the upper-right quadrant are oriented to a user-member who does, or potentially wants to do, something offline. Web sites in the lower-right quadrant are oriented to users who are active online. To the left side of the origin, by contrast, we find Web sites that are oriented not to members but to visitors. For example, Web sites in the bottom-left quadrant seem oriented to a visitor who uses a directory to gain information about other sites on the Web. Those in the upper-left-hand quadrant seem oriented to a user who visits sites to gain information related to donation (in Eastern Europe in 2002, this is still very much an offline activity).

Whereas Web sites to the left of the origin control what is posted on their sites, those to the right allow users to post materials by participating in chat rooms and uploading documents. But it would be mistaken to interpret the horizontal axis as

TABLE 4

LOGISTIC REGRESSION MODEL OF FORMS AND INCOMING LINKS (DEPENDENT VARIABLE: 30+ INDEGREE)

	Coefficient	Odds Ratio
INTERACTIVES	0.262	1.300
NEWSLETTERS	0.757°	2.131°
SOLICITATIONS	1.262°	3.532°
DIRECTORIES	0.588°	1.801°

NOTE: The reference category is the pure brochures. A significant positive coefficient means that the given genre has more incoming links than the pure brochures, the least visible category. $^{*}p < .05$.

"closed" versus "open." The sign-up feature is double-sided. On one hand, it indicates that users can sign up to join the organization and/or receive materials; on the other, it suggests that there might be filtering mechanisms. Not just anybody can post materials—only those who have registered, perhaps only those who have in some way been vetted. That is, more participatory Web sites might be more restrictive, even exclusionary. Building online communities, especially as havens for groups out of the mainstream, can require boundaries. By contrast, Web sites to the left of the origin are an open book. Indeed, to some extent, they open their books by posting documents such as annual reports, budgets, and so on. They are open with information, but if you visit the site, there is not much to do there. The sites with more online participation, however, are highly unlikely to post such documents. Open to participation, some of these nonconformist groups would justifiably reject the notion that they should give an open accounting to just anybody.

Accessibility Redux

After analyzing the construction process whereby civil society organizations build Web sites of emerging genre forms, we turn to larger construction processes that incorporate these civil society Web sites into the World Wide Web. We examined the number of hyperlinks pointing to each Web site (referred to variously as "backlinks" or "in-degree"). Studies of the structure of the hyperlink network on the Web overall have shown that there are extreme inequalities—following highly skewed, power-law distribution—among Web sites in terms of their hyperlink centrality (Barabási, Albert, and Jeong 2000). The distribution of in-degree hyperlinks in our population of East European civil society Web sites is very similar to the overall distribution found on the Web. The least central 90 percent of the sites have only 20 percent of all incoming links, and the top 10 percent receive all the rest.

Centrality scores are not simply an academic's way to assess visibility on the Web. Such scores have practical consequences. Users navigating the Web are more likely to come across a site if they can click on a link that points to it. More important, today, search engines (not only Google, the most popular, but many others as well) famously use hyperlinks (Hindman, Tsioutsiouliklis, and Johnson 2003). More incoming links increase the probability that search engine Web crawlers (software robots that roam the Web) will find a site to place in their directories. And the equation of hyperlink centrality and "authority" means that Web sites with higher centrality scores will rank higher on search engine result listings.

Search engine technology is search engine politics. The inclusion of hyperlinks and search engine robots as kinds of actors in the society of the Internet gives a new twist to the problem of accessibility. Whereas the Internet and Society paradigm focused on inequality of users' access to various aspects of the Web, we now add the problem of inequality in the accessibility of Web sites to potential users. On one side, users differ in their access; on the other, Web sites differ in their accessibility to the general public.

How do our Web site genre forms differ in their hyperlink centrality and, hence, accessibility? To answer this question, we ran a logistic regression model to test whether we could find statistical differences among the genre forms in terms of incoming links. Table 4 shows the relative probability (compared to brochure sites) that Web sites in the other four genres belong to the most central ones with more than thirty incoming links.

The directory, newsletter, and multilingual solicitation clusters are each more likely to be highly central than the brochure sites. Interactive platforms, the type that we might think of as making use of the most exciting affordances of the Web, are not the most central Web sites. These sites are not "rewarded" by the dominant metric of the web.

Shaping the Web of Civic Participation

In this article, we explored the coevolution of organizational forms and emergent technologies. We examined a new field of political representation organized by civic associations making new types of claims outside of electoral politics within a new representational medium. In asking how these organizations re-present themselves online, we were examining the technologies of politics. In charting the characteristic patterns of how particular features are combined, we have examined the organization of technology. The emerging organizational forms we found were not "inscribed" in the technology; neither were they stages toward the full realization of the promise of technology leading to the singular ideal "Web site of civic participation." To put it differently, the social is not exogenous to technology. In our inquiry, we found distinctive sociotechnological networks, genre forms that are diverging patterns of online civic organization based on the combination of technological features, actors, and types of acts.

Strongly linked to offline activities, the online field of civic organization is not a uniform new public sphere with universal visibility and accessibility but a field consisting of diverse specific publics. Inequalities in visibility are shaped by the actions of the editors of news portals and designers of search engines that—relating to the combinations of Web site features—sideline participatory Web sites. In the civic organization of the World Wide Web, active forms of participation and "de-territorialization" are largely separated. Web sites allowing for more active forms of participation are primarily addressed to domestic constituencies, while the Web sites most likely to be multilingual are the least likely to allow for direct forms of participation. Instead of an emerging de-territorialized and participatory "global civil society," the expectation of techno-romantic approaches, in the field we find diverse organizations of primarily domestic publics.

Notes

1. For example, Harvard and Stanford each has a center on "Internet and Society," and researchers in the University of Maryland's program on Scientific Research on the Internet edit the journal *IT&Society*. For exemplary contributions to the paradigm, see DiMaggio et al. (2001); Robinson, DiMaggio, and Hargittai (2003).

2. Here we are more charitable than Bruno Latour (1999, 15) who, criticizing the approach of which he was a founder, famously commented that there were only four things wrong with Actor-Network Theory— "the word actor, the word network, the word theory, and the hyphen!"

3. Attention to the paradigm's moniker would, of course, be trivial if the division that it denotes did not so deeply inform the approach.

4. Thus, in place of Internet and Society, it would already be better to study the society of the Internet. The simple terminological change suggests an expanded and more heterogeneous constellation of "actors"— not only millions of persons, but also Web sites, routers, servers, search engines, and the rapidly proliferating population of pieces of software code ("intelligent agents") coursing through the Internet, interacting with us and each other. Systematic study of the social dynamics of these interacting populations is an exciting opportunity for sociology.

5. Details on sample selection, coding protocols, measures, statistical tests, and other methodological questions are available from the authors upon request.

6. Students of political participation will recognize that we translate standard definitions of types of political participation such as "reading about," "getting in touch," "identifying with," and "actually participating in" specific actions.

7. Each feature is recorded as a dummy variable, that is, with a score of one if a given feature is present and zero if it is not found on the Web site.

8. Alternatively, one might argue that Web sites would adopt the state-of-the-art practice current at the time of their founding. In this case, newer sites would be the more interactive. Our tests reject this hypothesis as well. There is no significant correlation between age and genre form.

9. Readers in the field of cultural studies will recognize correspondence analysis from the writings of Pierre Bourdieu. Models that explain nearly 60 percent of the variance are rarely encountered in his work.

References

Agresti, Alan. 2002. *Categorical data analysis*. New York: John Wiley.

Barabási, Albert-László, Réka Albert, and Hawoong Jeong. 2000. Scale-free characteristics of random networks: The topology of the World Wide Web. *Physica A* 281:69-77.

Barley, Stephen. 1986. Technology as an occasion for structuring: Evidence from observations of CT scanners and the social order of radiology departments. *Administrative Science Quarterly* 31:78-108.

Boczkowski, Pablo J. 2004. *Digitizing the news: Innovation in online newspapers*. Cambridge, MA: MIT Press.

Callon, Michel. 1991. Techno-economic networks and irreversibility, In *A Sociology of monsters: Essays on power, technology, and domination*, ed. J. Law, 132-61. London: Routledge.

DiMaggio, Paul, Eszter Hargittai, W. Russell Neumann, and John. P. Robinson. 2001. Social implications of the Internet. *Annual Review of Sociology* 27:307-36.

Eisenstein, Elizabeth L. 1993. *The printing revolution in early modern Europe.* Cambridge: Cambridge University Press

Fischer, Claude S. 1992. *America calling: A social history of the telephone to 1940.* Berkeley: University of California Press.

Hand, Martin, and Barry Sandywell. 2002. E-topia as cosmopolis and citadel: On the democratizing and de-democratizing logics of the Internet, or, Toward a critique of the new technological fetishism. *Theory, Culture, and Society* 19 (1-2): 197-225.

Hindman, Matthew, Kostas Tsioutsiouliklis, and Judy A. Johnson. 2003. Googlearchy: How a few heavily-linked sites dominate politics on the Web. Paper presented at the annual meetings of the Midwest Political Science Association, Chicago.

Hutchins, Edwin. 1995. *Cognition in the wild.* Cambridge, MA: MIT Press.

Kuti, Eva. 2001. *A nonprofit szektor főbb statisztikai jellemzői.* Budapest, Hungary: Központi Statisztikai Hivatal.

Latour, Bruno. 1991. Technology is society made durable. In *A sociology of monsters: Essays on power, technology and domination*, ed. J. Law, 103-31. London: Routledge.

———. 1999. On recalling ANT. In *Actor network theory and after*, ed. John Law and John Hassard. Oxford, UK: Blackwell, the Sociological Review.

Orlikowski, Wanda J. 2000. Using technology and constituting structures: A practice lens for studying technology in organizations. *Organization Science* 11 (4): 404-28.

Robinson, John P., Paul DiMaggio, and Eszter Hargittai. 2003. New social survey perspectives on the digital divide. *IT&Society* 1 (5): 1-22.

Ward, Joe H., Jr. 1963. Hierarchical grouping to optimize an objective function. *Journal of the American Statistical Association* 58:236-44.

Yates, JoAnne. 1989. *Control through communication: The rise of the system of American management.* Baltimore: Johns Hopkins University Press.

The New Digital Media and Activist Networking within Anti–Corporate Globalization Movements

By
JEFFREY S. JURIS

This article examines how anti–corporate globalization activists have used new digital technologies to coordinate actions, build networks, practice media activism, and physically manifest their emerging political ideals. Since the World Trade Organization protests in Seattle, and through subsequent mobilizations against multilateral institutions and forums in Prague, Quebec, Genoa, Barcelona, and Porto Alegre, activists have used e-mail lists, Web pages, and open editing software to organize and coordinate actions, share information, and produce documents, reflecting a general growth in digital collaboration. Indymedia has provided an online forum for posting audio, video, and text files, while activists have also created temporary media hubs to generate alternative information, experiment with new technologies, and exchange ideas and resources. Influenced by anarchism and peer-to-peer networking logics, anti–corporate globalization activists have not only incorporated digital technologies as concrete tools, they have also used them to express alternative political imaginaries based on an emerging network ideal.

Keywords: transnational social movements; digital technologies; media activism; globalization; activist networking; cultural politics

Following a second day of street battles and police riots on July 21, 2001, at the anti-G8 protests in Genoa, I walked over to the media center at around 8 p.m. together with my Catalan friends to catch up on the latest news. The *Caribinieri* (Italian police) had just attacked a peaceful march of nearly three hundred thou-

Jeffrey S. Juris is a postdoctoral fellow at the University of Southern California Annenberg School for Communication. He received his Ph.D. in anthropology from the University of California, Berkeley, where his research focused on globalization, social movements, and transnational activism. He is currently writing a book based on his doctoral dissertation about the cultural logic and politics of transnational networking among anti–corporate globalization activists in Barcelona. He is also developing a comparative ethnographic project exploring the use of new digital technologies and emerging forms of collaborative practice among media activists in Europe and Latin America.

DOI: 10.1177/0002716204270338

sand demonstrators who had come together to challenge corporate globalization and denounce the murder of a young Italian activist killed the previous day. The center was teaming with protesters when we arrived, writing e-mails, conducting interviews, and posting audio and video clips. Pau, from the Catalan Movement for Global Resistance (MRG),[1] was still connected to the Internet via laptop sending out real-time updates, as he had been the entire week. He told us the buses would be leaving for Barcelona shortly, but I had planned to stay in Genoa for a few more days to take part in antirepression actions together with the Pink & Silver Bloc. Indeed, we had spent much of our time during the past two days running from baton charges and tear gas. Fortunately, protesters shot reams of digital footage documenting police abuses, which were compiled, edited, and uploaded at the Independent Media Center (IMC) on the floor above.

After the meeting, I went back to the computer lab to inform my Catalan friends that I had decided to stay. All of a sudden, we heard a terrible commotion in the streets, followed by loud banging on the media center gate out front. Several activists charged into the main room screaming, "Police, police!" Concerned about my pictures and field notes, I immediately grabbed my backpack and dragged it up to the fourth floor, where people were frantically running back and forth. As I wandered the hallway, two American direct action veterans threw me a sleeping bag and led me up to an empty room, where we hid under a table. As we waited in the dark, helicopters flew overhead, while the police began smashing computers and accessories at the IMC below. An Italian officer eventually entered the room and brought us to a second-floor corridor where police held us with roughly thirty others for nearly half an hour. Although dozens of activists were viciously beaten at the Diaz School across the way, the police left the media center as soon as they had destroyed large quantities of hardware and documentation. I was still somewhat rattled, so I ultimately decided to head back to Barcelona, joining a group of Catalans who had called for a taxi to bring them to a meeting point on the outskirts of town.

This anecdote suggests that government and police officials view Indymedia as a major threat. Indeed, there have been other similar incidents, though perhaps none so extreme. During the anti–Free Trade Area of the Americas (FTAA) protest in Quebec City in April 2001, for example, FBI agents appeared at the Seattle IMC demanding names and e-mail addresses of everyone who had visited the site during the previous two days. The following year, Spanish authorities monitored and tried to shut down several activist Web sites, including Indymedia, prior to the mobilization against the European Union (EU) in Barcelona. Finally, during November 2002, the police broke into IMCs throughout Italy after the European Social Forum in Florence. Riot cops have also repeatedly attacked media activists during protests, often leading to wider crackdowns. For example, at the beginning of a mobile street theater action during the anti-EU mobilization in Barcelona in March 2002, the police charged a group of video activists and then unsuccessfully tried to surround the larger crowd. The French police used a similar strategy with greater success to break up an immigrant rights action during a European No Border camp the following July.

The question thus arises as to why the forces of law and order specifically target media activists before, during, and after mass mobilizations? More generally, why do they consider independent media so threatening? On one hand, over the past few years Indymedia and other digital networks have helped mobilize hundreds of thousands of anti–corporate globalization[2] protesters around the world, while creating radical social movement publics for the circulation of alternative news and information. Clamping down on grassroots forms of media production, communication, and coordination thus has a practical effect. On the other hand, media activism and digital networking more generally are among the most important features of contemporary anti–corporate globalization movements, generating what Waterman (1998) has referred to as a "communications internationalism." Police are not only interested in collecting information and destroying evidence. Such attacks are also meant to intimidate, sending real-time shock waves through global activist networks, while targeting their most important symbolic expressions.

By significantly enhancing the speed, flexibility, and global reach of information flows, allowing for communication at a distance in real time, digital networks provide the technological infrastructure for the emergence of contemporary network-based social movement forms (cf. Arquilla and Ronfeldt 2001; Bennett 2003a, 2003b; Castells 1997; Cleaver 1995, 1999; Escobar 2004; Lins Ribeiro 1998). Regarding social networks more generally, Barry Wellman (2001) has argued that "computer-supported social networks" (CSSN) are profoundly transforming the nature of communities, sociality, and interpersonal relations. Although the proliferation of increasingly individualized, loosely bounded, and fragmentary community networks predates cyberspace, computer-mediated communications have reinforced such trends, allowing communities to sustain interactions across vast distances.

The Internet is also being incorporated into more routine aspects of daily social life, as virtual and physical activities become increasingly integrated (Miller and Slater 2000; Wellman 2001; Wellman and Haythornthwaite 2002). Despite the shrinking yet still formidable digital divide, the Internet facilitates global connectedness, even as it strengthens local ties within neighborhoods and households, leading to increasing "Glocalization" (Wellman 2001, 236; cf. Robertson 1995). Similar trends can also be detected at the level of political activity, where Internet use—including e-mail lists, interactive Web pages, and chat rooms—has facilitated new patterns of social engagement. Anti–corporate globalization movements thus belong to a particular class of CSSN: *computer-supported social movements*. Using the Internet as technological architecture, such movements operate at local, regional, and global levels, while activists move back and forth between online and offline political activity.

The horizontal networking logic facilitated by new digital technologies not only provides an effective method of social movement organizing, it also represents a broader model for creating alternative forms of social, political, and economic organization. For example, many activists specifically view the open source development process—where geographically dispersed computer programmers freely improve, adapt, and distribute new versions of software code through global communication networks—as potentially applicable within wider social spheres.[3] As Steven Weber (2004) suggests, open source could potentially revolutionize production within other information-based sectors, such as primary care medicine or genomics. Although Weber maintains a strict definition of open source as involving only those processes that entail a new conception of property as the right to distribute, not the right to exclude, many activists view open source as a broader metaphor (cf. Lovink 2003, 195), which might one day inspire postcapitalist forms of political and social organization at local, regional, and global scales.

The horizontal networking logic facilitated by new digital technologies not only provides an effective method of social movement organizing, it also represents a broader model for creating alternative forms of social, political, and economic organization.

This article examines the innovative ways that anti–corporate globalization activists have used new digital technologies to coordinate actions, build networks, practice media activism, and physically manifest their emerging political ideals. Since the protests against the World Trade Organization (WTO) in Seattle, and through subsequent mobilizations against multilateral institutions and forums in Prague, Quebec, Genoa, Barcelona, Porto Alegre, and other cities, activists have used e-mail lists, Web pages, and open editing software to organize actions, share information, collectively produce documents, and coordinate at a distance, reflecting a general growth in digital collaboration. Indymedia has provided an online forum for autonomously posting audio, video, and text files, while activists have also created temporary media hubs to generate alternative information, experiment with new technologies, and exchange ideas and resources. Influenced by anarchism and the logic of peer-to-peer networking, more radical anti–corporate globalization activists have thus not only incorporated new digital technologies as concrete networking tools, they have also used them to express alternative political imaginaries based on an emerging network ideal.

I have elsewhere explored the emergence of what I call the "cultural logic of networking" among anti–corporate globalization activists, or the broad guiding principles, shaped by the logic of informational capitalism, which are internalized by activists and generate concrete networking practices (Juris 2004).[4] This cultural logic specifically entails a series of deeply embedded and embodied social and cultural dispositions that orient actors toward (1) building horizontal ties and connections among diverse, autonomous elements; (2) the free and open circulation of information; (3) collaboration through decentralized coordination and directly democratic decision making; and (4) self-directed networking. It thus not only reflects the values associated with open source development, incorporated within GNU/Linux or the World Wide Web, it also forms part of a broader "Hacker Ethic" identified by Himanen (2001).[5]

This article is based on fourteen months of ethnographic research among Barcelona-based anti–corporate globalization activists, within Catalonia and the broader circuits through which they travel.[6] Specifically, I conducted participant observation during mass actions and gatherings in cities such as Barcelona, Genoa, Brussels, Leiden, Strasbourg, and Porto Alegre, and within sustained networking processes as a member of MRG's international working group. My research strategy thus involved situating myself within a specific node and following the transnational connections outward through virtual and physical formations, including Peoples Global Action (PGA) and the World Social Forum (WSF) process.[7] I had also carried out prior ethnographic research in Prague, Seattle, and among U.S.-based activist networks. My fieldwork was thus multisited but also rooted within specific network locales, constituting an example of what Burawoy (2000) calls a "grounded globalization," while affording me a strategic position from which to observe local, regional, and global networking practices. Finally, I also conducted qualitative interviews, media, and textual analysis as a complement to participant observation.

This article begins with an introduction to anti–corporate globalization movements and then continues with an exploration of how contemporary activists are appropriating new digital technologies as concrete networking tools. Next, I turn to the relationship between the Internet, decentralized network forms, and the cultural logic and politics of activist networking, with a specific emphasis on Spain and Catalonia. I then examine the new media activism, including independent media, culture jamming, and electronic civil disobedience. Finally, I conclude with some reflections about how new digital technologies and horizontal networking practices are generating new models of horizontal production and globally networked democracy.

The Rise of Anti–Corporate Globalization Movements

Nearly fifty thousand people took to the streets to protest corporate globalization at the WTO meetings in Seattle on November 30, 1999. A diverse coalition of environmental, labor, and economic justice activists succeeded in shutting down the meetings and preventing another round of trade liberalization talks. Media images of giant puppets, tear gas, and street clashes between protesters and the police were broadcast worldwide, bringing the WTO and a novel form of collective action into view. Seattle became a symbol and battle cry for a new generation of activists, as anti–globalization networks were energized around the globe.

On one hand, the "Battle of Seattle," packaged as a prime-time image event (Deluca 1999), cascaded through global mediascapes (Appadurai 1996), capturing the imagination of long-time activists and would-be postmodern revolutionaries alike. On the other hand, activists followed the events in Seattle and beyond through Internet-based distribution lists, Web sites, and the newly created IMC. New networks quickly emerged, such as the Continental Direct Action Network (DAN) in North America,[8] or MRG in Catalonia, while already existing global networks such as PGA, ATTAC, or Via Campesina also played crucial roles during these early formative stages. Although more diffuse, decentralized all-channel formations (Arquilla and Ronfeldt 2001), such as DAN or MRG, proved difficult to sustain over time, they provided concrete mechanisms for generating physical and virtual communication and coordination in real time among diverse movements, groups, and collectives.

Anti–corporate globalization movements have largely grown and expanded through the organization of mass mobilizations, including highly confrontational direct actions and countersummit forums against multilateral institutions. The anti-WTO protests were a huge success, and everywhere activists wanted to create the "next Seattle." Mass mobilizations offer concrete goals around which to organize, while they also provide physical spaces where activists meet, virtual networks are embodied, meanings and representations are produced and contested, and political values are ritually enacted. Public events can broadly be seen as "culturally constituted foci for information-processing" (Handelman 1990, 16), while direct actions, in particular, generate intense emotional energy (Collins 2001), stimulating ongoing networking within public and submerged spheres. Activists organized a second mass protest against the World Bank and International Monetary Fund (IMF) in Washington, D.C., on April 16, 2000, and went truly global during the subsequent mobilization against the World Bank/IMF in Prague on September 26, 2000. Protesters came from countries around Europe, such as Spain, Italy, Germany, and Britain, and other parts of the world, including the United States, Latin America, and South Asia. Solidarity actions were held in cities throughout Europe, North and South America, and parts of Asia and Africa.

The first WSF, organized in Porto Alegre, Brazil, in late January 2001, represented an important turning point, as activists began to more clearly emphasize specific alternatives. The success of the first WSF was magnified during the next two editions, which drew seventy thousand and one hundred thousand people, respectively. More than a conference, the WSF constitutes a dynamic process involving the convergence of multiple networks, movements, and organizations. Whereas PGA remains more radical, horizontal, and broadly libertarian,[9] the WSF is a wider political space, including both newer decentralized network-based movements and more hierarchical forces of the traditional Left. Meanwhile, mass actions continued to intensify and expand during spring and summer 2001, including the anti-FTAA protests in Quebec City and increasingly militant actions against the EU in Gothenburg, the World Bank in Barcelona, and the G8 in Genoa.

U.S.-based anti–corporate globalization movements, which were severely shaken by the September 11 attacks, reemerged when activists shifted their attention from the war in Iraq back toward corporate globalization, leading to mass mobilizations against the WTO in Cancun and the FTAA summit in Miami during fall 2003. In the rest of the world, mobilizations continued to grow after 9/11, including a half-million-person march against the EU in Barcelona in March 2002. Anti–globalization and anti–war in Iraq movements soon converged, leading to an antiwar protest of more than a million people during the European Social Forum in Florence in November. Meanwhile, the third edition of the WSF in Porto Alegre drew nearly one hundred thousand participants during January 2003. The following June, hundreds of thousands of anti–corporate globalization and antiwar activists descended on the border of France and Switzerland to protest the G8 summit in Evian, while the most recent World and European Social Forums were successfully organized in Paris in November 2003 and Mumbai, India, in January 2004.

Three broad features thus characterize anti–corporate globalization movements. First, although movement networks are locally rooted, they are *global* in scope. Coordinating and communicating through transnational networks, activists have engaged in institutional politics, such as global campaigns to defeat the Multilateral Agreement on Investments or abolish the foreign debt, and extrainstitutional strategies, including coordinated global days of action, international forums, and cross-border information sharing. Perhaps most important, activists *think* of themselves as belonging to global movements, discursively linking local activities to diverse struggles elsewhere. Second, anti–corporate globalization movements are *informational*. The various protest tactics employed by activists, despite emerging in different cultural contexts, all produce highly visible, theatrical images for mass mediated consumption. Finally, anti–corporate globalization movements are organized around a multiplicity of virtual and physical network forms.[10]

Computer-Supported Social Movements

Inspired by the pioneering use of the Internet by the Zapatistas (Castells 1997; Cleaver 1995, 1999; Olesen 2004; Ronfeldt et al. 1998) and early free trade campaigns (Ayres 1999; Smith and Smythe 2001), anti–corporate globalization activists have employed digital networks to organize direct actions, share information and resources, and coordinate activities. Activists have made particularly effective use of e-mail and electronic listservs, which facilitate open participation and horizontal communication. On one hand, given their speed, low cost, and geographic reach, e-mail lists have facilitated the organization of globally coordinated protests, such as the global days of action inspired by PGA. For example, the second PGA global day of action on June 18, 1999, involved demonstrations in more than forty countries around the world against the anti-G8 Summit in Cologne, while hundreds of thousands mobilized globally during the WTO Summit in Seattle the following November. On the other hand, the worldwide circulation of discourses, strategies, and tactics signals the emergence of a global web of alternative transnational counterpublics (Olesen 2004; cf. Fraser 1992).

Although anti–corporate globalization activists primarily use e-mail lists to facilitate planning and coordination, they also create temporary Web pages during mobilizations to provide information, resources, and contact lists; post documents and calls to action (cf. Van Aelst and Walgrave 2002); and sometimes house real-time discussion forums and Internet relay chat rooms. Indeed, interactive Web sites offering multiple tools for coordination are becoming increasingly popular. These include open publishing projects like Indymedia or sites that incorporate collaborative production software, such as the Infospace in Barcelona (see below). Moreover, particular movement networks and processes—such as PGA, the WSF, or ATTAC—have their own, more narrowly focused Web pages, where activists post reflections, analyses, updates, calls to action, and links along with more logistical information.

Internet use has complemented and facilitated face-to-face coordination and interaction, rather than replacing them. During my fieldwork in Barcelona, activists used listservs—both within broad convergence spaces (Routledge 2004), such as the campaigns against the World Bank and EU and within specific networks like MRG or the Citizens Network to Abolish the External Debt (XCADE)—to stay informed about activities and events and to perform concrete logistical tasks. However, complex planning, political discussions, and relationship building often took place within physical settings. My own time thus largely involved attending meetings nearly every evening, followed by long hours of online work late into the night. At the same time, the phone remained an important tool of communication. For example, after sending various e-mails back and forth between MRG International and activists from a Dutch collective during planning for a European PGA meeting, we had to pick up the phone on several occasions to work out disagreements, which were impossible to solve without interactive communication.

Despite these cautionary remarks, the Internet has proven absolutely crucial, allowing key "activist-hackers" (cf. Nelson 1996) to carry out relay and exchange operations, receiving, interpreting, and distributing information out to diverse network hubs and nodes.[11] For example, when an MRG-based activist developed a system for instantly sending messages out to hundreds of listservs around the world, he turned to me and exclaimed, "Now I can reach thousands of activists at the touch of a button every time we want to communicate something important!" Activist interviews further illustrated how the Internet has facilitated long-distance coordination and horizontal collaboration, as Joseba, from Indymedia-Barcelona, recalled:

> I learned how a group of people, some in the U.S., others in London, and others, who knows where, coordinated through a global listserv. Suddenly someone would send an e-mail saying, "I think this story is important, what do you think?" In less than a week, ten people had answered, one or two saying it wasn't clear; but most feeling it was important,

so we distributed the tasks: "I'll reduce it to so many characters," "I'll translate it into German," and "I'll do Italian." The next day we started working, and the messages began arriving: "Spanish translation done," "Italian done," "French done." Then someone sent a photo, "What do you think about this picture?" The comments went around, and then someone sent another picture, and suddenly we had created an article![12]

Digital Technologies and the Cultural Politics of Activist Networking

The Internet does not simply provide the technological infrastructure for computer-supported social movements; its reticulate network structure reinforces their organizational logic (Arquilla and Ronfeldt 2001; Bennett 2003a; Castells 1997; Cleaver 1995, 1999; Escobar 2004; Juris 2004). Decentralized, flexible local/ global networks constitute the dominant organizational forms within anti– corporate globalization movements. The absence of organizational centers within distributed networks makes them extremely adaptive, allowing activists to simply route around nodes that are no longer useful. Moreover, the introduction of new digital technologies significantly enhances the most radically decentralized all- channel network formations, facilitating transnational coordination and communication among contemporary movements.

For example, MRG-Catalonia, which grew up around the World Bank/IMF protests in Prague, was conceived as "a network of people and collectives against economic globalization and unitary thinking . . . a tool for providing local struggles with global content and extension."[13] Activists wanted to create a flexible mechanism for communication and coordination among diverse local struggles, including environmentalists, squatters, Zapatista supporters, solidarity and antidebt activists, and EU opponents. Rather than top-down command, activists preferred loose, flexible coordination among autonomous groups within a minimal structure involving periodic assemblies, logistical commissions surrounding concrete tasks, and several project areas, including a social movement observatory and resource exchange. In contrast to traditional leftist organizations, open participation was favored over representation: "MRG is a movement 'without members;' membership . . . leads to static, non-dynamic structures and to a clear and distinct, rather than a more diffuse sense of belonging."[14]

MRG activists also took part in broader regional and global networks, including PGA, which itself represents a diffuse all-channel network involving communication and coordination among diverse local movements around the world. Like MRG, PGA has no formal members but rather seeks to provide an instrument for coordination to help "the greatest number of persons and organizations to act against corporate domination through civil disobedience and people-oriented constructive actions."[15] Any person or collective can participate as long as they agree with the network hallmarks, which include a clear rejection of capitalism and all systems of domination, a confrontational attitude, a call to direct action and civil disobedience, and an organizational philosophy "based on decentralization and autonomy."[16]

Within movements such as MRG or PGA, networking logics have given rise to what many grassroots activists in Barcelona call a "new way of doing politics." While the command-oriented logic of leftist parties and unions is based on recruiting new members, developing unified strategies, political representation through vertical structures, and the pursuit of political hegemony, network-based politics involve the creation of broad umbrella spaces, where diverse organizations, collectives, and networks converge around common hallmarks while preserving their autonomy and specificity. Rather than recruitment, the objective becomes horizontal expansion and enhanced "connectivity" through articulating diverse movements within flexible, decentralized information structures allowing for maximal coordination and communication.

For example, when the Barcelona campaign against the World Bank was formed in early 2001, MRG-based activists brought their horizontal networking praxis to bear within this broader political space. Leftist parties and larger NGOs initially wanted their institutions to figure prominently within the campaign, which more grassroots activists interpreted as a strategy for gaining members or increasing electoral support. Formal organizations also favored structures based on representative voting, where influence would be determined by membership size rather than actual contribution. On the other hand, activists from MRG, XCADE, and other grassroots groups felt the best way to encourage broader and more active participation was to create open, assembly-based structures where everyone would have an equal say through consensus decision making, while establishing a rotating group of spokespersons to issue public declarations. This open networking model ultimately won out, but it did not lead to an absence of conflict. Rather, collective decisions would be restricted as much as possible to technical coordination as opposed to abstract political debates, allowing diverse actors to organize within a common platform.

Networking logics are thus unevenly distributed, as more established organizations tend to incorporate new digital technologies into existing communication routines, while smaller, resource-poor organizations often use technologies more innovatively, taking advantage of their low cost to forge horizontal linkages (Bennett 2003a). What many observers view as a single anti–corporate globalization movement is actually a congeries of competing, yet sometimes overlapping, social movement networks that differ according to issue addressed, political subjectivity, ideological framework, political culture, and organizational logic. Struggles within and among different networks, which I call the "cultural politics of networking," largely shape the way specific networks are produced, how they develop, and how they relate to one another within broader social movement fields.

For example, following the mobilization against the World Bank in Barcelona, the more institutional sectors created their own representative structure called the Barcelona Social Forum. Meanwhile, many traditional Marxists wanted the broader campaign to become a permanent statewide platform. Activists associated with MRG and XCADE opposed this idea, arguing against what they considered a return to more traditional organizational forms. They felt it was important to maintain open spaces for communication and coordination but that such spaces should facilitate the continual reconfiguration of fluid ties. The assembly finally agreed to bring the World Bank campaign to a close in September 2001, giving rise to a new coordinating space later that fall to plan for the upcoming mobilization against the EU. Moreover, militant squatters, who had created an anticapitalist platform against the World Bank, would take part within the wider campaign this time around, as parties and unions had forged a space of their own.

[N]etwork-based politics involve the creation of broad umbrella spaces, where diverse organizations, collectives, and networks converge around common hallmarks while preserving their autonomy and specificity.

Radical anticapitalists thus face a continual dilemma about whether to operate within more strictly defined political formations, at the risk of being marginalized, or participate within broader spaces involving more reformist and traditional actors. Complex patterns of shifting alliances also operate at the transnational scale. For example, activists associated with PGA and other radical grassroots networks often create "autonomous spaces" during the world and regional social forums, conceived as "separate, yet connected" to official events. However, specific networks will move between the larger forums, autonomous spaces, or not participating at all, depending on the political context. Digitally powered social movement networks are thus "rhizomatic" (Cleaver 1999; cf. Deleuze and Guatarri 1987)—constantly emerging, fusing together, and hiving off—yet it is important to consider how such contradictory processes are actually generated in practice through concrete networking politics, which are always entangled within complex relationships of power rendered visible through long-term ethnographic research.

W. Lance Bennett (2003a, 154) has argued that contemporary Internet-driven campaigns are not only flexible and diverse, they are also "ideologically thin," allowing "different political perspectives to co-exist without the conflicts that such differences might create in more centralized coalitions." Although Bennett is right to highlight diversity within such campaigns, he may overstate their internal cohesion and ideological thinness. At the very least, these features will vary according to political culture and context. For example, his case studies involve U.S.-based corporate campaigns against Microsoft and Nike. My own research among broader anti–corporate globalization spaces revealed somewhat different dynamics. For example, activists generated a great deal of ideological discourse within the Barcelona campaigns against the World Bank and EU, or the world and regional social forums more generally, but decision making tended to involve practical matters, while political debates were often coded as conflicts over organizational form. Indeed, activists increasingly express their utopian imaginaries directly through concrete political, organizational, and technological practice, as Geert Lovink (2002, 34) suggests: "Ideas that matter are hardwired into software and network architectures."

The New Digital Media Activism

Contemporary independent media activists have made particularly effective use of new technologies through alternative and tactical forms of digital media production (cf. Meikle 2002). Alternative media constitute independent sources of news and information beyond the corporate logic of the mainstream press. John Downing (2003, v) defined what he called "radical media" as diverse small-scale outlets that "express an alternative vision to hegemonic policies, priorities, and perspectives." Such alternative or radical media also tend to be independently operated and self-managed through horizontal participation rather than top-down command. Not only do they incorporate a broader networking logic, they are also increasingly Internet based.

Alternative media. Indymedia is perhaps the most emblematic of the new alternative digital media projects (Downing 2003; Halleck 2002; Kidd 2003; Meikle 2002). Using open publishing software developed by Australian programmer Mathew Arnison, the first IMC was established during the anti-WTO mobilization in Seattle. Indymedia journalists reported directly from the streets, while activists uploaded their own text, audio, video, and image files. Indymedia sites would soon be up and running in Philadelphia, Portland, Vancouver, Boston, and Washington, D.C., while the network quickly expanded on a global scale to places like Prague, Barcelona, Amsterdam, Sao Paolo, and Buenos Aires. There are now more than 120 local sites around the world, while the global network receives up to 2 million page views per day.[17]

During mass actions and gatherings, Indymedia centers become dynamic communication hubs, particularly among more radical sectors. During the December 2001 mobilization against the EU in Brussels, for example, the official convergence center was situated in a large open-air tent, which principally housed NGO information tables, generating an institutional feel. The IMC, on the other hand, was organized in an old squatted theater in the center of town. The main computer lab buzzed with activity as media activists and protesters uploaded images and audio files, swapped reports and information online, and edited video files. Meanwhile, the entire floor below was transformed into a project called Radio Bruxxel, which featured 24-hour programming about the EU, immigration, economic exclusion, war, and self-management.

Such temporary spaces of digital production provide a crucial terrain where activists carry out several concrete tasks. First, they send e-mails to each other and to their friends and families, facilitating action coordination, while rapidly circulating information about events on the ground. Second, activists generate formal updates, which are instantly posted and distributed through global distribution lists. Third, protesters can also immediately upload and disseminate video and image files. Fourth, IMCs also provide workshops for carrying out more complex operations, including live video and audio streaming as well as documentary film editing. While in the past activists had to rely on experts and the mass media to circulate their messages, largely due to high transaction costs and time constraints, they can now use new digital technologies to take on much of this work themselves, assuming greater control over the media production process, while enhancing the speed of information flow. Finally, such temporary media labs have also facilitated the exchange of information, ideas, and resources, as well as experimentation with new digital technologies through which media activists inscribe their emerging political ideals within new forms of networked space, a practice I call "informational utopics."[18]

During mass actions, hundreds of media activists thus take to the streets to record video footage, snap digital photos, and conduct interviews. At the mobilization against the EU in Barcelona during March 2002, for example, Meri, from MRG, exclaimed, "Everyone is filming everyone else!" Indeed, contemporary social movements are uniquely self-reflexive (Giddens 1991), as activists circulate their own texts and images through global networks in real time. Moreover, activists have also used digital technologies to help plan and organize mass direct actions themselves. Beyond e-mail lists, protesters have also made innovative use of cell phone technology to coordinate tactical positions, report on police activities, and provide real-time updates. However, the use of cell phones should not be exaggerated. For example, even though organizers created an intricate communications structure in Prague, the system broke down when the Czech police blocked cellular transmissions. Activists have certainly used mobile phones, but not with the "military-like" tactical precision often suggested in more popular accounts.

Beyond specific mobilizations, Indymedia also incorporates a broader networking logic, as open publishing software allows activists to independently create, post, and distribute their own news stories regarding concrete actions, ongoing campaigns, and thematic issues. Open publishing reverses the implicit hierarchy dividing author and consumer, empowering grassroots users to freely participate in the production process, as programmer Evan Henshaw-Plath pointed out: "It's all about using technology to disintermediate the authority and power structure of the editor."[19] The refusal of editorial control allows users to draw their own conclusions about the veracity and relevance of particular posts. Moreover, the open publish-

ing process facilitates active participation through the provision of concrete networking tools and nonhierarchical infrastructures, as Henshaw-Plath explained: "I
see my task as building technological systems where people can exert power
through egalitarian systems that will reproduce horizontal cooperative social relations and institutions."[20] Open editing thus represents an important example of
informational utopics, as broader values related to horizontal collaboration, open
access, and direct democracy are physically inscribed into Indymedia's network
architecture.

Tactical media. Rather than creating alternative counterpublics, tactical media
aim to creatively intervene along dominant media terrains (Lovink 2002, 254-75;
Meikle 2002, 113-72). This can involve either the juxtaposition of incommensurate
elements to generate subversive meanings, as in "guerrilla communication"
(Grupo Autónomo A.f.r.i.k.a. et al. 2000), or the playful parodying of corporate
advertisements and logos to produce critical messages, which activists call "culture
jamming" (cf. Klein 2000, 279-310; Lasn 2000). First theorized and put into practice during the "Next 5 Minutes" festivals in the Netherlands (Meikle 2002, 119),
tactical media emphasize the use of new technologies, mobility, and flexibility.
Geert Lovink (2002, 265), activist and Internet critic, put it in the following terms:
"It is above all mobility that most characterizes the tactical practitioner. . . . To cross
borders, connecting and re-wiring a variety of disciplines and always taking full
advantage of the free spaces in the media."

Tactical media interventions do not necessarily take place in cyberspace, but
new digital technologies are almost always crucial. For example, the Canadian-
based Adbusters, founded by Kalle Lasn, provides multimedia culture jamming
resources online, allowing local participants to download materials and participate
in global campaigns, including Buy Nothing Day. Anti–corporate globalization
activists have built clone sites like the "World Trade Organization/GATT Home
Page" during the anti-WTO protests in Seattle. After the WTO secretary general
publicly denounced the clone site, the story was picked up by CNN (Meikle 2002,
118), involving what Bennett (2003a, 161) called "micro-to-mass media crossover."

Within Catalan anti–corporate globalization movements, the "Agencies," a Barcelona-based political art and media collective, has developed numerous tactical
media projects using digital technologies to produce and distribute physical and
virtual materials, including posters, flyers, stickers, and videos. Its latest project,
called "YOMANGO," combines guerrilla communication, culture jamming, civil
disobedience, and sabotage. "Mango" is a Spanish-owned multinational clothing
chain, while the slang "Yo Mango" also means "I steal." The campaign provides
materials and information encouraging people to steal clothing and other items
from transnational corporations. YOMANGO also involves public events including
collective shoplifts and banquets featuring stolen food. Reflecting an open networking logic, the project aims to create "tools and dynamics that flow and prolifer-
ate, in order to be re-appropriated and circulate,"[21] Moreover, the project ironically promotes, "the free circulation of goods!"[22]

"Hacktivism" or "electronic civil disobedience" constitutes a final dimension of tactical media (Meikle 2002, 140-72; Wray 1998). Just as power moves through nomadic electronic circuits, Critical Art Ensemble (CAE; 1996) argued that activists should also operate along virtual terrains, using digital trespass and blockade tactics. Whereas CAE insisted that electronic civil disobedience should remain underground, Electronic Disturbance Theater (EDT) and its principal theorist Stefan Wray have promoted a more public approach to digital protest (Meikle 2002, 141). During the "virtual sit-in," for example, activists gather at a preannounced Web site and are automatically transferred en masse via FloodNet software to a target site, overwhelming its server. EDT has staged successful sit-ins against the Mexican government in support of the Zapatistas, while the "Electrohippies" flooded the WTO Web site during the protests in Seattle. Other digital tactics include the "e-mail bomb" and the "hijack," where surfers are automatically redirected from one Web site to another. Virtual actions rarely succeed in completely shutting down their targets, but they often generate significant media attention (Meikle 2002, 154-55).

Beyond specific tactical objectives, alternative and tactical media both involve ongoing experimentation with new technologies, forming part of an emerging digital activist networking culture. Moreover, grassroots media activists increasingly express their broader political values by projecting them onto both physical and virtual terrains through horizontal forms of digital collaboration. Contemporary activist gatherings, including No Border camps, PGA conferences, or the world and regional social forums, thus also provide concrete spaces for the practice of informational utopics. For example, the July 2002 Strasbourg No Border camp was specifically designed to challenge the nearby Schengen Information System (SIS), which tracks movement across EU space, but the camp was also conceived as a broader experiment in collective living and grassroots self-management. Activists transformed an empty swath of parkland along the Rhine River into a bustling two-thousand-person tent city, involving mobile kitchens; makeshift showers and latrines; video zones; dance spaces; and domes for logistical, first-aid, legal, security, and action planning. Organizers also devised a directly democratic decision-making structure based on autonomous neighborhoods that coordinated through larger assemblies. The scheme often broke down in practice, yet it represented an attempt to manifest a horizontal networking logic in the design and management of social space.

The alternative media center, ironically called "Silicon Valley," was among the most vibrant zones in the camp, housing an IMC, an Internet café running open source software, a radio tent, Web-based news and radio, and a double-decker tactical media bus from Vienna called the Publix Theater Caravan, which itself featured video screening, Internet access and streaming, and a bar and lounge. Pau and I first visited the media space on the second day of the camp and immediately ran into Karl, a friend from Indymedia-Berlin, who was typing something on his laptop outside the Internet café. He explained the entire zone was equipped with WiFi (wireless) connection and that he was sending e-mail. He then took us over to the radio tent, which was equipped with a fifty-watt transmitter and produced 24-hour simultaneous Web and broadcasts.

There were also numerous workshops within a project called d.sec (database systems to enforce control), which explored links between freedom of movement and communication, as well as physical and virtual struggles against growing mechanisms of control. Specific themes included open source, guerrilla communication, technology and the body, and media activism. More generally, d.sec was conceived as a space for experimentation with open networking, self-organization, and horizontal collaboration, as the project flyer explained:

> d.sec . . . an open structure where activists, anti-racists, migrants, hackers, techs, artists and many more put their knowledge and practices into self-organized interaction: a space to discuss and network, skill share, and produce collaborative knowledge. A laboratory to try out ways to hack the streets and reclaim cyberspace with crowds in pink and silver; experiment with virtual identities, Linux, and open source . . . explore the embodiment of technology, learn about the meanings of physical and virtual border crossing.

d.sec was a platform for generating new ideas and practices that physically embodied an emerging network ideal. Moreover, together with the broader media zone, which featured always-ready Internet connection, live audio and video streaming, and interactive peer-to-peer file sharing, activists had created an innovative, networked terrain fusing the "space of flows" and the "space of places" (cf. Castells 1996). If revolutions are characterized by their production of new spatial forms (Lefebvre 1991), then informational utopics also constitute a concrete mechanism for imagining and experimenting with alternative digital age geographies.

Conclusion: Digitally Networking Democracy?

Anti–corporate globalization movements have not only generated widespread visibility surrounding issues related to global economic justice and democracy, they have also pioneered in the use of new digital technologies. On one hand, grassroots activists have developed highly advanced forms of computer-mediated alternative and tactical media, including Indymedia, culture jamming, hacktivism, and electronic civil disobedience. These practices have facilitated the emergence of globally coordinated transnational counterpublics while providing creative mechanisms for flexibly intervening within dominant communication circuits. On the other hand, activists have appropriated the Internet into their everyday routines, largely through e-mail lists and Web sites, favoring the rise of highly flexible and decentralized network forms. At the same time, the network has also emerged as a broader cultural ideal, as digital technologies generate new political values and vocabularies (cf. Wilson and Peterson 2002, 453), which are often directly inscribed into organizational and technological network architectures, suggesting a powerful dialectic among technology, norm, and form, mediated by human practice. Finally, activists are building a new digital media culture through the practice of informational utopics, involving experimentation with new technologies and the projection of utopian ideals regarding open participation and horizontal collaboration onto emerging forms of networked space.

Beyond specific tactical objectives, alternative and tactical media both involve ongoing experimentation with new technologies, forming part of an emerging digital activist networking culture.

Although the use of new digital technologies has helped mobilize hundreds of thousands of people around the world in opposition to corporate globalization, it remains to be seen whether new horizontal networking practices can be incorporated into more everyday forms of social, economic, and political life. This was precisely the motivation behind the development of a new media project by anti–corporate globalization activists in Barcelona called the "Infospace," which combines virtual tools, including an Internet server and social movement directory, with physical tools, including publishing and editing services; activist research and documentation; a solidarity economy project; and a physical storefront housing reception, meeting, and digital workspace. The physical and virtual are thus completely intertwined. For example, activists use Internet-based collaborative software (twiki) to collectively produce documents regarding real-world initiatives, while virtual projects are coordinated through both online and offline interaction.[23] Regarding the project's long-term goal, Pau had this to say: "We are building autonomous counterpower . . . by networking movements . . . and creating our own alternatives without waiting for the government . . . and helping others to achieve them as well."

Activists in Barcelona and elsewhere are thus increasingly turning to technological paradigms as a way to promote social transformation. Many specifically view open source as a harbinger of new self-organized forms of horizontal collaboration coordinated at multiple scales. For example, theorists associated with the German-based Oekonux project have debated how open software principles might potentially "migrate" into other contexts, perhaps leading to postcapitalist forms of economic production (cf. Lovink 2003, 194-223).[24] At the political level, electronic democracy advocates are interested in how "the technical possibilities of cyberspace make innovative forms of large-scale direct democracy practical," not via Internet alone, but rather through "collective and continuous elaboration of problems and their cooperative, concrete resolution by those affected" (Lévy 2001, 176). Anti–corporate globalization activists have similarly developed the European Social Consulta as a way to build political alternatives and exchange resources among local assemblies coordinated regionally through digital networks.[25]

Although such long-term networking projects, and the practice of informational utopics more generally, may not produce immediate results, they should be seen in another light. Indeed, as Alberto Melucci (1989, 75) once argued, new social movements are cultural innovators that challenge dominant cultural codes while also developing new "models of behavior and social relationships that enter into everyday life." Beyond the production of alternative values, discourses, and identities, however, contemporary anti–corporate globalization movements are perhaps best understood as social laboratories, generating new cultural practices and political imaginaries for a digital age.

Notes

1. The Catalan Movement for Global Resistance (MRG) was ultimately "self-dissolved" in January 2003 as a response to declining participation and a broader political statement against the reproduction of rigid structures. Pseudonyms have been used throughout to hide activist identities.

2. I use "anti–corporate globalization" here to emphasize that most activists do not oppose globalization per se but rather those forms of economic globalization viewed as benefiting transnational corporations. "Global justice" is increasingly preferred by English-speaking activists but is not common elsewhere.

3. Open software is based on the "copyleft" principle, requiring that original source code be released and distributed with new program versions (cf. Himanen 2001; Raymond 1999; Lovink 2003, 194-223).

4. I adapt this term from Jameson (1991), who refers to postmodernism as the cultural logic of late capitalism; and Ong (1999), who explores a specific type of late capitalist cultural logic-transnationality.

5. Citing the hackers' jargon file, Himanen (2001, vii-viii) defined hackers as "people who 'program enthusiastically' and who believe that 'information-sharing is a powerful positive good.' "

6. Barcelona-based fieldwork was carried out from June 2001 to August 2002 for my doctoral dissertation titled "The Cultural Logic of Networking: Transational Activism and the Movement for Global Resistance in Barcelona," supported by the Wenner-Gren Foundation for Anthropological Research and the Social Science Research Council (with Andrew W. Mellon funding).

7. MRG was a co-convener of Peoples Global Action (PGA) Europe, while MRG-based activists also took part in the social forums.

8. The Continental Direct Action Network (DAN) process came to a standstill during the year after Seattle.

9. This brand of left-wing "libertarianism" should be distinguished from the variety prevalent in the United States. The former involves a radical critique of both the market and the state, while the latter is oriented toward limiting the role of the state in order to unleash the dynamic potential of the free market.

10. These include hierarchical circle patterns, intermediate wheel formations, and the most decentralized all-channel configurations (Kapferer 1973, 87), which refer to those where every node is connected to every other (Arquilla and Ronfeldt 2001). Networks can be defined more generally as sets of "interconnected nodes" (Castells 1996, 469).

11. Diane Nelson (1996) employed the term "Maya-Hacker" to characterize Mayan activists engaged in cultural activism and transnational networking.

12. Unless otherwise stated, quotations are from personal interviews.

13. Cited from "La Organización del MRG" in *EIMA* (February-March 2001), a Catalan activist journal.

14. Cited from a document sent to the global@ldist.ct.upc.es listserv on October 18, 2000.

15. See PGA Network Organizational Principles (www.nadir.org/nadir/initiativ/agp/cocha/principles.htm).

16. See PGA Hallmarks (www.nadir.org/nadir/initiativ/agp/gender/desire/nutshell.htm).

17. See Indymedia FAQ page, retrieved from http://process.indymedia.org/faq.php3 on March 14, 2004.

18. With regard to radical activism more generally, Hetherington (1998, 123) refers to the spatial practice of "utopics," whereby "a utopian outlook on society and the moral order that it wishes to project, are translated into practice through the attachment of ideas about the good society onto particular places."

19. Interview with Evan Henshaw-Plath: http://lists.indymedia.org/mailman/public/mediapolitics/2001-November/000041.html, retrieved on March 18, 2004.

20. Ibid.

21. Cited from http://www.sindominio.net/lasagencias/yomango/ES/textos/10sugerencias.html, retrieved on March 15, 2004.

22. Cited from www.sindominio.net/lasagencias/yomango/ES/acciones/presentacion_1.html, retrieved on March 15, 2004.

23. "Tiki Wiki" is an open source content management system based on Wiki technology, which allows users to collaboratively create and edit content using any Web browser (http://tikiwiki.org).

24. See http://www.oekonux.org/. Also, see King (2004) for a critical perspective regarding the idea of openness as an organizing principle for social movements and other aspects of society.

25. This more ambitious version of the European Social Consulta has not yet generated widespread support around Europe, but Spanish and Catalan activists decided to move forward with a statewide referendum during the 2004 European parliamentary elections. See www.consultaeuropea.org.

References

Appadurai, Arjun. 1996. *Modernity at large*. Minneapolis: University of Minnesota Press.

Arquilla, John, and David Ronfeldt. 2001. *Networks and netwars*. Santa Monica, CA: Rand.

Ayres, Jeffrey M. 1999. From the streets to the Internet. *Annals of the American Academy of Political and Social Science* 566:132-43.

Bennett, W. Lance. 2003a. Communicating global activism. *Information, Communication & Society* 6 (2): 143-68.

———. 2003b. New media power. In *Contesting media power*, ed. Nick Couldry and James Curran. Lanham, MD: Rowman & Littlefield.

Burawoy, Michael. 2000. Grounding globalization. In *Global Ethnography*, ed. Michael Burawoy, Joseph A. Blum, Sheba George, Zsuzsa Gille, Teresa Gowan, Lynne Haney, Maren Klawiter, Steve H. Lopez, Sean Riain, and Millie Thayer. Berkeley: University of California Press.

Castells, Manuel. 1996. *The rise of the network society*. Oxford, UK: Blackwell.

———. 1997. *The power of identity*. Oxford, UK: Blackwell.

Cleaver, Harry. 1995. The Zapatistas and the electronic fabric of struggle. http://www.eco.utexas.edu/faculty/Cleaver/zaps.html (accessed March 18, 2004).

———. 1999. Computer-linked social movements and the threat to global capitalism. http://www.eco.utexas.edu/faculty/Cleaver/polnet.html (accessed April 1, 2004).

Collins, Randall. 2001. Social movements and the focus of emotional attention. In *Passionate politics*, ed. Francesca Polletta, James M. Jasper, and Jeff Goodwin. Chicago: University of Chicago Press.

Critical Art Ensemble. 1996. *Electronic civil disobedience*. Brooklyn, NY: Autonomedia.

Deluca, Kevin Michael.1999. *Image politics*. New York: Guilford.

Delueze, Gilles, and Felix Guatarri. 1987. *A thousand plateaus*. Minneapolis: University of Minnesota Press.

Downing, John D. H. 2003. The Independent Media Center movement. In *Contesting media power*, ed. Nick Couldry and James Curran. Lanham, MD: Rowman & Littlefield.

Escobar, Arturo. 2004. Actors, networks, and new knowledge producers. In *Para Além das Guerras da Ciência*, ed. Boaventura de Sousa Santos. Porto, Portugal: Afrontamento.

Fraser, Nancy. 1992. Rethinking the public sphere. In *Habermas and the public sphere*, ed. Craig Calhoun. Cambridge, MA: MIT Press.

Giddens, Anthony. 1991. *The consequences of modernity*. Palo Alto, CA: Stanford University Press.

Grupo Autónomo A.f.r.i.k.a. et al. 2000. *Manual de Guerrilla de la Comunicación*. Barcelona, Spain: Virus.

Halleck, DeeDee. 2002. *Hand-held visions*. New York: Fordham University Press.

Handelman, Don. 1990. *Models and mirrors*. Cambridge: Cambridge University Press.

Hetherington, Kevin. 1998. *Expressions of identity: Space, performance, politics*. London: Sage.

Himanen, Pekka. 2001. *The hacker ethic*. New York: Random House.

Jameson, Fredric. 1991. *Postmodernism*. Durham, NC: Duke University Press.

Juris, Jeffrey S. 2004. Networked social movements. In *The network society*, ed. Manuel Castells. London: Edward Elgar.

Kapferer, Bruce. 1973. Social network and conjugal role. In *Network Analysis*, ed. Jeremy Boissevain and J. Clyde Mitchell. The Hague, the Netherlands: Mouton.

Kidd, Dorothy. 2003. Indymedia.org. In *Cyberactivism*, ed. Martha McCaughey and Michael D. Ayers. New York: Routledge.

King, Jamie. 2004. The packet gang. *Metamute* 27. http://www.metamute.com (accessed March 18, 2004).

Klein, Naomi. 2000. *No logo*. New York: Picador.

Lasn, Kalle. 2000. *Culture jam*. New York: Quill.

Lefebvre, Henri. 1991. *The production of space*. Oxford: Oxford University Press.

Lévy, Pierre. 2001. *Cyberculture*. Minneapolis: University of Minnesota Press.

Lins Ribeiro, Gustavo. 1998. Cybercultural politics. In *Cultures of politics, politics of cultures*, ed. Sonia E. Alvarez, Evelina Dagnino, and Arturo Escobar. Boulder, CO: Westview.

Lovink, Geert. 2002. *Dark fiber*. Cambridge, MA: MIT Press.

———. 2003. *My first recession*. Rotterdam, The Netherlands: V2_/NAi Publishers.

Meikle, Graham. 2002. *Future active: Media activism and the Internet*. New York: Routledge.

Melucci, Alberto. 1989. *Nomads of the present*. Philadelphia: Temple University Press.

Miller, Daniel, and Don Slater. 2000. *The Internet: An ethnographic approach*. Oxford, UK: Berg.

Nelson, Diane M. 1996. Maya hackers and the cyberspatialized nation-state. *Cultural Anthropology* 11 (3): 287-308.

Olesen, Thomas. 2004. *Long distance Zapatismo*. London: Zed Books.

Ong, Aihwa. 1999. *Flexible citizenship*. Durham, NC: Duke University Press.

Raymond, Eric. 1999. *The cathedral and the bazaar*. Cambridge, MA: O'Reilly.

Robertson, Roland. 1995. Glocalization. In *Global modernities*, ed. Mike Featherstone, Scott M. Lash, and Roland Robertson. London: Sage.

Ronfeldt, David, John Arquilla, Graham E. Fuller, and Melissa Fuller. 1998. *The Zapatista "social netwar" in Mexico*. Santa Monica, CA: Rand.

Routledge, Paul. 2004. Convergence of commons. *The Commoner*, Autumn/Winter. www.thecommmoner.org (accessed March 18, 2004).

Smith, Peter Jay, and Elizabeth Smythe. 2001. Globalisation, citizenship and technology. In *Culture and politics in the information age*, ed. Frank Webster. London: Routledge.

Van Aelst, Peter, and Stefaan Walgrave. 2002. New media, new movements? The role of the Internet in shaping the "anti-globalisation" movement. *Information, Communication & Society* 5 (4): 465-93.

Waterman, Peter. 1998. *Globalization, social movements, and the new internationalisms*. London: Mansell.

Weber, Steven. 2004. *The success of open source*. Cambridge, MA: Harvard University Press.

Wellman, Barry. 2001. Physical place and cyberplace. *International Journal of Urban and Regional Research* 25 (2): 227-52.

Wellman, Barry, and Caroline Haythornthwaite, eds. 2002. *The Internet in everyday life*. Malden, MA: Blackwell.

Wilson, Samuel M., and Leighton C. Peterson. 2002. The anthropology of online communities. *Annual Review of Anthropology* 31:449-67.

Wray, Stefan. 1998. On electronic civil disobedience. http://cristine.org/borders/Wray_Essay.html (accessed March 18, 2004).

Pablo J. Boczkowski. 2004. *Digitizing the News: Innovation in Online Newspapers*. Cambridge, MA: MIT Press. 264 pp. $30.00. ISBN 0262025590.

Simon Head. 2003. *The New Ruthless Economy: Work and Power in the Digital Age*. Oxford: Oxford University Press. 240 pp. $13.95 (paperback). ISBN 0195179838.

Lawrence Lessig. 2004. *Free Culture: How Big Media Uses Technology and the Law to Lock Down Culture and Control Creativity*. New York: Penguin. 240 pp. $24.95. ISBN 1594200068.

A Digital Revolution? A Reassessment of New Media and Cultural Production in the Digital Age

By
DAVID GRAZIAN

Reassessing the Production of Culture in the Digital Age

A great deal of past research explores new media consumption through common questions: Who uses the Internet and what kinds of activities do they pursue while online? Does Internet use facilitate or compete with offline forms of cultural consumption? Finally, do disparities in digital literacy and/or access to new media suggestive of a "digital divide" reproduce established social inequalities, whether among socioeconomic classes or between core and periphery nations? The answers to these questions are vital to understanding how consumers incorporate new media into the texture of their everyday lives. Yet Internet-oriented research sometimes demonstrates a tendency to treat

David Grazian is an assistant professor of sociology at the University of Pennsylvania and the author of Blue Chicago: The Search for Authenticity in Urban Blues Clubs *(Chicago: University of Chicago Press, 2003). His research and teaching interests include the study of mass media and popular culture, urban sociology, symbolic interaction, and ethnographic methods. His current research examines the production and consumption of urban nightlife in Philadelphia.*

DOI: 10.1177/0002716204270286

technological advancement uncritically without exploring the tentative and evolutionary nature of digital production itself.

In contrast, contemporary developments in the fields of anthropology, sociology, business management, and law demonstrate how the online production of recorded music, advertising, and hypertext occurs across changing institutional and legal boundaries, inconsistently applied organizational norms, shifting market forces, and competing definitions of creative merit and occupational identity. By directing our attention away from consumption and toward the *production* of new media and other forms of alternative culture, we can begin to map out the dynamic technological flows and flashpoints of contestation that lend shape to the digital environment as an unpredictable space of social interaction and meaning making. In the interests of exploring these issues in greater depth, in this review essay I examine three recent studies of new media and cultural production in the digital age.

[O]nline newspapers increasingly offer user-centered options such as reader forums, personal weblogs, and direct e-mail exchanges with reporters, thus encouraging a shift from passive reception to active participation on the part of news consumers.

Refocusing the discussion is crucial if we are to establish not only a sufficient sociological account of the digital age but an objective assessment of its social impact as well. Contemporary promoters of the digital age celebrate the rise of information technology, online banking, and friendship network applications without much hesitation or critical reflection. This boosterism becomes commonplace in journalistic features chronicling the ascendance of new media and its rebellious heroes: the kid-genius programmer of the dot-com explosion; the hotshot Internet CEO and his expensive toys (Lewis 2000; Patterson 2000); the adolescent online investor (Lewis 2001); the Web-savvy volunteer of the once-promising Howard Dean presidential campaign (Shapiro 2003); and the industrious teen ripping, burning, and mixing music files in her bedroom.

The excitement surrounding the digital age relies on four widely held but questionable assumptions. First, like Marx's rendering of the emergence of capitalism itself, the digital age is assumed to represent a *revolutionary* moment that promises to reorganize established social relations and inequities: fixed, fast frozen, and otherwise. Second, recent technological advances *determine* social changes in the postmodern fabric of tomorrow. Third, these technological changes encourage the greater *creativity, innovativeness, autonomy,* and *power* of individual cultural producers, from Web-based gossip columnists to grassroots political operatives. Finally, the rise of digital technology will ultimately promote the nation's shift to a better-connected and more *democratic* society.

Recent work on new media calls each of these assumptions into question. First, contrary to overblown narratives describing the sweeping upheavals of the digital "revolution," technological change typically progresses in a more gradual and *evolutionary* manner. The development of new media has occurred in a piecemeal fashion over the past several decades as cultural producers have experimented with alternative technologies ranging from analog-based telecommunications to early forays into flexible manufacturing processes. Rather than driving the reinvention of society, the specific uses of digital technology in the production of culture suggest an extension of already established workplace norms, including traditional divisions of editorial and artistic labor and the employment of scientific management strategies of worker control (see below).

Second, discourses surrounding the rise of the digital age commonly emphasize the taken-for-granted nature of technology and its highly deterministic impact on the production of culture. This type of technological determinism, however, should be tempered by two long-standing sociological findings: first, while culture-producing activities are certainly shaped by the technological contexts in which they are embedded, they are not shaped *only* by such factors but by an array of social, cultural, and material forces, including localized norms of behavior, preconfigured institutional strategies, organizational structures, legal constraints (both de facto and de jure), and the dictates of the commercial marketplace.[1] Also, while the increased popularity of the Internet has contributed to the emergence of Web-based media, it has also been put to a variety of innovative and unforeseen uses. This leads to a second caveat: different social actors will respond to this aforementioned constellation of variables by embarking on notably divergent paths to success and failure (and sometimes both).

Third, although some celebrants praise the digital age for its significance as an empowering era in which individual cultural producers can harness this new technology to tap into their own resources of keen artistic creativity and wild innovation, the record suggests a more ambiguous set of results. Undoubtedly, its potential benefits are unquestionable. To take just one example, the proliferation of peer-to-peer file sharing contributes innumerable value-added resources to our cultural economy: (1) increased consumer access to independent music and film, internationally produced pop culture, and otherwise unavailable cultural products (i.e., old recordings no longer in commercial circulation); (2) the facilitation of omnivorous cultural consumption (Peterson 1992) through the increased exposure to a wide variety of cultural genres and styles; (3) the greater ease of manipulating audio and visual files as a means of revising and reinterpreting older cultural objects; and ultimately (4) the transformation of passive *consumers* into active *pro-ducers* within their own art worlds and fields of creativity. It is equally clear, how-ever, that digital technologies can also be deployed by call center managers to mon-itor and punish their employees for taking restroom breaks, and Web page builders censor themselves out of fear of being sued for pirating work that should be in the public domain. This is hardly the dawning of a new enlightened age of cultural innovation and creative freedom: in fact, in the digital age it is increasingly labori-ous for amateur cultural producers to circumvent roadblocks erected by media conglomerates and even more difficult for professionals to subvert the unrelenting demands of the commercial marketplace, much less push its cultural boundaries to the bleeding edge.

Finally, the political ramifications of the emergent digital age are mixed at best. Of course, Internet-based activities have the potential to enable various modes of political communication among citizens (whether via listservs, political blogs, or online media sites) as well as increase access to public information ranging from government-collected data to electoral information and the voting records of legis-lators. Nevertheless, technology can be deployed in multiple context-dependent ways and can therefore be appropriated for exclusionary and hegemonic purposes as well as prosocial causes. Given the evolutionary nature of technological prog-ress, there is probable cause to wonder whether what were once hailed (without irony) as the so-called "killer" applications of the digital age may simply represent new tools of domination for achieving a familiar set of ends.

Pablo J. Boczkowski, Simon Head, and Lawrence Lessig show that a scholarly analysis of cultural production in the digital age must begin by critically assessing the most popular assumptions of the era: (1) the revolutionary distinctiveness of recent advances in digital production processes; (2) the determinism of computer-based technology; (3) the links between the rise of digitized culture and the innovativeness and autonomy of individual creators and cultural workers; and (4) the optimistic belief that the meteoric rise of virtual realities, network expansion, software development, and interconnectivity will lead toward the creation of a more participatory democracy. In the interests of employing contemporary social science to explore these twenty-first-century assumptions regarding the digital age, I will now take each of the aforementioned authors' arguments in turn.

Innovation and the Production of New Media

Boczkowski presents a sobering perspective in his excellent book, *Digitizing the News*, which uses ethnographic and archival data to explore the evolutionary development of online newspapers and the workplace processes that structure the production of digital journalism. Newspapers have experimented for decades with electronic alternatives to print, including audiotext, videotext, and fax technolo-gies. Boczkowski uses case studies to show that media companies took divergent paths to harness the tools of digital technology, particularly with regard to their varied emphases on user participation through public forums, chat rooms, and other attempts to disseminate relatively unfiltered reader-based content.

Despite the creative technological possibilities provided by digital media, online newspapers tend to operate in a conservative fashion by consistently choosing strategies of hedging to minimize risk, such as repackaging old articles as new online content. These strategies are notable for three reasons: First, they emulate safe and proven successes rather than untested innovations and thus tend to be timid and reactive rather than creatively daring. Second, even seemingly intrepid forays into the digital world tend to serve as defensive moves intended to bolster parent print publications, rather than showcase alternative forms of media. Third, these strategies often promote the adoption of technologies that lead to short-term gains while discouraging investment in experimental ventures that may eventually lead to significantly longer-term success. In this context, decisions to appropriate technological innovations are inevitably constrained by their perceived commercial viability.

Boczkowski elaborates upon these themes in his illuminating cases studies of three ethnographic research sites: the Technology Desk of *The New York Times* on the Web; Virtual Voyager, a Web-only multimedia features section of HoustonChronicle.com; and Community Connection, a site run by New Jersey Online (the online presence of the *Newark Star-Ledger, Trenton Times*, and *Jersey Journal*), on which nonprofit groups post Web pages to promote their services to readers. Carefully researched, each case presents evidence of the overall conditions affecting the evolution of online newspaper development, while stark differences among the three cases emphasize the nondeterministic nature of technology in the context of cultural production.

Boczkowski's case study of *The New York Times* on the Web is a portrait of the conservatism of established media organizations as they attempt to achieve an online presence. Although reporters, writers, and editors at the Technology Desk had the resources of the most so-called "revolutionary" media tools since the telegraph at their disposal—including audio, video, computer animation, and 360-degree digital photography—most of the content of the site consisted of "repurposed" stories simply appropriated from the paper's print editions. The paperless medium allows for the publication of very long journalistic features and analyses (due to the "limitless hole" of cyberspace) and a flexible publication cycle, yet writers strictly adhered to traditional seven hundred to twelve hundred word limits on articles and a relatively fixed schedule. Even from a superficial, stylistic point of view, the site's award-winning design seems staid, as it merely replicates the six-column cover-page layout of the print edition. Overall, the cautious moderation displayed by the *Times* on the Web demonstrates the gradually evolving character of online innovation, as well as the way increases in the technological capabilities available within an occupational field do not necessarily lead to changes in workplace norms and practices.

Compared to the *Times* on the Web, the staff of Virtual Voyager appears to embody the revolutionary enthusiasm evoked by new media. The Virtual Voyager site incorporates video, text, and sound into the day-to-day reporting of excursions ranging from western swing concert tours to elaborate boating expeditions. But as an unfortunate result, the site winds up blurring the already muddied boundaries between news and entertainment. A Web-based extension of the *Houston Chronicle*, Virtual Voyager prioritizes individual stories not on their newsworthiness but on their expected financial contribution to the organization through advertising revenue, a relative rarity among print newspapers of merit. Increasingly, editorial decisions are informed by the site's marketing and advertising departments, thus diminishing what has traditionally been a separation of the business and editorial functions of media companies. This places enormous commercial constraints on the professional standards of journalists, writers, and editors and leads to an escalating emphasis on Web design and onscreen pyrotechnics over critical substance. Meanwhile, the use of amateur reporters, coupled with the dilution of duties among print journalists who are increasingly required to incorporate digital photography, audio, and video into their stories, has contributed to the de-skilling of the journalism profession as a whole.

Finally, New Jersey Online's Community Connection allows nonprofit groups to set up Web pages that promote their services. In a certain sense, this venture is inherently populist since it provides self-publishing tools to thousands of volunteer and community-based service organizations free of charge. Still, it is difficult to see the journalistic value in such an enterprise. In fact, many of Boczkowski's informants argue that the program operates more as a marketing scheme designed to attract readers to New Jersey Online's Web site and increase its traffic among users. His interview with Sara Glines, New Jersey Online's editor, is particularly revealing:

> Sara Glines told me that the business plan behind Community Connection was "to make our site sticky. We want people to come and use it and have a reason to stay and come back tomorrow, and when they are here we want them to feel tied to our site." Hence, "what better way to do that than let them build their site on your site? Now they're going to keep coming back, and will feel a certain amount of ownership in New Jersey Online." (p. 161)

This suggests far more than a playful blurring of boundaries between the site's editorial and marketing functions but the wholesale replacement of editorial content with revenue-generating strategies. According to Glines, Community Connection "has begun to shape my image of what editorial per se is. . . . Editorial now is web sites built by nonprofit groups, the content in our forums, whatever happens in our chat rooms, in addition to the newspaper stories and our polls" (p. 159). Given journalism's traditional role as a government watchdog and distributor of vital information to the body politic, this drastic redefinition of editorial content with regard to online newspaper publishing suggests that the political promise of new media may be premature. Rather, it highlights how media companies rely on digital technologies to advance the same business agenda they pursue in all of their enterprises, journalistic and otherwise.

Still, Boczkowski can be critical without resorting to cynicism, as his account does acknowledge how digital media have facilitated innovation in cultural production. As suggested above, online newspapers increasingly offer user-centered options such as reader forums, personal weblogs, and direct e-mail exchanges with reporters, thus encouraging a shift from passive reception to active participation on the part of news consumers. By redirecting the one-way communication flows of traditional media, online sites create the potential for the expression of a greater variety of viewpoints, and their flexibility can refocus editorial content toward a more localized community of readers. As Boczkowski reminds us in his conclusion, however, the consequences of these innovations have yet to be determined. While "the construction of online newspapers has challenged the boundaries that separate the once neatly divided territories of print, broadcast, and telecommunications, this does not mean that this will lead to a world without borders, but probably to one with different boundaries and more cross-boundary work" (p. 181).

Reproducing Power in the Digital Age

Whereas we typically associate cultural production in the digital age with media technologies, hyperflexible product design and information-based services represent rapidly growing fields of cultural production in the new economy as well. In *The New Ruthless Economy*, Simon Head analyzes the organization of newly reengineered postindustrial workspaces from Nissan plants to American Airlines reservation centers. As an empirical reassessment of the reputed consequences of producer-based technologies (including eased flexibility of workplace norms and the creation of a newly skilled and thus empowered workforce), his research uncovers an alternative and more dire set of findings.

First, contrary to the pretensions of new-age management theories promoted in books with lofty titles such as *The Reengineering Revolution* (Hammer and Stanton 1995) and *Reengineering the Corporation: A Manifesto for Business Revolution* (Hammer and Champy 2001), the reengineered workplace simply represents an extension of age-old principles of scientific management invented at the turn of the twentieth century by Henry Ford and Frederick Winslow Taylor and subsequently developed by William Henry Feffingwell, who converted his protocols of factory efficiency to office workplaces and the white-collar service economy. Like their predecessors, postindustrial managers employ digital technology to further segment manufacturing procedures into highly routinized and repetitive tasks to be speedily completed at the physiological limits of human capacity. At Nissan, so-called flexible manufacturing allows assembly line laborers to build customized cars while still adhering to a Fordist regime of mass production. According to Head,

> Attached to the front bumper of each car body as it reached the head of the assembly line was a small, plastic box shaped like a playing card. The box contained an electronic device

that communicated with a nearby computer. On receiving the box's message, the computer printed out a legal-sized document that was then attached to the car's body.

The document told the assemblers which among a variety of seats, dashboards, radios, carpets, or door handles was to be fitted to that particular car. The plant's system of supply ensured that the right variety of components reached the right point on the assembly line at exactly the right time. Nissan's design engineers explained to me that this "mass customization" of their automobiles was always governed by the principle of "manufacturability." Manufacturability meant that every variety of seat, dashboard, door handle, or radio had to be designed in such a way as to minimize any variation in the assembler's routine as he or she installed that particular component. (p. 44)

This process of mass customization provides infinite variety for the consumers of automobiles but simultaneously decreases the set of choices available to shop-floor workers whose speed and efficiency are "achieved through the endless repetition of simple tasks, and not through the enhancement of worker training and skills" (p. 45). While it may be user-friendly, digitized manufacturing further alienates workers from the final product of their labor by minimizing their creativity, autonomy, and control. This de-skilling of automobile workers in the digital age parallels that of the emasculated Boston bread bakers described in Richard Sennett's (1998) *The Corrosion of Character*: as former artisans who today are reduced to simply clicking on touch-screen Windows-styled icons of French and Italian loaves in computerized kitchens, they are bakers who "no longer actually know how to bake bread" (p. 68).

Moving from auto manufacturing to high-tech customer services, Head shows us how call centers incorporate digital technology into the structure of interpersonal encounters between agents and clients and management's control over employees. Typically, agents are required to model all their verbal interactions with callers according to elaborate scripts provided by customer-relations management (CRM) software. From their desktop monitors, pop-up windows display routines calibrated according to the specific demographic profile of each caller; employees juggle among a series of multiple-choice-based options to progress from screen to screen, each providing yet another formulaic reply to every contingency that arises over the course of a call. By reducing their customer interactions to a mind-numbing sequence of "prescribed action responses," and restraining even the most experienced of employees from drawing on their expertise when handling outgoing sales pitches and incoming service requests, CRM represents micromanagement at its most absurd.

These protocols are effectively enforced through the same mechanisms used to achieve discipline among workers on Ford's automated high-speed assembly lines: the expectations set for each point in the labor process are built into the technology itself, making noncompliance an unavailable option for all but the most conspicuous of offending workers. Moreover, as an evolved counterpart to panoptic surveillance techniques barely imagined by Foucault, new monitoring software applications ruthlessly evaluate the volume and duration of employees' calls (as well as their "problem resolution speed"), their demeanor and politeness while conversing with customers, and perhaps most important, how well the agent adheres to

FOR MORE INFORMATION ABOUT THIS JOURNAL, TO VIEW A SAMPLE COPY ONLINE, OR TO ORDER THIS JOURNAL ONLINE, PLEASE VISIT: http://ann.sagepub.com OR FILL OUT THIS POST CARD AND RETURN IT TO ⑤ SAGE PUBLICATIONS.

THE ANNALS OF THE AMERICAN ACADEMY OF POLITICAL AND SOCIAL SCIENCE

Frequency: 6 Times/Year

Please start my subscription to The Annals of the American Academy of Political and Social Science- Clothbound

(C295) ISSN: 0002-7162

In the North America, South America, Central America, the Caribbean, and Asia

☐ $45 (Single Copy) ☐ $615 (Institutions) – *Price includes print & e-access. Print only or e-access only also are available. For these prices, please visit www.sagepub.com/resources/librarians.aspx?sc.1.*

In the United Kingdom, Europe, Australasia, the Middle East, and Africa

☐ £72 (Single Copy) ☐ £410 (Institutions) – *Price includes print & e-access. Print only or e-access only also are available. For these prices, please visit www.sagepub.com/resources/librarians.aspx?sc.1.*

All member individual subscriptions are handled through the American Academy of Political and Social Science at www.aapss.org.

Name _____

Title/Department _____

Address _____

Address _____

City/State or Province / Zip or Postal Code / Country _____

Phone _____   E-mail _____

Subscriptions will begin with the current issue, unless otherwise specified. Prices are quoted in U.S. dollars and are subject to change. Customers outside of the United States will receive their publications via air-speeded delivery.

their computer-generated script while on the phone with clients. With the aid of "stealth monitoring" processes that employ the use of compressed digital files, managers can easily retrieve an agent's past phone recordings and computer sessions for performance review without their knowledge. Statistical software programs can then convert these individual-based evaluations into quantifiable data to be compared across a company's workforce to ensure maximum worker efficiency and subordination.

Head successfully demonstrates how the incorporation of digital technology into the customer-relations field has neither eased the flexibility of workplace norms nor led to the creation of a newly empowered skilled workforce.

As a result, digital workplaces often engender what business consultants describe as a "negative call center culture" marked by extreme psychological, emotional, and physical stress. Dispelling the fantasy conjured up by the 1990s dot-com dream world of work as play (the relaxing of formal dress policies, the lunchtime ping-pong tournaments, the all-night coding/pizza parties), Head reveals the coercive and mean-spirited workplace regulations encountered by the customer service workers of the digital age. At Teletech, an Arizona telemarketing firm, managers enforce strict dress codes, even though call center employees "never actually come into physical contact with their clients and the dress habits of the Southwest are notably relaxed" (p. 104). At such companies, draconian regulations regarding punctuality and work breaks are applied across the board, even to employees who have sustained injuries on the job. Perhaps not surprisingly, managers rely on digital technologies to monitor and enforce these types of decidedly inflexible workplace norms as well.

Head successfully demonstrates how the incorporation of digital technology into the customer-relations field has neither eased the flexibility of workplace norms nor led to the creation of a newly empowered skilled workforce, but on other issues he appears less convincing. Moving away from the ethnographic grounding of his earlier findings, he overstates his case by arguing that the workplace technologies of the digitized call center may ultimately lead to increased inefficiencies in production. He cites two reasons: first, the causal relationship between the call center's insufferable work environment and its high levels of employee turnover.[2] Second, the new technology itself undermines the call center's efficiency. CRM software relies on a meticulously organized language to interact with customers who speak in all-too-human tones, contradictory and inarticulate. According to Head, the demands placed on agents to translate their customers' utterances into the inflexible grammar of computerized logic replace more traditional worker efficiencies with new costs to productivity.

While these latter assumptions may seem intuitive, they fail to cohere with the ethnographic realities of Head's case studies. Are the companies that employ CRM software sacrificing profit for technological prowess? If so, what is the response of management in such instances? Moreover, the recent exportation of call center jobs oversees to Bangalore and New Delhi demonstrates the ease with which the global hiring strategies of American firms more than compensate for the inefficiencies created by employee turnover at home. (These tactics may seem heartless or unpatriotic, but they are hardly inefficient.) While Head presents a corrective to the reengineering manifestos popularized in management self-help guides, his polemical approach sometimes lacks the social scientific rigor necessary for the empirical evaluation of his cases.

Creativity and Control in the Production of Culture

In *Free Culture*, Lawrence Lessig's principal argument is that intellectual property and copyright law constrain cultural production by taking valuable creative works out of the public domain. According to Lessig, the health of any democratic society requires that its cultural products and ideas be available for unfettered distribution, commentary, and eventual innovation and appropriation to ensure their rejuvenation and evolution over time. He suggests that the availability of unprotected cultural objects contributed to the richness of twentieth-century American popular culture, from Disney's appropriation of classic films and fairy tales to the rise of open-source software. Lessig recommends revising intellectual property law to ensure that future artists, scholars, and fans have access to cultural products (i.e. films, recordings, visual images, software) while still enabling creators to financially benefit from their own efforts for a limited period of time. We place limitations on the extension of patents to promote scientific progress, and the fecundity of our cultural landscape requires similar guarantees.

Currently, though, intellectual property law and the litigious impulses of a consolidated media industry with unlimited financial resources and political influence prevent cultural creators from borrowing corporate-controlled images and reproductions, even for seemingly "fair use" purposes. To take just one of his many examples, Lessig introduces the reader to Jon Else, a documentary filmmaker who encounters trouble while directing a film about the San Francisco Opera. During a performance of Wagner's Ring Cycle, Else captures a deliciously ironic shot of the hall's stagehands playing checkers in their lounge below the stage while *The Simpsons* airs on a television in the corner of the room, thus wonderfully blurring the distinctions between classical art and mass culture. Although both *Simpsons* creator Matt Groening and Gracie Productions granted Else permission to use the 4.5 seconds of the indirect shot of the program, Gracie's parent company Fox demanded that the director pay $10,000 for the privilege or else face a possible lawsuit and an injunction prohibiting him from releasing the film. Faced with these unattractive options, Else censored his own work by cutting the image from the shot, even though his actions might have reasonably been covered under fair use protection.

According to Lessig, the health of any democratic society requires that its cultural products and ideas be available for unfettered distribution, commentary, and eventual innovation and appropriation to ensure their rejuvenation and evolution over time.

The threat of litigation restricts contemporary artists who choose self-censorship over sinking into debt to fight off lawsuits from corporate giants like Fox, even winnable ones; in such cases, what is legally considered de jure fair use and thus permissible by statute can hardly be acknowledged as de facto fair use in any practical sense. According to Lessig, the rise of new media technologies only exacerbates this problem by choking the options of consumers and creators. According to current copyright law, it is within one's rights as the purchaser of a compact disc, paperback novel, or newspaper to lend it to friends, sell it to a secondhand shop, or give it a third and fourth listen or read oneself, as these activities constitute fair use. In a digitized format, however, doing any of these things with a cultural object under copyright protection can be illegal since using even a fragment of a digitized text (such as a downloaded photograph or an excerpt from an electronically published book or journal article) always involves making a new electronic copy of the material in question, whether by pulling up one's own file, sending an e-mail to a friend, or accessing a family member's Web site.

In certain cases, each use can constitute an entirely separate alleged offense, as Rensselaer Polytechnic Institute freshman Jesse Jordan learned the hard way when he modified a preexisting search engine built for his school's network, allowing students to access one another's publicly available computer files, including those containing music. The following year the Recording Industry Association of America (RIAA) sued Jordan for "willfully" violating copyright law and demanded statutory damages of $150,000 per infringement. RIAA alleged that each use of a music file constituted a separate infringement and cited more than one hundred individual acts of illegality. According to RIAA, Jordan owed $15 million in damages.

Stories such as these symbolize the profiteering behavior of culture industries in the digital age, demonstrating that while in theory the rise of new media offers cultural workers the autonomy to produce original art, in practice it is difficult to harness new technologies for sampling the products or challenging the dominance of global conglomerates. In fact, in most cases independent creators cannot gain permission to use logos, cartoon characters, and other images that *promote* corporate-controlled merchandise (Klein 1999). While digital technologies allow for an unprecedented abuse of preexisting copyright law, the tools provided by Web-based search engines allow major media companies to efficiently monitor the Internet landscape and identify violators for harassment and legal action. As Naomi Klein (1999, 178) argues, "The underlying message is that culture is something that happens to you. You buy it at the Virgin Megastore or Toys 'R' Us and rent it at Blockbuster Video. It is not something in which you participate, or to which you have the right to respond."

Of course, the technological architecture of the digital age is hardly deterministic. As Lessig himself contends, technological advances must compete with shifting trends in the law, the commercial market, and changing social norms. Likewise, the protectionism brought about by technological change is an old and familiar tale. While the Internet has provoked anxiety among industry leaders that its "revolutionary" nature may lead to the wholesale destruction of commercial mass media through peer-to-peer file sharing, audio sampling, and other forms of "piracy," similarly alarmist suspicions have historically surfaced in instances when a new technology has gained popularity, including FM radio, audiotape, videocassette recording, and now digital reproduction. When confronted with the emergence of high-fidelity FM radio as a viable alternative to its AM dominion, in 1936 RCA used its influence with the Federal Communications Commission (FCC) to effectively undermine FM's development for decades to come. After Sony introduced its Betamax video recorder, Disney and Universal sued the company for manufacturing a device that enabled users to duplicate copyright-protected films and television programs. Lessig describes the now-laughable panic expressed by Motion Picture Association of America (MPAA) president Jack Valenti during his 1982 testimony before the U.S. Senate Judiciary Committee: "When there are 20, 30, 40 million of these VCRs in the land, we will be invaded by millions of 'tapeworms,' eating away at the very heart and essence of the most precious asset the copyright owner has, his copyright" (p. 76).

In addition, the vilified behavior attributed to teenage users of file-sharing services like Napster hardly seems rebellious when compared to the zealous acts of piracy historically committed by more established media enterprises throughout the twentieth century. Independent film companies fled to Hollywood during the first decades of the century to evade federal policing over the unlicensed use of Thomas Edison's patented technologies. Prior to 1909, the recording industry routinely appropriated the works of composers without offering remuneration, while radio stations currently compensate songwriters for airing their records but not the recording artists themselves. In the postwar era, the first cable television companies sold access to the content of broadcasters to viewers without actually paying for it themselves, and twice the Supreme Court ruled that the copyright holders of this rebroadcast content did not deserve compensation. As Lessig points out, "Cable companies were thus Napsterizing broadcasters' content, but more egregiously than anything Napster ever did—Napster never charged for the content it enabled others to give away" (pp. 59-60).

Lessig demonstrates the evolutionary, nondeterministic progress of digitizing cultural production and suggests some of the more disturbing social and political ramifications of new media in its current forms. But at times his argument suggests the same extremism expressed by more effusive celebrants of the digital age: presumably, not all cultural innovators suffer the same consequences as Jon Else, Jesse Jordan, and the other victims of corporate power celebrated by Lessig in *Free Culture*. How do less newsworthy cultural workers sustain both their livelihoods and creativity in the face of existing challenges? Given the legal, social, and commercial constraints Lessig identifies as hindrances for the development of otherwise inventive cultural work, what kinds of daily strategies do they implement in their given professions to bypass such inconveniences? Do professionals working in computer graphics and animation, synthesized audio, software design, electronic book publishing, and other related fields of digitized art and communication negotiate these stumbling blocks in the same manner, or do they rely on more distinct methods of evasion and accommodation? These are empirical questions and require further social scientific investigation. Nevertheless, Lessig's *Free Culture*, along with Boczkowski's *Digitizing the News* and Head's *The New Ruthless Economy*, provides a careful reassessment of the so-called revolutionary consequences of new media and cultural production in the digital age.

Notes

1. A similar critique of technological determinism is suggested by the "new institutionalism" perspective in sociology and other culturally oriented approaches to organizational behavior, including ethnographic studies of technology-based firms and agencies (Powell and DiMaggio 1991; Kunda 1992; Vaughan 1996). On the impact of marketplace demands on artistic and cultural production, see Becker (1982), Fine (1996), Peterson (1997), and Grazian (2003, 2004).

2. As Head argues, when seasoned agents quit, they are inevitably replaced by inexperienced workers who are incapable of retaining clients at the same rate as their longer-term counterparts. In addition, new hires require rounds of costly on-the-job training and are typically less efficient and confident workers than their more senior coworkers. They also generate a lower yield of high-quality employee referrals.

References

Becker, Howard S. 1982. *Art worlds*. Berkeley: University of California Press.

Fine, Gary Alan. 1996. *Kitchens: The culture of restaurant work*. Berkeley: University of California Press.

Grazian, David. 2003. *Blue Chicago: The search for authenticity in urban blues clubs*. Chicago: University of Chicago Press.

———. 2004. The production of popular music as a confidence game: The case of the Chicago blues. *Qualitative Sociology* 27 (2): 137-58.

Hammer, Michael, and James Champy. 2001. *Reengineering the corporation: A manifesto for business revolution*. New York: HarperCollins.

Hammer, Michael, and Steven A. Stanton. 1995. *The reengineering revolution*. New York: HarperCollins.

Klein, Naomi. 1999. *No logo: Taking aim at the brand bullies*. New York: Picador.

Kunda, Gideon. 1992. *Engineering culture: Control and commitment in a high-tech corporation*. Philadelphia: Temple University Press.

Lewis, Michael. 2000. *The new new thing: A Silicon Valley story*. New York: Norton.

———. 2001. *Next: The future just happened*. New York: Norton.

Patterson, Randall. 2000. The idled workaholic. *The New York Times Magazine*, March 5, p. 64.

Peterson, Richard A. 1992. Understanding audience segmentation: From elite and mass to omnivore and univore. *Poetics* 21:243-58.

———. 1997. *Creating country music: Fabricating authenticity*. Chicago: University of Chicago Press.

Powell, Walter W., and Paul J. DiMaggio, eds. 1991. *The new institutionalism in organizational analysis*. Chicago: University of Chicago Press.

Sennett, Richard. 1998. *The corrosion of character: The personal consequences of work in the new capitalism*. New York: Norton.

Shapiro, Samantha M. 2003. The Dean connection. *The New York Times Magazine*, December 7.

Vaughan, Diane. 1996. *The Challenger launch decision: Risky technology, culture, and deviance at NASA*. Chicago: University of Chicago Press.

QUICK READ SYNOPSIS

Cultural Production in a Digital Age

Special Editor: ERIC KLINENBERG
New York University

Volume 597, January 2005

Prepared by Herb Fayer (Consultant)

Global Networks and the Effects on Culture

Alexander R. Galloway, New York University

Protocols	At the core of networked computing is the concept of protocols.

- The protocols that govern much of the Internet are contained in what are called RFC (Request for Comments) documents.
- The RFCs are published by the Internet Engineering Task Force (IETF) and are used predominantly by engineers who wish to build hardware or software that meet common specifications.
- The IETF is affiliated with the Internet Society, an altruistic, technocratic organization that wishes to ensure the open development, evolution, and use of the Internet for the benefit of all people.
- Many of the Web's protocols are governed by the World Wide Web Consortium (W3C).
- Protocols refer specifically to standards governing the implementation of specific technologies.
  - Computer protocols establish points necessary to enact an agreed-upon standard of action.
  - Computer protocols govern how specific technologies are agreed to, adopted, implemented, and ultimately used by people around the world.

NOTE: These regulations always operate at the level of coding—they encode packets of information so they may be transported, documents so they may be effectively parsed, and communications so local devices may effectively communicate with foreign devices.

Internet Scientists	Technical protocols and standards are established by a self-selected oligarchy of scientists consisting largely of electrical engineers and computer specialists.

- This technocratic elite toils away, mostly voluntarily, to hammer out solutions to advancements in technology.
- This group is described as an ad-hocracy of well-meaning geniuses.

- To keep the system working, the protocol designers built into the system several key characteristics:
  - The Internet protocols are designed to accommodate massive contingency.
  - The general principle is be conservative in what you do and be liberal in what you accept from others.

ANSI

ANSI, the American National Standards Institute, is responsible for aggregating and coordinating the standards creation process in the United States.
- It is a conduit for federally accredited organizations in the field that are developing technical standards.
- ANSI verifies that the rules have been followed before a proposed standard is adopted.
- ANSI is also responsible for articulating a national standards strategy for the United States—it is the only organization that can approve standards as American national standards.
- ANSI standards are voluntary, which means that no one is bound by law to adopt them.
  - The burden of a standard's success lies in the marketplace.
  - While most technical standards today are voluntary, this does not mean they are haphazardly or infrequently adopted. In fact, the core standards of the Internet are some of the most universally adopted technologies in history.

Effects of Standards

What are the social and cultural effects of universal network standards?
- The principles of flexibility and robustness have changed everything from economic supply chains to buying a book on Amazon.
- Its worth looking at computer viruses:
  - Computer viruses thrive in environments that have low levels of diversity. Whenever a technology has a monopoly, such as Microsoft's Windows, you will find viruses.
  - Computer viruses are able to propagate far and wide in computer networks by leveraging a single vulnerability from computer to computer. Diversity would kill out viruses overnight.

NOTE: The various internal characteristics of the Internet can be leveraged in powerful ways by malicious code because the Internet is so highly standardized. Viruses can route around problems and stoppages because of the robustness of the Internet. Because the Internet is so decentralized, it is virtually impossible to kill viruses once they are released.

Political Challenges

The Internet was invented to avoid certain vulnerabilities of nuclear attack.
- In the original vision, the organizational design of the Internet involved a high degree of redundancy to avoid a total wipeout.
- The Internet can survive attacks not because it is stronger than the opposition, but precisely because it is weaker—it is the opposite design of a pinpoint nuclear blast.
- Destruction of a network has to be an all-or-nothing game or it survives.
- Networks can be used for good or bad.
  - Drug cartels, terror groups, and underworld figures all take advantage of it.
  - Yet both corporations and grassroots activist groups make productive use of the Internet also.

Cultural
Production

The author offers a few instructions for those interested in the effects of global computer networks on cultural production.

- First is the principle of openness to leverage the swelling mass of social momentum.
- Second, build social institutions that can "route around" problems just like core protocols do.
- Third, a warning: following the robustness principle, networking technology will tend to standardize rather than diversify.

NOTE: Cultural producers will become more and more encumbered by technologies that exploit standardized systems, such as spam, e-mail worms, and viruses.

- Those interested in cultural production must understand the political import of networks.
- The powers that be have finally come to understand networks, and what was previously liberating about networks may not be liberating in the future.

Q
R
S

Multiple Media, Convergent Processes, and Divergent Products: Organizational Innovation in Digital Media Production at a European Firm

Pablo J. Boczkowski and José A. Ferris,
MIT Sloan School of Management

Background

This article explores the role of technology in news work and the processes that shape media convergence and its consequences.

- Previous research has suggested that the digitization of information erases the boundaries that separate print, radio, television, and online technologies and by implication or assumption lead to the production of homogeneous news products.
- This article examines the dynamics of a large European media firm from 1994 to 2003 to paint a more complex portrait of change.
- The study shows that understanding the technological dimension of news production is critical to making sense of editorial dynamics. Technical considerations affect who gets to tell the story, what kinds of stories are told, how they are told, and to what public they are addressed.

GMS History

GMS—a fictional name for the firm being examined—was born in 1990 from the merger of five publishing and related companies. It began as a print publisher and added broadcast and online media in the past ten years.

- Digital media's position within GMS changed dramatically during this period. It went from being a secondary function, to becoming the primary strategic focus, to being integrated with other media. Different organizational structures were created to reflect and enable these changes in function and status.
- At the end of 1995, the Electronic Extensions Department was created to centralize digital media development.
  - It was seen as a secondary function—an extension to the core print business.

- Personnel assigned to create online publications were located in the newsrooms but reported to Electronic Extensions.
- Their status was subordinate to traditional journalists, who viewed new hires in digital media as computer experts with no understanding of journalism.
- The first Web pages reproduced the newspaper content; added online-only features were seen as secondary to the print products.

GMS Prepares At the end of the 1990s, GMS executives prepared to take the company public.
to Go Public
- They decided to make the Internet Department into a company within the company and make the whole of GMS revolve around the Internet Department.
- This department was to oversee all the content of the online publications and
  - develop and implement new tools to support these publications,
  - pursue new opportunities in the nonprint business, and
  - infuse the company with a new media ethos.
- Traditional newsrooms moved into Internet departments.
- The Internet Department generated online publications that drew content originally created for the traditional media but added information and services that took advantage of the Web.
  - They wrote shorter story versions for print and longer versions for the Internet.
  - They built online, searchable archives.

Newsroom   The Internet bust of the late 1990s shattered people's faith in the central role
Integration of the Internet department with the firm.
- They reoriented GMS from a media company to a content company.
- They created three divisions: Sports, Business, and Other.
- And they renamed the Internet Department as the Digital Media Department.
- Traditional editors assumed control of online content.
- Digital Media became a unit supporting GMS online publications, developing new tools, and seeking new business opportunities.
- A given reporter could now write a radio story, rewrite it for the Web, and then again rewrite the story for the next day's newspaper.
- A newspaper now works to increase its counterpart radio audience and number of visitors to an accompanying Web page while those departments' staffs do the same for the newspaper.
- Editors sit next to each other at a new location, while reporters are grouped according to areas of specialization.
- A single newsroom produces content for multiple media.

Conclusion   Studies of cultural production in digital media have often emphasized the product homogenization that results from media convergence. The story at GMS, however, presents a more complicated picture.
- Digital media moved from being a secondary endeavor to the very axis of content production, converging with the print and broadcast units to form a single system of production.
- But content, format, and functionality of products remains diverse, as a result of differences in technology and differences in background, expertise, and orientation of traditional and new media personnel.

Convergence: News Production in a Digital Age

Eric Klinenberg, New York University

Q
R
S

Background

Lacking current research, critics are left to guess about strategies, practices, and interests that shape major news corporations; determine the content of news products; and produce the "symbolic power" of publicly defining, delimiting, and framing key issues and events.
- This article examines the point of journalistic production in one major news organization (Metro News) and shows how reporters and editors manage constraints of time, space, and market pressure in companies producing content for multiple types of media such as radio, print, TV, and the Internet.

Changes in the Journalistic Field

Changes in the journalistic field, particularly new technologies and the corporate integration of news companies, have led to double fragmentation:
- First, for newsmakers, whose daily work has been interrupted and rearranged by additional responsibilities and new pressures of time and space.
- Second, for news audiences, whom marketers have segmented into narrow groups based on commercial considerations.

Metro News

Media evolution in a company like Metro News has gone through four key development strategies.
- Going from private to public companies with a bottom-line demand from stockholders.
- Streamlining production systems in the newsroom and reducing labor costs.
- Making massive investments in digital communications technologies.
- Establishing lines of horizontal integration, which meant acquiring other content providers and distributors, such as TV stations, Internet companies, and magazines and also linking the marketing and news divisions across these diverse media companies—reporters had to learn to produce content useable in all media.
    - Each media segment uses the products of the others to enhance its offerings and cross promote its brands.
    - Sales people can work for all the segments and can create special packages of media.
    - News bureaus can be streamlined and combined—reporters in Los Angeles or New York find their work being used by different papers and other media at once.
    - Freelancers can broker deals with a corporate network to provide content across media lines.
    - Each branch of the operation produces content for several media at once—staffs of different media segments share information and content.

Organizational Changes

The organizational transformation of Metro News has produced changes in the physical and social space of its offices.
- Journalists can move freely between print, broadcast, and Internet departments to meet the demands of the new environment.
- Newspaper staff worry that the mission is determined by the production values of TV news. But they are interested because TV represents a route to celebrity, wealth, and influence for journalists in these big media companies.

- The new environment has forced newspaper journalists to take on additional responsibilities in the same work period, which has consequences for cultural production.
- Instead of twenty-four-hour newspaper deadlines, the time cycle for news making is radically different: it is an unending news "cyclone" that works around the clock to fulfill twenty-four-hour news programming.
- In the new media newsroom, journalists have to become flexible laborers, reskilled to meet demands from several media at once.
  - They learn that content does not move easily from one medium to the next. They have to work to adapt material.
  - Being flexible adds to employee value within organization.
- The editorial staff has less time to research, report, and even to think about their work.
  - Concerns about efficiency can push journalists to rely on the most easily accessible information—online information.
  - Errors from lack of confirmation and use of misinformation become more likely.
  - Production of the easiest to produce content becomes the norm and reduces investigative type journalism.

Target Marketing

Digital news systems have enabled media organizations to push the principles of target marketing to new levels so they can appeal to narrow groups of consumers that can be sold by one advertising staff.

- The mass audience has been fragmented to give each segment what they want in news and entertainment.
- The strategy is to locate and target affluent audiences in the suburbs at the expense of poorer rural and inner-city areas so advertising rates can be raised.

Convergence Production

Sharing resources and staff helps companies expand the scope of their reporting.

- The Internet, rather than TV or print, offers the most exciting possibilities for creating new forms of journalism with advanced technology and convergence production.
  - The Internet is ideal for deepening coverage with interactive links to video, text, and graphics where you can produce a new kind of content.
- Print staff can help improve the quality of TV news since TV staffs are small and print reporters bring depth to their offerings.
- Print journalists are concerned that visual information is promoted at the expense of text and that production forms of TV will take over newspaper style.
- When news organizations do cover national and international events, journalists are encouraged to illustrate why news far from home is relevant to the local community.
- Target marketing and convergence production have helped to create informational islands of communities who receive specialized news products.

Consequences

The consequences of the emergent journalistic and managerial practices are already visible.

- Convergence news companies expect their staff to be flexible and fast.
- Editors and managers are revaluing their workers, considering multimedia skills in their assignments. Some hiring and retention decisions are based on these skills.
- Time available to report, research, write, and reflect on stories has shrunk.

- An elite group of reporters are able to do investigative work, and the rest have more responsibilities than ever.

Conclusion The penetration of market principles and marketing projects into the editorial divisions of news organizations is one of the most dramatic changes in journalism.
- Editors work hard to produce more marketable and profitable products.
- Corporate managers and advertisers are the now active participants in editorial decision making, and their interests now structure the form and content of news to unprecedented levels.
- Extensive research is used to learn what kinds of content consumers want, which has made important qualitative changes in their offerings to meet market demand.
- Digital technologies have changed journalistic production, but not according to the journalists' preferences—the goal is productivity, efficiency, and profitability.
- Technology is used to facilitate the process of multimedia work and to increase the capacity to repackage articles from platform to platform.
NOTE: Digital systems in major news companies remain in the early stages, and their direction for growth will be determined by the political economy, cultural conventions, and regulatory restrictions.

Q
R
S

Digital Gambling: The Coincidence of Desire and Design

Natasha Dow Schull,
Institute for Social and Economic Research and Policy

Background Digitally enhanced gambling machines, rather than traditional forms of gambling, now drive the gambling industry. In Las Vegas, machines garner twice the combined revenue of all other games. This turn to technology has consequences for player experience. More broadly, the case illuminates distinctive characteristics of the "digital age."

Game Design Digital gambling machines are designed to increase profit by increasing "time on device" or *duration* of play, and by ensuring *speed* and *continuity* of play.
- To increase time spent playing, single machines are programmed with many gaming opportunities such that players can explore, browse, and experiment from a selection of games without leaving their seats.
  - Some systems allow players to view TV shows and closed-circuit events; others allow players to print bingo tickets.
  - From their game terminals, players can place requests for change, drinks, a mechanic, etc.
  - Mobile ATMs, wireless units, and portable credit card advance systems function to keep money flowing to the player. Players can even transfer funds directly from a checking account to add to their machine credit.
- To speed up play, machines feature push buttons instead of pull handles, and bill acceptors reduce the time-consuming process of coin feeding.

Digital game design exploits the psychological principles of learning and conditioning.
- Digitized games intensify the variable intermittent reinforcement schedule with frequent small wins and near misses.
- The option to play off credit rather than to play coin by coin allows rapid replay and little consideration of financial loss.
- Multiple payout lines and the option to bet numerous coins on each play increases the machine productivity for the house.
  - These machines give the perception of winning on every pull even though the winnings are most times less than the total amount bet per "pull."
- Visual and auditory features (or "second-order conditioning") create a sense of winning and add another level of reinforcement to play.
- As game designers have learned how to "teach" players to stay at machines, they have learned how to adapt their technologies to the playing rhythms and reward preferences of individual players.
  - Some machines automatically adjust the pace and the game to the pace of the player—the faster one plays a machine, the faster the machine lets one play.
  - Some games feature reward schedules designed to appeal to low-denomination players seeking frequent small wins; other games appeal to high-denomination players seeking big wins.

Game Play Interaction with the digitally enhanced features of new games sustain a dissociated subjective state that gamblers call the "zone."
- The zone is a trance-like state that depends on isolation, noninterruption, speed, a sense of choice or control, and flow.
  - Digital gambling machines are designed to facilitate these elements by protecting gamblers from interruption, allowing continuous and rapid play, and lending gamblers a sense of autonomy to increase their investment in play.
- The zone suspends social, bodily, temporal, and monetary parameters of existence.
  - In the zone, players feel removed from their bodies.
  - Money loses its value for players—they play to stay in the zone, not to win.
  - Players lose a sense of "clock time."
  - Players have a sense of merging with the machines they play.
- The fact that machine design responds ever more immediately to player desire for the zone challenges the idea that digital enhancements in game design allow for greater player *entertainment*, suggesting instead that they allow for greater player *absorption*.
  - Some machines in Australia carry a feature called "auto play" that allows players to load the machine with credits and then simply sit and watch it play game after game for them, removing all sense of interactivity or autonomy in play.

Reflections Like their predecessors, digital gambling machines aim to harness space and time to financially generative ends. They do not abandon strategies of modern discipline and value extraction such as fragmentation, regimentation, and discontinuity, yet they refine these to a point where player experience becomes one of continuous flow. The fact that the continuous flow of play translates into "continuous productivity" for the gambling industry raises troubling questions about the use to which digital capabilities are put in contemporary consumer technology design.

Mobilizing Fun in the Production and Consumption of Children's Software

Mizuko Ito, University of Southern California

Background and Framework

From the late 1970s to the end of the 1990s, a new set of cultural, economic, technological, and social relations emerged in the United States, centered on using computers to create entertaining learning experiences for young children.

- PCs held out the promise of interactive, child-driven, entertaining, and open-ended learning environments that differed from the top-down structure of traditional classroom instruction.
- Children's software development is part of broader trends toward engineering play through the design of media targeted to children.

Contemporary childhood in the United States is produced through a variety of social, cultural, and economic negotiations where media industries and technologies play an increasingly central role.

- "Education" and "entertainment" or a central polarity in the construction of children's culture and society.
- Discourse of digital kids promises to cross the divide between "passive" entertainment and "active" learning media.
- In practice, the distinctions between passive and active, top-down and democratic, entertainment and educational media are not so clear-cut.

The Children's Software Industry

Multimedia united the lowbrow appeal of popular visual culture with the highbrow promise of the PC and the educational ideal of child-centered learning.

- Early developers shared an educational reform orientation, seeking to enrich children's learning as well as liberate it from the dry, serious, and often alienating culture of the classroom.
- The 1990s saw graphics and visual appeal become central to software design.
- These new ventures were not under the same constraints as classroom software and were given more freedom to have content that appealed directly to children—a shift from a pedagogy to entertainment.
- Entertainment was an expanding site of negotiation and struggle between the interests of educators, entertainers, programmers, artists, and businesspeople, with entertainment gaining a strong voice.
- The market for children's software is being polarized between a hodgepodge of school-coded content and wholesome entertainment titles that are marketed as an alternative to action games.
  - Ads for this software portray children as ecstatic and pleasure-seeking rather than reflective and brainy.
  - Ads play on parents' desires to indulge their children's pleasures.
  - They show that entertainment products can compete with TV and videos and still have some educational value.
- "Edutainment" titles are generally linear and make much of achieving certain levels and scores, while entertainment software are exploratory, often repetitive, and open-ended.

Field Sites: The 5thD is an activity system where elementary-aged children and under-
5thD Clubs   graduates from a local university come together to play with educational soft-
ware in an after-school setting.
- There is a commitment to a collaborative and child-centered approach to learning, mixing of participants of different ages, and the use of PCs.
- In software programs like *The Magic School Bus*, kids learn through a chaotic and dizzying set of encounters where characters in a story careen from one scene to another—representing the shift towards entertainment.
- In the 5thD, an orientation to fun is actively encouraged—fun indicates authentic engagement and is celebrated to the extent it happens in the context of a prosocial learning task.
- The 5thD accommodates both child and adult agendas, creating opportunities for cross-generational negotiation and shared discourse.

Spectacle and   Visual effects are used to keep attention.
Special Effects   • Recordings of kids at play with graphically advanced games is punctuated by their reactions to on-screen eye candy that testifies to their appreciation of visual aesthetics of one kind or another.

Mobilizing Fun   The interactional and auditory special effects serve to give the experience of being able to control and manipulate the production of the effect.
- A sound effect is a result of a particular action and, when initiated by the player, is often the occasion for delight and repeated activation.
- Pleasure in this interaction can be understood as a kind of computer holding power that creates a brief but tight interactional coupling of player and game.
- The interactive special effect is somewhat antisocial, relying on a tight coupling of player and machine, often at the expense of other people in the setting.
- Interactional effects are similar to the manipulations of clay and finger paints but are mediated by a program that uniquely amplifies and embellishes the actions of the user—a momentary and aesthetic pleasure.

Adults use "fun" to describe engagement, and kids use it to describe spectacular and no-instrumental activity.
- "Fun" becomes a tool for kids to define a kid-centered social and cultural space defined against adult goals, such as when a child plays extensively with the disaster function of *SimCity 2000*.

Conclusion   Fun and spectacle is an important focus for kid peer solidarity that is structurally defined in opposition to educational goals and institutions.
- Entertainment industries are allied with kids in creating these kid cultures.

Although children's software was founded on a challenge to existing idioms of education and entertainment, existing discursive, social, and political alignments across sites of production, distribution, marketing, and consumption have tempered this transformative promise.
- As alternative models for software production and distribution take hold, we may find that children's software can truly redefine cultural logics of contemporary childhood established in the TV era.

Q
R
S

Audience Construction and Culture Production: Marketing Surveillance in the Digital Age

Joseph Turow, University of Pennsylvania

Background

The digital world being built by marketers has as a core belief that success will come from seducing customers to provide personal data in return for rewarding relationships with media and marketers.

- Marketers would like to ensure that their target views targeted, even customized, commercials on the Web or TV.
- Valued targets may be offered discounts, special programming, and custom messages.
  - Such seemingly benign relationships can lead to feelings of discrimination if other viewers believe they are not getting the discounts or special materials.
  - Customer relationship management (CRM) specialists have learned to make the above feelings a private issue resulting from the rules of collaboration.
  - Good customers try to show by their purchases that they deserve more and those that exit the relationship may suit the company just fine (being less valued customers).
- Efficient marketing means managing the customer roster—rewarding some, getting rid of others, improving the value of each of them.
- Critics say that media firms fundamentally shape the main streams of entertainment and news.
  - Audience definitions lead to the creation of certain kinds of media materials—the production of certain kinds of culture and not others.
  - Audience constructions are not derived from the social world, but the attributes they choose to highlight relate directly to industrial needs and provide justification for industrial activities.

Relationship Building

An emerging strategic logic encourages media firms and marketers to cultivate consumers' trust so audiences will not object when companies want to track their activities.

- The goal is to store personal and lifestyle information to be used to reward the best customers with discounts and even story lines designed for them.
- Advocacy groups decry this practice and push for alternatives.
- An ad-sponsored universe has profound implications for the production of entertainment, news, and information. The material must be successful in attracting audiences that advertisers want and getting them in a buying mood.

NOTE: It seems clear that important aspects of media culture will result from the strategies being laid out now under the rubric of giving the (industrially constructed) audience what it wants.

Issues Affecting Advertisers

There is a need to understand how changes affecting media and marketing organizations are interactively affecting construction of audience and media culture.

- The large number of media channels (created by cable TV and the Web) is making it difficult to reach potential customers efficiently with traditional advertising.
- Consumers are using technology to escape ads and keep content.
- Marketers are trying to figure how to cultivate customers via media in coming decades, which is pushing the production of media culture toward audience surveillance.
  - There are concerns for information privacy and ad-induced anxieties.
  - The model is based on CRM melded with direct marketing.

Customer Value   A major reason CRM attracts marketers is that it focuses on the quantifiable value of known individuals rooted in two insights:
- A small number of current customers contribute to most of the profit (focus 80 percent of your effort on the top 20 percent of your customers).
- It is almost always more expensive to gain new customers than to keep current ones who have a substantial lifetime value.
  - Marketers' ability to discriminate based on a customer's contribution to profit has become a badge of honor.
  - Privacy issues have forced companies to get permission to gather data from each customer.
  - Advertisers are experimenting with ways to insert themselves in customers' lives in ways that encourage surveillance and tailored relationships.

Direct   Direct marketers are at the forefront of where everyone in advertising is going
Marketing   to be.
- Customized media will apply the concepts of one-on-one marketing to gain the loyalty and trust of desirable audience members.
  - They are turning to the Web to cultivate relationships and collect data for targeting ads.

Walled Gardens   To generate new revenue streams to help pay for customized permission marketing, many online practitioners have used the "walled garden" approach.
- A walled garden is an environment where consumers go for information, communications, and commerce services. This setting discourages them from leaving for a larger digital world.
  - Consumers are enticed to enter, and then their activities are tracked.
  - The firm running it can charge for this service.
  - They offer incentives to stay, such as faster access to high-end applications and to premium content that others cannot see.
  - They claim to protect their users from things like spam, viruses, pop-ups, etc.
  - An example is Bell South getting $4.95 for fast access to add-on content from ABC.
- Interactive television is another service that can provide incentives and collect data in return.

NOTE: The emerging strategic logic of mainstream marketing and media organizations is to present their activities not as privacy invasion but as two-way relationships, not as commercial intrusion but as pinpoint selling help.

Remote Control:
The Rise of Electronic Cultural Policy

Siva Vaidhyanathan, New York University

Q
R
S

Background

Since the early 1990s, the United States has been formulating, executing, and imposing on the rest of the world a form of "electronic cultural policy." This includes:
- Policies to mandate design standards for electronic devices in ways that would dictate a set of cultural choices.
- The goal would be to encourage and enable "remote control."
  - Such mandates shift decisions over the manipulation of content from the user to the vendor with built-in regulating devices in digital hardware of all kinds.
  - Their potential has created a whole new set of forms of cultural domination by a handful of powerful global institutions.

NOTE: Fortunately, these efforts have been clumsy and incompetent—most are utter failures or have been hacked into irrelevancy. These policies have ignited global indignation and disobedience.

Reimagineering

Powerful forces have acted to reengineer or reimagineer the way individuals handle media and manipulate texts and images.
- This electronic cultural policy guides the architecture of interfaces, networks, standards, protocols, and formats that house and deliver cultural products.
- Individuals have been employing tools that allow them to evade some of the most powerful instruments of cultural policy.
  - They have spurred powerful interests to demand more expansive means of enforcement.
  - The commercial film industry and the governments that do its bidding are willing to go to extreme measures to preserve their global cultural and commercial standing—this is "cultural imperialism."

Cultural Policy

The battle over formats and terms of delivery and distribution date back to the struggles to regulate early radio in the United States.
- Major industry players were wise to enact regulations to limit competition.
- This model of industry-state synergy extended to television, cable, and telecommunication.
- The exception is the Internet, which has minimal state oversight and no dominant firms dictating policy.
- Panic over the radical democracy of Internet use has pushed established content producers to try to rein in the freedom of use of PCs and the Internet.
- The leaders of copyright-producing industries started a movement to shift the site of regulation from the courts to the machines themselves with the use of chips and software.
- The developed world pushed for the establishment of the World Intellectual Property Organization (WIPO) and the Trade Related Aspects of Intellectual Property Rights (TRIPS) accord.
  - Members may, through the World Trade Organization (WTO) enforcement mechanisms, seek retribution for violations.

• The United States used the WTO to force nations that sought favorable trade in other areas to sign with TRIPS and follow a set of regulations on global minimum standards for copyright, patent, trade secret, trademark, etc.

• Many developing nations stood their ground against these dictates and made it clear that the United States and Europe could not dictate terms of intellectual policy.

  • Concerns that these nations are havens for software and video pirates has kept pressure on their governments to adopt U.S.-style laws.

NOTE: Many countries including the United States have laws forbidding the distribution of any technologies that might crack access or copy control mechanisms for digital materials. These laws take us from the realm of human judgment to a technocratic regime of enforcement.

Copyright Changes

Where once users could assume wide latitude in their private, noncommercial uses, now a layer of enforcement code (U.S. Digital Millennium Copyright Act [DMCA]) stands in the way of access to the work itself, preventing a variety of harmless uses.

• Access controls allow content providers to totally regulate use in their own terms.

• Copyright laws now can, against the intent of such laws, allow infinite time of protection. Many providers work over and above real copyright law with their own software-based protections.

• The DMCA ensures that producers may exercise editorial control over the uses of their materials.

  • They can automatically restrict parody and criticism.
  • They can automatically restrict reuse of facts or ideas.

Global Broadcasting

The most ambitious attempt at imposing electronic cultural policy considered by the WIPO is to allow broadcasters, not copyright holders, to control video distribution rights.

• Consumers would have no rights to copy or edit videos for home use.

• Such regulations would shut down independent recording firms like TiVO and replace them with recorders owned, controlled, and monitored by broadcasters.

• These standards would require manufacturers to build into TVs a device that would regulate access to and the copying of encrypted materials.

• Another bill introduced in Congress would allow copyright holders to hack in and disrupt a computer's ability to communicate with others if they suspect violations.

• There is a clamoring for more intrusive and restrictive measures, which has caused a creative and political backlash.

Conclusion

Global information regulatory systems are absurd.

• Such absurdity stems from a widespread anxiety that digitization and networking will wreak havoc on cultural industries.

• Participating in a pirate economy is easier than ever. Participating in a legitimate, competitive economy is easier than ever.

• But participating in a legitimate information or cultural economy is harder and more expensive than ever under new regulations.

• The spread of top-down global electronic cultural policy has the potential to chill both technological and cultural experimentation.

The Changing Place of Cultural Production: The Location of Social Networks in a Digital Media Industry

Gina Neff, University of California, San Diego

Background

Scholars have pointed to the social ties that link companies together across a geographic region as the foundation of innovative, creative, and emergent industries, with social networking being the process to get people together to share ideas, information, and feelings.

- An industry's parties, seminars, and informal gatherings form its social backbone and allow the rapid dissemination of information.
- The Internet industry owes much to networking and networking affects where people choose to live. People in the industry prefer access the social network—being where the action is, is important.
- This article looks at the social networks in New York City's Silicon Alley, the home base of Internet companies in New York.

Geographic Clustering

Even within a digital media industry that relies on the technologies that enable distance work, social networks can lead to tight geographic clustering.

Social Networks

Social networks provide workers with a type of job security in which personal connections serve as conduits for information about new jobs and new technologies.

- Workers unable to access these networks may be at a disadvantage.
- In Silicon Alley, the absence of other organizational supports meant one's network became the main source for maintaining employability.
- Networks encourage collaboration, keep people up to date, and build environments of innovation.
- "Noise" (rumors, impressions, recommendations, trade folklore, strategic misinformation) may tie the workforce together through a process of negotiating meaning and of sense-making.
  - Noise socializes and enculturates workers, transmitting the norms, practices, and stories of the work community.
  - Telecommunication advances that increased information may make the instinctual interpretation of noise even more important.

Venues of Creativity

Neighborhoods with the reputation for fostering artistic production provide individual cultural producers with resources that facilitate creative activity.

- The art galleries, bars, restaurants, and other nightlife venues are new intersections of consumption and production.
- These venues make it easier for cultural producers to recognize and establish contact with one another.
- Silicon Alley became a thriving cultural space and incorporated the creative values of its workforce into industry practice through the nightlife events.
- The intensified social networking that occurred suggests that the events themselves become an important place of production within creative industries.

- New York had one of the country's highest concentration of commercial Internet domains—this concentration is reflected in the clustering of industry nightlife events.

Social Reporting

Social events reporting (gossip columns) is underused for collecting data.
- Event reporting formed a who's who of Silicon Alley.
- Events also provided companies with access to potential employees and clients, as well as access to people in other industries such as arts and media and business and finance.
- Reporting of who hosted and attended events showed who was part of the industry in Silicon Alley.
- Social networking became an industry with event planners and event management companies hired to handle parties.
- Being close to the nighttime action was important for positioning a company within Silicon Alley.

Conclusion

City and business leaders looking to foster creative industries should consider how to encourage the formation of ties across organizations as a way to harness innovation.
- Some spaces will be more important and more central to the process of social networking and should be identified.
- Employees could face severe disadvantages if they are unable to participate in the frenzy of nighttime activity.
NOTE: If we are to fully understand markets and economic processes as "tangible social construction," then the relational richness of social ties must be studied simultaneously with the structures that organize industries. Studying the emergence of informal organization across industry players is one mechanism for research.

Deep Democracy, Thin Citizenship:
The Impact of Digital Media
in Political Campaign Strategy

Philip N. Howard, University of Washington

Background

Analyzing how political campaigns produce political content and how citizens consume this content may be the best way to assess the health of the public sphere, the space where people exchange ideas and challenge opinions.
- First, it requires shared text and content about political campaigns and public policy options.
- Second, it requires conversation about political affairs.
- Third, it requires a place for action: legislatures, courts, voting booths, etc.
NOTE: Increasingly digital technologies allow for both the production and consumption of political content.

Databases and Predictive Models

Both campaigns and citizens buy databases online that match voter's names and addresses with voter registration records, credit card purchases, and more.

- Anybody involved in a campaign is always concerned about control, but chat is difficult to control, so managers have very specific uses for the online tools they build.
- Campaign consultants use models to predict political outcomes, and the new technologies help improve their accuracy—they make reliable calculations about elections or legislative votes on issues important to their members.
- Digital technologies make possible a refined science of campaigning with ever more predictable electoral or legislative outcomes.

Consultants　　Political consultants usually offer three kinds of services.
- When lobby groups form, consultants build legitimacy for the cause by identifying members unaware of the need for representation.
- These firms do direct-inference public policy polling.
- These firms also do indirect-inference polling from surveys, demographic data, credit card purchases, Internet activity, or voter registration files.

New Media　　With new media tools, political campaigns amass data from so many sources in
Tools　　complex relational databases that are used to extrapolate political information without ever directly contacting anyone.
- When they do contact people, they sample exactly who they want to sample.
- Today's commercially available political information is multisourced, nuanced, and scaled from named individuals and households to residential blocks, zip codes, and electoral districts.

Political　　The market for political information now includes advertising and public rela-
Information　　tions agencies, media and entertainment companies, university research institutes, pollsters, nonprofits, political parties, Internet service providers, and PACs.
- Most of these organizations associate with academic research institutions to appear more legitimate—they use university names liberally in business plans and literature.
- The cost of polling has dropped and is now available to anyone who wants to spend the money for it.
- Most campaigns use informational products to try to narrowcast their messages by sending particular messages to particular people.
NOTE: The Internet is an integral part of campaign communications and a significant portion of the population uses it to learn about politics.

Political News　　There are several interesting changes in the way we produce and consume political news.
- The proportion of people who never look for political news has diminished.
- A sizeable number consult at least two types of media for political news.
- The number who consult three or four other kinds of media has increased steadily.
- Outside of news providers, six types of Web sites provide political content: special interest groups, office holders, candidates, partisan groups, nonpartisan groups, and community activist groups.
  - The Web sites of special interest groups capture most of the attention.

The Internet　　Although television is still the dominant medium for election news, those who have used the Internet for political information report why they prefer it as a medium.

- They find it more convenient, feel other media do not provide enough news, get information not available elsewhere, and find that online news sources reflect their personal interests.
- Mass media had distinct roles for the elite producers of content and the mass consumers of content, while digital communication is networked and can narrowcast.

Role for New Media

One of the most important roles for new media in politics has been in opening up the market for political information.
- Several companies now amass and market detailed profiles of citizens using traditional survey and data mining but have also developed powerful new media tools.
  - Their spider programs crawl through the Web, automatically collecting Web site content, such as personal contacts or press releases.
  - They use unsolicited e-mails to gather or spread information.
  - They use spyware covertly on a user's computer to record activities and political preferences.
- Most digital campaigns claim to share aggregated, not personally identifiable, information, but there is leakage.
  - In the 2000 campaign, several politicians altered their Web sites' privacy policy when they realized they had collected politically and commercially valuable data from their supporters.
- Consultants mislead people into surrendering personal information and often get permission to install spyware, which many panelists forget is on their machines.
- Political information now circulates in a marketplace where it is priced, trademarked, and sold.

Database Sources

Many political databases came from companies that provided free e-mail service and required subscribers to fill out questionnaires.
- Spyware is used to supplement this data.
- The largest databases now include information on more than 150 million registered voters.
- Personal information is secretly added to these databases without explicit or informed consent.
- PACs, as nonprofits, are able to access voter registration records and add this to databases.

Customized Messages

The combined relational databases are used to serve the private interests of political candidates or lobbyists—to uniquely customize messages to manipulate certain responses from particular individuals.
- Both political organizations and commercial industry are able to drive traffic to their Web sites by directing customized banner and e-mail ads via the political, demographic, and commercial characteristic profiles of members of the database.
  - Partner or affinity campaigns share data on sympathizers, members of the public, and elected officials.
  - Information is also now being collected globally.
- Both political and commercial organizations now conduct surveillance of citizen opinion on public policy questions.

Shared Text?

The competition between political campaigns results in smaller pieces of text being shared by smaller and smaller groups of people.

- Experienced Internet users self-segment by programming their news services to provide particular content—random encounters with political content is prevented for users and nonusers of the Internet.
  - Content is designed to entrench a citizen's political norms through software that privileges some content over other content.
  - Some of us identify our preferences by where we go for political information on the Internet or where we go to become members of organizations like the National Rifle Association, Sierra Club, or the Christian Coalition.
  - The campaign managers of these organizations take great interest in preparing content for their membership by reducing exposure to content from competing political agendas and editorializing the context.
  - These managers have developed tricks to direct the results of search engines to specific content.
- Digital technologies remove the random distribution of content, the kind of content that people casually pick up from newspapers and television.
- A healthy public needs shared text and acts of conversation, yet Americans increasingly use digital tools to research politics, which is increasingly fragmented for particular people whose interest have been secretly encoded.

Organizing Technologies:
Genre Forms of Online Civic Association
in Eastern Europe

Balázs Vedres, Central European University, László Bruszt, European University Institute (Florence), and David Stark, Columbia University

Background   Some believe that new information technologies will overcome the one-to-many character of the once-dominant mass media in favor of free flow, unmonitored connections among global citizens.
- Technology like the Internet wakes the dormant public by creating new domains of deliberation and participation.
- The cyber-citizen will be a user and producer of information and news and online debates.
- The public sphere will become virtual and global.

But are such visions likely to be realized? This article examines Web sites of emerging nongovernmental organizations (NGOs) in Eastern Europe for the likely outcomes of tomorrow's civil society.

Online Genres   An examination of 1,585 of these Web sites reveals five different archetypes or genres:
- Newsletters
  - typically include calendars of events and information about meetings and comprise nearly one-third of the NGO Web sites.
- Interactive Platforms
  - often allow the user to join the organization online and sign up for various services, are most likely not to provide information for offline reachability, are least likely to provide things like annual reports, and characterize about 20 percent of the NGO Web sites.

- Multilingual Solicitations
  - are likely to post reports that establish their legitimacy, are least likely to provide online means for joining, and characterize about 15 percent of the NGO sites.
- Directories
  - are least likely to have information about conferences and meetings, provide virtual directories, and characterize about 12 percent of NGO sites.
- Digital Brochures
  - provide offline reachability information, have very few links, are usually in one language, and characterize about 18 percent of NGO sites.

Analysis

These archetypical NGO Web sites are not aligned across stages of development from simple to sophisticated, as an analysis of the age of the Web sites reveals. Newer Web sites are actually more likely to have features that are typical of the genre to which they belong. Several of these genres are also more likely to have links pointing to them from other Web sites, increasing their accessibility and visibility to potential users through the technology of search engines. The Directory, Newsletter, and Multilingual Solicitation sites are more central to the Web in this regard than are the Brochure and Interactive Platforms.

Conclusion

The world of online civic organizations serves diverse specific publics through different levels and types of civic engagement that appear not to be converging on a single model. Inequalities in their visibility are shaped in part by the editors of news portals and designers of search engines that will likely sideline interactive Web sites and give greater voice to solicitations and newsletters.

The New Digital Media and Activist Networking within Anti–Corporate Globalization Movements

Jeffrey S. Juris, University of Southern California
Annenberg School for Communication

Background

A diverse coalition of environmental, labor, and economic justice activists succeeded in shutting down the meetings of the WTO in Seattle in 1999.
- Seattle became a symbol and battle cry for a new generation of activists, as antiglobalization networks were energized around the globe.
- Activists followed the events in Seattle and beyond through Internet-based distribution lists, Web sites, and the newly created Independent Media Center (IMC).
- Activist networks provided concrete mechanisms for communication and coordination in real time among diverse movements, groups, and collectives.

The WSF

The first World Social Forum (WSF) represented an important turning point, as activists began to more clearly emphasize specific alternatives.
- The WSF constitutes a dynamic process involving the convergence of multiple networks, movements, and organizations.

• Whereas Peoples Global Action remains more radical, the WSF is a wider political space including newer decentralized network-based movements and the more hierarchical traditional Left.

Anti–Corporate
Globalization

Three broad features characterize anti–corporate globalization movements:
• Although locally rooted, they are global in scope.
• They are informational.
• They are organized around a multiplicity of virtual and physical network forms.

Activists' Use of
the Internet

Anti–corporate globalization activists have employed digital networks to organize actions, share information and resources, and coordinate activities.
• They have made effective use of e-mail and electronic lists, which facilitate open participation and coordinate global protests.
• They create temporary Web pages during mobilizations to provide information and contact lists and post documents and calls to action.
NOTE: Internet use has complemented and facilitated face-to-face coordination and interaction, rather than replacing them.

Internet Value

The Internet does not simply provide the infrastructure for computer-supported social movements, it reinforces their organizational logic.
• Decentralized, flexible local/global networks constitute the dominant organizational forms within anti–corporate globalization movements.
• The absence of organizational centers within networks makes them adaptive, allowing activists to simply route around nodes that are no longer useful.
• Technology enhances the most radically decentralized movements by facilitating transnational coordination and communication.
• Within movements, networking logics have given rise to what many grassroots activists call a new way of doing politics—network-based politics involve the creation of broad umbrella spaces, where diverse organizations converge around common hallmarks while preserving their autonomy and specificity.

Shifting
Alliances

Radical anticapitalists face a continual dilemma about whether to operate within more strictly defined political formations, at the risk of being marginalized, or participate within broader spaces.
• Complex patterns of shifting alliances operate at local, regional, and transnational scales.
• Specific networks move between larger forums or do not participate at all, depending on the political context.
• Digitally powered social movement networks are rhizomatic: constantly fusing together and hiving off, driven by complex cultural politics within specific contexts.

Alternative
Media

Contemporary independent media activists have made effective use of new technology through alternative and tactical forms of digital media production.
• Alternative media constitute independent sources of news and information beyond the mainstream press.
• Such alternative or radical media also tend to be independently operated and self-managed rather than involving top-down command.

Indymedia

Indymedia is perhaps most typical of the new alternative digital media projects with more than 120 local sites networked worldwide.

- During mass actions and gatherings, Indymedia centers become communication hubs, particularly among more radical sectors.
- These temporary spaces of digital production provide a crucial terrain where activists carry out several concrete tasks:
  - Using e-mail to coordinate action and send information.
  - Generating formal updates.
  - Providing video and image files.
- Providing workshops to carry out complex operations.
  - Creating innovative activist uses for new technologies.
- Protesters have also made innovative use of cell phone technology to coordinate, report, and provide real-time updates.
- Indymedia incorporates a broad networking logic, as open publishing software allows activists to independently create, post, and distribute their own news stories. Absence of editorial control allows users to draw their own conclusions about the truth and relevance of reports.

Tactical Media   Rather than creating alternative counterpublics, tactical media aim to creatively intervene with dominant media spheres.

- Tactical media interventions do not necessarily take place in cyberspace, but new digital technologies are almost always crucial.
- "Culture jamming" involves the playful parodying of corporate advertisements and logos to produce critical messages.
- "Hacktivism" or "electronic civil disobedience" constitutes a final dimension of tactical media using digital trespass or blockade tactics. This often generates significant media attention.

Conclusion   Anti–corporate globalization movements have not only generated widespread visibility surrounding issues related to global economic justice and democracy; they have also pioneered in the use of new technology.

- Their practices have facilitated the emergence of globally coordinated transnational counterpublics, while providing creative mechanisms for flexibly intervening with dominant communication circuits.
- At the same time, the network has also emerged as a broader cultural ideal, as digital technologies generate new political values and vocabularies.
- Activists are building a new digital media culture using open participation and horizontal collaboration.
- Anti–corporate globalization movements are best understood as social laboratories, generating new cultural practices and political imaginaries for a digital age.

ERRATUM

The following biographical information for the author was inadvertently omitted from the article "Family-Friendly Workplace Reform: Prospects for Change" published in *THE ANNALS* 596:36-61, November 2004:

Amy L. Wax is a professor of law at the University of Pennsylvania Law School; she holds an MD from Harvard and a JD from Columbia. She trained as a neurologist at New York Hospital in the early 1980s; served as a law clerk to Judge Abner J. Mikva on the D.C. Circuit Court of Appeals; and from 1988 to 1994 worked as an attorney in the Office of the Solicitor General at the Department of Justice, where she argued fifteen cases before the U.S. Supreme Court. She taught at the University of Virginia Law School before coming to Penn in 2001. Her areas of teaching and research include civil procedure, remedies, social welfare law, and the law and economics of work and family. Published works include "Evolution and the Bounds of Human Nature," Law & Philosophy *(November 2004) and "The Political Psychology of Redistribution: Implications for Welfare Reform," in* The Politics of Welfare Reform *(2004).*